# Managing High Risk Sex Offenders in the Community

D0744916

The management of sex offenders in the community is of paramount concern to the general public, and this is reflected in the numerous recent changes to public protection procedures.

*Managing High Risk Sex Offenders in the Community* covers both the assessment and management of high risk sex offenders in the community, with an emphasis on evidence-based approaches. The reader will be able to access the most widely used actuarial approaches to risk assessment and understand the clinical themes that underpin such variables. The book answers questions including:

- Are sex offenders likely to escalate their behaviour if not stopped?
- Is the risk on the streets or at home?
- Can we differentiate between those offenders who will and those who will not reoffend?

This book links psychologically-based theoretical principles with practical considerations for professionals in the field. By demystifying the current state of knowledge on risk posed by sex offenders, practitioners will be well placed to engage in defensible decision-making and strive for best practice in the community.

**Jackie Craissati** is Head of Forensic Clinical Psychology services with Oxleas NHS Trust, Kent and author of *Child Sexual Abusers*.

# Managing High Risk Sex Offenders in the Community

A psychological approach

Jackie Craissati

Brunner-Routledge
Taylor & Francis Group

HOVE AND NEW YORK

First published 2004
by Brunner-Routledge
27 Church Road, Hove, East Sussex BN3 2FA

Simultaneously published in the USA and Canada
by Brunner-Routledge
29 West 35th Street, New York NY 10001

*Brunner-Routledge is an imprint of the Taylor & Francis Group*

Copyright © 2004 Jackie Craissati

Typeset in Times by RefineCatch Ltd, Bungay, Suffolk
Printed and bound in Great Britain by TJ International Ltd, Padstow,
Cornwall
Paperback cover design by Richard Massing

This publication has been produced with paper manufactured to
strict environmental standards and with pulp derived from
sustainable forests.

*British Library Cataloguing-in-Publication Data*
A catalogue record for this book is available from the British Library

*Library of Congress Cataloging-in-Publication Data*
Craissati, Jackie.
   Managing high risk sex offenders in the community : a
psychological approach / Jackie Craissati.
      p. ; cm.
   Includes bibliographical references.
   ISBN 1-58391-157-X (hbk)—ISBN 1-58391-158-8 (pbk)
   1. Sex offenders—Mental health. 2. Sex offenders—Rehabilitation.
3. Psychosexual disorders—Treatment. 4. Risk management.
5. Community mental health services.   I. Title.
   [DNLM: 1. Paraphilias—rehabilitation—Case Report. 2. Risk
Management—methods—Case Report. 3. Sex Offenses—prevention
& control—Case Report. WM 610 C886m 2004]
RC560.S47C736 2004
616.85'83—dc22                                    2003024561

ISBN 1-58391-157-X (hbk)
ISBN 1-58391-158-8 (pbk)

# Contents

# List of contributors

**Jackie Craissati** is a Consultant Forensic and Clinical Psychologist and Head of Forensic Psychology with Oxleas NHS Trust in South East London. She has been working with mentally disordered offenders for the past 13 years, and is known for her work with sex offenders. She has considerable experience in assessing and treating sex offenders in the community, in partnership with the Probation Service. An adviser to the Department of Health, she trains practitioners across London and lectures widely on the subject. She is the author of *Child Sexual Abusers: A Community Treatment Approach* (Psychology Press 1998).

**Joanna Hall** is a practising barrister with 29 years' experience. She specialises in the law relating to children and much of her practice is in public law cases. She has also led workshops for lawyers and childcare professionals on children's law and related issues.

**Geraldine Gavin** is currently one of three operational directors for the newly constituted London Probation Area, which is an amalgamation of the five former Probation Services across London. Having originally been a teacher, she joined the Probation Service in 1981 and held a variety of posts in case management delivery before moving into management in December 1992. Since 1996 Geraldine has developed expertise in the public protection arena. As well as operational responsibilities across London, she holds the portfolio for community protection in London.

# Acknowledgements

The seeds of this book were first sown over ten years ago, when we sat as a group of clinicians and probation officers and decided to run a treatment group for child molesters. With time the service expanded, and in doing so allowed me to gain invaluable experience. Throughout, the Probation Service has been entirely supportive in all treatment and research efforts on my part, and I am wholly indebted to the local service, in particular, for their unfailing support over the years.

My employers, Oxleas NHS Trust, have provided me with time and library support, for which I am grateful. There are also particular individuals who have gone out of their way to respond to my queries and assist me with technical aspects of the work. I would like to thank Carol Paton, Rob Hale and Kevin Browne in this respect. Over the last five years, Tony Beech has kept me up to date with the recidivism literature, and provided endless support in helping me to complete my PhD and this book.

# Chapter I

# Introduction

Detectives hunting for missing eight-year-old Sarah Payne today found the body of a young girl north of Littlehampton. The body was found near the grounds of Brinsbury agricultural college, in Pulborough, West Sussex, about ten miles from the area where Sarah disappeared on July 1.

*Guardian*, Monday 17 July 2000

Police confirmed yesterday that the body of a girl found in a field in West Sussex was that of eight-year-old Sarah Payne ... Detectives said the body was naked but would not say if there was evidence that the girl, who had been missing since the start of the month, had been sexually assaulted.

*Guardian*, Wednesday 19 July 2000

There must be no hiding place for the evil perverts who prey on our children. For too long the nation has endured the pain of seeing innocents such as Sarah Payne snatched from streets to become victims of paedophiles.

*News of the World*, Sunday 23 July 2000

The people of Britain have been given their chance to speak on the subject of child sex offenders in a significant MORI poll commissioned by the *News of the World*. Its conclusions below show a gulf between us and our lawmakers. It must not be ignored by our politicians, our police or our courts. The British public has voiced huge support for the *News of the World*'s proposals to identify all paedophiles. In an eye-opening public opinion poll: 88 per cent of those questioned say parents should be told if a child sex offender is living in their area; 75 per cent say perverts jailed for life for sex crimes against children should never go free; 82 per cent believe paedophiles should be chemically castrated – their sex drives suppressed by drugs.

> Charles Begley, *News of the World*,
> Sunday 23 July 2000

Today, in a groundbreaking edition of the *Irish News of the World*, we begin the biggest public record of child sex offenders ever seen. We do so in memory of Sarah Payne, whose murder broke so many hearts. There are 110,000 proven paedophiles roaming free in the UK, one for every square mile of the country. Today we begin naming them. Week in, week out, we will add to the list of shame.

> Terenia Taras and Paul McMullan, *Irish News of the World*,
> Sunday 23 July 2000

An uneasy truce was declared yesterday by seething protesters fighting to drive alleged paedophiles off a troubled council estate. Demo leaders announced they were suspending their campaign for one day of talks with local officials. The move followed seven nights of violent protests on the Paulsgrove Estate, Portsmouth, Hants. Five families have fled as mobs of up to 300 people fire-bombed cars and stoned houses of suspected perverts. Action group Peaceful Protesters of Paulsgrove claim to have a list of 20 paedophiles on the estate and say they will be targeted until they leave. However there are only two known sex offenders on the estate and police say four families who fled had 'nothing to do' with child sex.

> Stewart Whittingham, *News of the World*,
> Friday 11 August 2000

Violence has also flared in Plymouth, a man was chased by a mob in Whitley, Berkshire, and two men accused of child sex offences have committed suicide. Police said a millionaire businessman ... arrested over child sex charges, had been found on Sunday night shot dead at his Kent home ... what they've [*News of the World*] created is an atmosphere of fear among members of the public, among parents and among sex offenders ...

> Vikram Dodd, *Guardian*, Thursday 10 August 2000

These extracts from British newspaper clippings highlight a train of events which was sparked off on 1 July 2000 by the disappearance of an 8-year-old girl, Sarah Payne. On 17 July, a girl's body was found, and two days later it was confirmed to be that of Sarah. The nation was undoubtedly horrified, and moved by the dignified presence of Sarah's family in the media. Less than a week later, the *News of the World* – a popular national tabloid newspaper – launched a controversial campaign to 'name and shame' all the known paedophiles in Britain. By 4 August 2000, there was public unrest, most notably in an estate near Portsmouth, where protests to move paedophiles away from the locality erupted in violence for a period of a week. The 'name and shame' campaign was dropped by the *News of the World* in favour of a more muted lobbying for 'Sarah's Law', which focused on empowering parents and victims, and improving prevention of sex offences.

This was a highly emotional three weeks for all concerned – the public, the media and sex offenders themselves. Yet, for all the drama and controversy, this example raises very meaningful questions about the nature of the risk posed by sex offenders, and the most effective means of managing that risk in the community. Such questions might include

- Is the risk on the streets or at home?
- Are women as unsafe as children?
- Does action arising from sexually motivated child murders help us in managing other types of sex offender?
- Are sex offenders likely to escalate in their behaviour if not stopped?
- Is there any form of treatment which can be guaranteed to be effective?
- Can we differentiate between those offenders who will and those who will not reoffend?
- What role can the community play in the management of sex offenders?
- Is current legislation and statutory practice ineffective?
- Does community notification always lead to vigilante behaviour?

Clearly, there are not answers to all these questions, and those answers that there are may be equivocal. Nevertheless, the following pages attempt to provide the reader with a range of practical and evidence-based information to enable them to gain confidence in their risk management practice with sex offenders.

## The scope of the book

This book is aimed at a range of practitioners working in a range of agencies. It is assumed that there will be a variety of skills and knowledge bases among readers, and this is taken into account. However, so much has been written and spoken about sexual offenders that it is important to set some boundaries to the scope of the book, in order to retain its focus. The decision was made to focus on *contact sexual offences, the adult men who commit such offences, and in particular those individuals who pose the highest risk of sexual reoffending.* This is a pragmatic approach, reflecting public concern with behaviour which is problematic in terms of its apparent frequency and its likely impact on others. Although much of the material is relevant to specialist groups of offenders, there are inevitable omissions: learning disability is briefly discussed in Chapters 3 and 6, but is not extensively reviewed in terms of community management approaches. Non-contact sexual behaviours – indecent exposure and pornography use – are discussed in terms of their potential contribution to risk assessment in contact sex offenders; however, current public interest in internet pornography offences as a subject in its own right is not reflected in this book and the reader may wish to seek out specialist material on this relatively new subject (see Cooper 2002; Taylor & Quayle 2003).

However, work on adolescent sex offenders and, to a lesser extent, female sex offenders, has become more mainstream, and these two groups are discussed in greater detail. Common sense would suggest that there is some overlap between the approach to adult male sex offenders and other groups, but the evidence base is not yet sufficiently sophisticated to support this premise. Some introductory comments about adolescent and female offenders are set out below.

A further restriction of the book is the area of risk upon which the primary focus rests; that is, there are many possible forms of risk. Whatever the limitations of such an approach, this book has largely restricted itself to consideration of risk to others, with a particular emphasis on the likelihood of sexual reoffending. Victim impact – the subject of much research and commentary – is not discussed in any detail. Table 1.1 lays out a simple framework for risk assessment which suggests that key risk areas include the likelihood of reoffending, the seriousness of victim impact and public interest. This latter area includes professional and institutional risk when failures in the community occur. Clearly, an offender may lie at

*Table 1.1* Risk table

|  | Likelihood of reoffending | Seriousness of impact | Public interest |
|---|---|---|---|
| **Low risk**<br>**Medium risk**<br>**High risk** |  |  |  |

different risk levels in terms of offending probability, victim impact and professional/institutional/public consequences.

In terms of the use of terminology in this book, a *sexual offender* refers to an individual who has engaged in illegal sexual behaviour, whether or not he or she has been convicted. An *index offence* relates to the most recent (sexual) conviction and *sexual reoffending* – perpetrating another illegal sexual act (whether caught or not) – is labelled *sexual reconviction* or *sexual recidivism* when a further conviction is obtained. However, when a study makes clear that arrests and charges are considered as well as convictions, sexual recidivism is used. Offenders against children (under the age of 16) are called *child molesters*, and offenders against adults – women victims unless specified – are called *rapists*. This is admittedly something of a shorthand, which does not relate to the conviction but to the age of the victim. Unless otherwise stated, the use of the male prefix reflects the emphasis on male sex offenders. If any of the research cited in the book differs markedly in its use of terminology, this is made clear at the time.

## The extent of the problem

Determining the extent of the problem is fraught with difficulties. Randomised retrospective surveys of the general adult population estimate that 12 per cent of females and 8 per cent of males have experienced unwanted contact before the age of 16 (Baker & Duncan 1985). However, figures vary according to the style of survey (whether or not non-contact behaviours are included) and the numbers of victims are unlikely to reflect the number of perpetrators, some of whom will have engaged in prolific illegal sexual activity (Abel, Becker, Mittelman, Cunningham-Rathner, Rouleau, & Murphy 1987). Determining the prevalence of sexual offenders who have never been convicted is particularly problematic. Social services child protection teams manage families where children have been identified as being at serious risk of sexual abuse, although the majority of alleged perpetrators have not been prosecuted. For example, McClurg and Craissati (1999) found that between 0 and 8 per cent of these alleged perpetrators in two London boroughs were convicted as a result of the allegations.

In terms of adult victims, the British Crime Survey (BCS) (Myhill & Allen 2002) found that 0.4 per cent of women aged 16 to 59 in England and Wales said they had been raped in the year preceding the 2000 BCS, which was estimated at 61,000 victims. Around 5 per cent of women said they had been raped since the age of 16, while 10 per cent of women said they had experienced some form of sexual victimisation in that time (including rape). Approximately 20 per cent of sexual victimisation incidents in the preceding year came to the attention of the police (an estimated 12,000).

However, if we then turn to official crime statistics in the year 2000/1 (Simmons et al. 2002), there were 41,425 recorded sexual offences, of which 9,743 were for rape (9,008 of which were against a female), and 21,765 were for indecent assault on a female. Although offence categories do not necessarily allow for the differentiation between child and adult victims, these figures would suggest that it is reasonable to presume that only one fifth of sexual offences are actually reported to the police.

With regard to the offenders, in 1995 in England and Wales, 4,600 men and 100 women were sentenced by the courts for indictable sexual offences and a further 2,250 were cautioned. Of these, 2,554 convictions were for sexual offences against children (aged less than 16), 19 of whom were female offenders. By the age of 40, Marshall (1997) estimated that 1.1 per cent of men born in 1953 had a conviction for a serious sexual offence, 0.7 per cent of whom clearly had a child victim (0.6 per cent a girl victim and 0.1 per cent a boy victim). Estimating the population of sex offenders, 260,000 men had a conviction for any sexual offence, of which 165,000 had a conviction for a serious sexual offence, and 110,000 had a conviction for an offence against a child.

Official recording figures of crime are very different to conviction figures. There are many intervening factors, not least the possibility that no crime has been committed, or that no suspect is found or charged. Even when a conviction is obtained, the type of conviction may not reflect the extent or nature of the sexually abusive behaviour. Some homicide, harassment and false imprisonment offences may contain a predominantly sexual element. It is well understood that the criminal justice process also distorts the picture: offenders may only be convicted of 'specimen' charges when abuse has occurred over a lengthy period or with a number of victims; charges are likely to be dropped or reduced in order to secure a conviction or avoid a trial. A study of convicted child molesters in South East London (Craissati 1994) showed that charges were more than twice as likely to be dropped when child victims were under the age of 10; 47 per cent of initial vaginal and anal rape charges were dropped/reduced to indecent assault before trial. The criminal justice response to allegations of rape is clearly described in Harris and Grace's (1999) interesting study, and it is worth examining their findings in more detail. They followed up all 483 cases initially recorded as rape in 1996 and compared their findings to a similar study in 1985. They found the following:

- Stranger rapes dropped from 30 per cent in 1985 to 12 per cent in 1996, while the number of recorded rape offences increased more than threefold – thus the number of stranger rapes has remained similar; in 66 per cent of crimed stranger cases, no suspect was caught despite advances in forensic science. Once detected, stranger attacks were the most likely to be crimed, but the low detection rate meant that they were the least likely to be prosecuted.
- Although only 5 per cent of complainants were aged over 45, they were the most likely to have reported being raped by a stranger; just over one quarter of complainants were aged less than 16 and 58 per cent of the total were aged 16 to 35.
- In 82 per cent of cases, there was some degree of consensual contact immediately prior to the attack (compared with 37 per cent of cases in 1985).
- Cases where there was no evidence of any violence, or the threat of violence, towards the complainant were more likely to be no-crimed, the most common reason being retraction by the complainant (36 per cent of 106 no-crimed cases). It was felt that sometimes withdrawal happened because the complainant was reunited with the suspect, although emotional and financial dependence was felt to be a common reason. Although a quarter of cases were no-crimed, this was much lower than in the previous study and the main reason was a police decision that the complaint was false or malicious (43 per cent).

- Cases involving particularly young complainants (<12) or older complainants (>45) were those most likely to be proceeded with by the Crown Prosecution Service (CPS), and 88 per cent of cases reaching the Crown Court involving complainants <13 led to a conviction.

- A quarter of the original sample of cases was discontinued and only a quarter reached Crown Court. Nine per cent of the original sample of 299 suspects for crimed rapes were convicted of rape/attempted rape; of the remaining 36, 17 were convicted of indecent assault and 12 for unlawful sexual intercourse, and a further 22 were acquitted (7 per cent of the original sample).

- Once convicted of rape, the sentences were severe, with half incurring a custodial sentence of over six years and up to life, and just under 30 per cent incurring sentences of between four and six years.

The study goes on to highlight the difficulties in the system and makes recommendations for change. These include improved training for police, greater support to complainants throughout the criminal justice process and improved evidence-gathering, particularly where there is evidence of violence.

## Adolescent sex offenders

The growing body of research on adolescent sex offenders has been beset with methodological limitations: small sample sizes, discrepancies between samples of incarcerated and community-based offenders, a low base rate for sexual reoffending and a failure to distinguish between child molesters, rapists and exhibitionists.

Definitions of what constitutes sexual abuse by adolescents have been put forward. For example, Vizard, Monck and Misch (1995) suggest that there are three aspects: the use of coercion or force, sexual interactions which are age inappropriate for the partner and partners who are not peers. Ryan (1997) suggests that sexually abusive behaviour be defined as sexual interaction that is against the victim's will, without consent and/or in an aggressive, exploitative, manipulative or threatening manner.

The real discrepancies emerge when researchers attempt to subdivide their samples. This is illustrated by two research approaches, both deploying different types of subgrouping. Richardson, Kelly,

Bhate and Graham (1997) described four subgroups in their sample of adolescent sex offenders:

- a *child group* who abused a victim four or more years younger than themselves;
- an *incest group* who abused siblings;
- a *peer group* who abused similar or older aged victims;
- a *mixed group*.

Prentky, Harris, Rizzell and Righthand (2000) classified their sample as follows:

- *child molesters*, whose victims were aged less than 11 and the offender was at least five years older;
- *rapists*, whose victims were aged 12 or older and there was less than a five-year age difference between the offender and youngest victim;
- *sexually reactive children*, where the offender and all victims were under 11;
- *fondlers*, where all sexual acts were limited to fondling/caressing/frottage and the same age criteria as for rapists;
- *paraphilic* offenders, where there was no physical contact with the victim.

Very little of the literature on adolescent sex offenders is related to risk prediction. For this reason, the actuarially-based approach to assessment by Prentky *et al.* (2000) has been emphasised, despite being in the preliminary stages of development. Chapters 2 and 3 outline what little is known, and Chapter 6 provides some guidelines for treatment, where adolescent approaches differ markedly from those developed with adults.

## Female sex offenders

In recent years there has been increasing attention paid to female sex offenders and an attempt has been made to reflect this in the following chapters. However, the academic literature is strikingly limited, both in terms of methodological limitations – very small sample sizes, lack of comparison groups, sampling biases in favour of convicted and incarcerated offenders – and relevance to risk prediction. In terms of pragmatic considerations, female sex offenders continue to pose few demands in terms of resource implications or community concerns in comparison to their male counterparts. Practitioners in the community rarely assess, supervise or treat more than a handful of female sex offenders over the course of their working life. Consideration has been given to the apparent lack of attention paid to convicted female sex offenders, and this is summarised by Atkinson (2000). Theories include elements such as preconceptions of women as non-violent nurturers, the greater freedom of women/mothers to touch children, the reluctance of children (particularly boys) to report abuse perpetrated by women on whom they are dependent, and the possibility that female perpetrators may be more likely to accompany their children when in the presence of other adults (e.g. the doctor or health visitor). Legally, men have been regarded as being physically incapable of being sexually abused by women, and male physiological responses contradict notions of unwanted sexual contact. Some authors have suggested that women are less likely to act out psychological conflicts on others (Welldon 1988), turning aggressive impulses inwards in terms of self-harm, self-mutilation and a tendency for somatisation of distress. This view is supported by Mathews, Hunter and Vuz's (1997) research on adolescent female sex offenders, in which they concluded that

> biological and socialization factors create a higher threshold for the externalization of experienced developmental trauma in females than males. In this regard, it may be that females are generally less likely than males to manifest the effects of maltreatment in the form of interpersonal aggression or violence and that females who develop such patterns of behavior are generally those who have experienced remarkably high levels of such developmental trauma in the absence of environmental support for recovery and the presence of healthy female role models.
>
> (p. 194)

Readers will find little of direct relevance to risk prediction in female sex offenders in Chapter 2, as there is an almost total lack of attention to detail on questions of risk. However, the descriptive evidence thus far has led to a reasonably consistent picture regarding the characteristics and typologies of women perpetrators, and these are described in Chapter 3. Treatment for women has been discussed in the literature – without reference to evidence-based change and its relevance to risk in the community – and this is addressed in Chapter 6.

## The case studies and the local context

Five case studies are discussed throughout the book, and their stories are presented in full in Chapter 7. Each case study is an amalgamation of two or more real individuals, designed both to ensure confidentiality and to demonstrate core features and difficulties which challenge practitioners in the field. It is important to note that these cases are not necessarily representative in terms of risk, as this book is predominantly focused on high risk sex offenders.

*Stephen* is a 30-year-old man, referred by social services due to concerns regarding the potential risk he may pose to his step-daughter. As the only unconvicted case and, in principle, a low risk sex offender, he was chosen to highlight some of the dilemmas which face child protection agencies when a low risk offender is placed in a potentially high risk situation.

*Anthony*, aged 30, was referred by his probation officer for assessment and treatment shortly after his release from prison on non-parole date licence. He had served four years of a seven-year sentence for the rape of a 21-year-old woman. He remained in total denial of his index offence. He was recalled to prison after breaching the rules of his licence (but not reoffending), but was later released. At follow up he was apparently doing well in the community.

*James*, aged 60, was released into the community on a life licence, having been convicted 25 years earlier for the murder of a 50-year-old woman. Although there was a history of sadistic sexual interests, he had made extremely good progress and appeared to do well in the community. However, 18 months after his release, he committed a further seriously violent offence against an adult woman and received a further life sentence.

*Peter* was aged 25 when he was referred by his probation officer, prior to his discharge from prison on automatic conditional release. He had served 22 months of a 44-month sentence for the indecent assault of a 14-year-old boy. Despite considerable resistance, Peter made good progress in a community treatment programme and at follow up three years later appeared to be doing well in the community.

*Martin*, aged 45, was referred for an assessment prior to his parole hearing. He was serving a five-year sentence following a conviction for indecent assault on a 9-year-old boy. Despite constructive engagement in the prison sex offender group programme, there were continuing concerns regarding his potential to offend and media interest in his release. His management in the community was hampered by Martin's chaotic presentation, which was reflected in the developing tensions between agencies. Ultimately he was recalled to prison, following his confession to having committed another offence against a boy. This was subsequently retracted by him and there were universal doubts that any offence had in fact occurred.

The temptation, when discussing good practice, is to emphasise the successes rather than the failures. Yet it is undoubtedly true that the impetus to learn and improve is driven by the desire to avoid failure, and that it is failures which predominantly trigger change. Not one of these case examples was straightforward to manage in the community. Those who had been released from prison posed difficulties which had been almost entirely dormant within the prison system; this is understandable, given the high levels of structure within a prison which provide both physical and emotional containment for damaged individuals. While the management of Anthony and Martin could as easily be considered a partial success as a partial failure – no offence apparently having been committed – James' failure was spectacularly disastrous, predominantly for the victim who suffered terrible physical and emotional harm, but also for the practitioners and agencies involved.

The case studies need to be considered within the context of the overall rate of success and failure for sex offenders in the community. Risk and reconviction is discussed in great detail in Chapters 2 and 3, and treatment effectiveness is presented in Chapter 6. However, there is a local context to the cases, which are drawn from a sample of 310 convicted sex offenders, assessed over a period of seven years in a discrete urban geographical area: the Challenge Project is an assessment and treatment programme for sex offenders in the community, which has been extensively evaluated (see e.g. Craissati & Beech 2001; Craissati & Beech forthcoming). Of the 310 subjects, 273 were at risk in the community (64 rapists and 209 child molesters) for an average period of 51 months. The sample was representative of all levels of risk and types of sex offender. There were 37 (13 per cent) failures – recalled/breached or any reconviction – but only nine sex offenders (2 per cent) were reconvicted for sexual offences – six (3 per cent) child molesters and three (5 per cent) rapists. Even when sexual recidivism was expanded to include any 'sexually risky behaviour' (behavioural precursors to relapse, arrests and allegations, see Craissati & Beech 2003), only 27 (10 per cent) sex offenders failed. Thus, after four years at risk, 90 per cent of sex offenders – including the majority of high risk offenders – were apparently successfully rehabilitated. Clearly, there is likely to be an unknown amount of undetected sexual offending, but nevertheless, these are encouraging figures.

## The public response

It seems indisputable that there is enormous public interest in sexual offenders, represented by (or fuelled by) media coverage. A cursory look at the coverage over the past five years would suggest that no amount of research, education or careful management can assuage profoundly held public beliefs about the nature of sex offenders – monstrous individuals who prey incessantly on children and are impervious to punishment or rehabilitation. That this view is overly simplistic and an incomplete picture is clearly shown throughout this book. Yet the public interest should not be summarily dismissed, for many reasons: the public can jeopardise the resettlement of a sex offender, leading to social exclusion and raised risk; the public have opportunities to identify potential victims and potential offenders if they remain appropriately vigilant; and the public may perceive some fundamental truth about sex offenders to which practitioners in the field become inured. For these reasons, it seems important to try and understand the nature of the public response to sex offenders.

Now that the impact of child sexual abuse and rape is understood more clearly, there is little moral ambiguity about the nature of the offence. Yet this does not seem to be sufficient to explain the public response. Other serious violent offences – for example, domestic violence and perhaps most obviously homicide – also have little moral ambiguity, yet do not evoke the same outcry and fears. Many women fear rape by a stranger, and this was confirmed by the BCS (Simmons et al. 2002) where 25 per cent of women reported being very worried about being raped. Yet women are most likely to be sexually attacked by someone they know, current partners being responsible for 45 per cent of the attacks reported (Myhill & Allen

2002). The same is true for child sexual abuse. In considering the media coverage, it is important to distinguish between child molesters and rapists, as the latter group of offenders are often relatively ignored by the press and the public. There has been a phenomenon over the past five to ten years of intensive and intrusive media coverage of sexually motivated stranger killings of children. Horrified, we watch transfixed as distraught and pleading parents face the press to beg the offender to return their child; we enter the life of the child via home video clips, repeated again and again, and the child becomes very real in everyone's life, bringing a more personal sense of tragedy and loss. This personalised experience distorts the reality of the danger. Not only does one automatically think of rape and killing when thinking of sex offenders, it seems incredible that the number of such killings should have remained remarkably stable over the years. Yet a look at the official statistics confirms it. Figures from 1991 onwards (Flood-Page & Taylor 2003) clearly show that on average 70–80 children under the age of 16 are killed every year, approximately 10 per cent by strangers (most of which will probably be sexually motivated). What should be more shocking to a public which believes in protecting children is that 60–80 per cent of the child victims are killed by their parents, and that children under the age of 1 are the most at risk of homicide across all age groups.

Aside from changes in the media and its influence, commentators might also point out hypocrisy in our apparently relaxed attitude to the eroticisation of children on the one hand and our prudish denial of the inherently sensual nature of young children and the comfort derived from physical contact with them on the other. The capacity to differentiate between the sensual and sexual nature of children is central to an understanding of child sexual abuse and a core distortion of child molesters. Perhaps the public understands the central but precarious nature of this divide, and takes up an extreme position in order to distance themselves, creating the image of a monstrous and unknown child molester who lives beyond the home.

## What is a psychological approach?

Psychological thinking is certainly not exclusive to the profession of psychology, but falls within the general domain. It relates to the individual processes – thoughts and feelings – which are shaped by internal and external influences and which underpin behaviour.

Sexual offending is undoubtedly a complex behaviour with multi-faceted personal, social and cultural influences; yet broadly psychological theories (Craissati 1998) dominate in terms of causal and treatment models. As scientist-practitioners, psychologists – both forensic and clinical – are concerned to ground their understanding of an individual offender within a coherent theoretical framework. This understanding (or formulation) of the individual forms the basis of all assessment and subsequent management, including treatment approaches. Testing out hypotheses allows for theoretical frameworks to be reviewed and revised. Without a conceptual and theoretical framework, the apparently irrational and abhorrent behaviour of sex offenders can overwhelm the practitioner, as it does the public. Management approaches which attempt to control behaviour without understanding it are more likely to fail or to meet resistance from the offender; limited resources may be misdirected.

At its simplest, and without adherence to any particular theoretical model, a framework for the management of sexual offenders needs to consider the interpersonal dimension of the behaviour at its core – the 'relationship' (real or symbolic) between perpetrator and victim. This entails an understanding of the details of the offending behaviour in the context of an individual's psychological and social functioning – that is, the interplay between an individual's internal state of emotional and cognitive functioning and his relationship to those in the world around him. This book is based on this framework, with an emphasis on the evidence base and its practical implications for the successful management of high risk offenders.

# Chapter 2

# Actuarial approaches to risk assessment

## Introduction

Actuarial assessment involves predicting an individual's behaviour on the basis of how others have acted in similar situations. Such assessments are based on statistical models which examine the relationship between types of offender, their personal and offending characteristics and their subsequent rate of failure (or reconviction). This chapter aims to review the key elements of the research literature on sex offender recidivism, and to discuss the strengths and weaknesses of the current risk prediction instruments.

## Professional and ethical issues

There is little doubt that professionals – both experienced and inexperienced – can often feel undermined by actuarial approaches to risk assessment. They may feel, quite wrongly, that their contribution is redundant, that they have been surpassed by a checklist. Furthermore, it may seem incredible that such an apparently complex and serious issue as risk assessment could be condensed into a few variables. However, as many researchers repeatedly point out, actuarial risk assessment is only part of the process – albeit a crucial part – which anchors clinical judgement. Throughout this chapter, the focus will be on the *likelihood of reoffending*. However, it is important to highlight that all the actuarial approaches referred to in this chapter are based on research with convicted sex offenders, the outcome of interest being a further sexual conviction or arrest.

The research evidence is clear: actuarial approaches are nearly always shown to be superior to clinical judgement. This holds true for different types of offender in both an institutional and community setting, across countries and agencies, for health professionals as well as criminal justice professionals. Specifically, for sex offenders, Hanson and Bussiere (1998) found that professional judgement to predict sex offence recidivism was only slightly better than chance (average $r = .10$).

Given the vagaries of clinical judgement, there are a number of ethical issues to be considered, the most prevalent of which are laid out below:

- Is your opinion subject to personal biases? For example, a moral view that sex offenders, by the very nature of their crime, have divested themselves of their human rights.
- Is your opinion subject to irrelevant biases? For example, a sex offender's lack of sincere remorse renders him a high risk.
- Are you basing your opinion on a broad range of experience, or the last case you held which went wrong? For example, the police often used to believe that all sex offenders reoffend because they only come across reoffenders more than once.
- Do you know the base rates for sexual recidivism? That is, the general rates of reconviction among sex offenders in the community.
- In summary, are you qualified to give an opinion, based on accurate knowledge, given the implications for both the offender and his potential victims?

It is worth examining the question of base rates and accuracy in some detail. Risk predictions fall into four categories:

1  *True positives* (a prediction of reoffending was borne out).
2  *True negatives* (a prediction of not reoffending was borne out).
3  *False positives* (a prediction of reoffending was not followed by an offence).
4  *False negatives* (a prediction of not reoffending was wrong and the individual committed a new offence).

We all worry about false negatives, and these anxieties are heightened when the social and political climate is intensely preoccupied with the issue of sex offenders. An unanticipated reoffence is likely to come under the scrutiny of managers and potentially leads to professional criticism, quite apart from the self-doubt it engenders and concern for the victim. Such a case – *James* – is discussed throughout this book. False positives also raise strong ethical dilemmas, although in the case of sex offenders these are often dismissed as a necessary by-product of public protection. When predicting any form of violence – indeed a wide range of behaviours – most studies show that professionals and lay people tend to falsely predict risk in a ratio of 3:1: for every three people thought to be at risk of future violence, only one of them will actually be violent. It is easy to understand the psychological bias to 'playing it safe' which, taken in combination with an ignorance of base rates, leads to this over-prediction. The extent of this difficulty is nicely illustrated by Campbell (1995): let us assume that a test instrument has an 80 per cent correct classification rate for sex offenders, both for predicting who will and who will not be reconvicted for a further sexual offence; let us also assume that there are three different base rates for reconviction in different types of sex offender (10 per cent for intrafamilial child molesters; 20 per cent for rapists and 60 per cent for extrafamilial child molesters with male victims). In fact these hypothesised base rates are probably fairly accurate, as discussed later in the chapter. Table 2.1 lays out the false positive and false negative rates for each subgroup of sex offenders.

If we consider the intrafamilial child molesters first, we would expect 10 out of 100 to be reconvicted. With a correct classification rate of 80 per cent, we would correctly identify eight of those reconvicted and 72 of those not reconvicted. That means there will be two reoffenders missed (false negatives) and 18 non-offenders incorrectly classified as reconvicted (false positives). Overall, we managed to correctly identify 8 out of 26 offenders (38 per cent) and 72 out of 74 non-offenders (97 per cent). As with so many studies, we were wrong two out of three times in predicting reoffending. If similar calculations are undertaken with the estimated base rate for rapists at 20 per cent, we were at least able to identify 50 per cent of reoffenders, but it is only when the base rate rises to over 50 per cent that we are able to correctly classify the majority of offenders reconvicted for further sexual offences.

The question is whether professionals – or the public – are in any way perturbed about these difficulties. Arguably, there are very significant implications for intrafamilial child molesters if they are so frequently falsely assessed as high risk, as they may be prevented from being rehabilitated into the family, from entering new families with children, or have future children taken from them and placed in care. This does have to be balanced against the paramount concern

Table 2.1 Correct classification rates for different base rates

| Test with correct classification rate of 80% N = 100 | Sex offenders reconvicted (%) | Sex offenders not reconvicted (%) |
|---|---|---|
| **Sex offender base rate 10%** | | |
| Anticipated rate | 10 | 90 |
| No. correctly classified | 8 | 72 |
| False negatives | 2 | 0 |
| False positives | 0 | 18 |
| Correctly classified | 38 | 97 |
| **Sex offender base rate 20%** | | |
| Anticipated rate | 20 | 80 |
| No. correctly classified | 16 | 64 |
| False negatives | 4 | 0 |
| False positives | 0 | 16 |
| Correctly classified | 50 | 94 |
| **Sex offender base rate 60%** | | |
| Anticipated rate | 60 | 40 |
| No. correctly classified | 48 | 32 |
| False negatives | 12 | 0 |
| False positives | 0 | 8 |
| Correctly classified | 86 | 73 |

of protecting children. Perhaps, in summary, the importance for maintaining professional integrity is to be explicit about the dilemmas and honest in acknowledging the possible error rate.

## Recidivism rates for sex offenders

As outlined in Chapter 1, there are numerous inadequacies in the published research literature on sex offenders. Sampling bias, length of follow up and failure to distinguish between subgroups of sex offender and different types of recidivism are probably the main limitations of the recidivism literature. However, over the past ten years sufficient data has been accumulated to provide us with a reasonably confident estimate of base rates. Some of the studies have not specified whether treatment was implemented, but if it is then the figures cited are for untreated groups of sex offenders. The comparison of recidivism for treated and untreated sex offenders is an important element of risk research and this issue will be discussed fully in Chapter 6. Three studies are of particular note – Marshall and Barbaree (1988), Alexander (1999) and Hanson and Bussiere (1998) – as they have produced figures from an analysis of accumulated studies. Such reviews of recidivism set criteria for adding published research data into their analysis, and the large sample size allows for the biased effects of individual studies to be reduced. In summary, the sexual reconviction rate for child molesters appears to range from 6 to 52 per cent, while their reconviction rate for violence ranges from 2 to 37 per cent. On the other hand, 10 to 39 per cent of rapists reoffend sexually and 15 to 49 per cent reoffend violently; all but one of the studies found that rapists were more likely to reoffend violently than sexually.

The question remains as to whether there are further divisions to be made, for either child molesters or rapists, which assist us in determining recidivism rates.

### Child molesters

Thornton and Hanson (1996) examined the gender and relationship specificity in sex offenders and found that 41 to 45 per cent of men with an index offence against a male child reoffended as compared to 9 to 19 per cent of men with an index offence against a female child. Alexander (1999) also found a different recidivism rate for incest offenders (12.5 per cent), child molesters with female victims (15.7 per cent) and with male victims (34.1 per cent). Quinsey, Lalumier, Rice and Harris (1995), in summarising 17 independent samples (n = 4,483) of child molesters, found that the weighted average sexual reconviction rates were:

- incest offenders: 8.5 per cent;
- female victims (excluding incest): 18.3 per cent;
- male victims (excluding incest: 35.2 per cent.

### Rapists

Very few studies differentiate between victim gender or relationship in samples of rapists. Thornton and Hanson (1996) found that 31 per cent of rapists with a male victim reoffended as compared to 28 per cent of rapists with a female victim.

## Adolescent sex offenders

The literature on risk and recidivism in adolescent sex offenders is a good deal more sparse than that relating to adult sex offenders. However, it is comprehensively reviewed by the following authors: Bourgon, Worling, Wormith and Kulik (1999) who are project workers for an evaluation of specialised treatment for adolescent sexual offenders on behalf of the Network for Research on Crime and Justice, Canada; Righthand and Welch (2001), on behalf of the US Department of Justice, have reviewed the professional literature; and Prentky *et al.* (2000) who have devised and reported on an actuarial procedure for assessing risk with juvenile sex offenders – detailed later in this chapter.

In England and Wales, approximately one third of all convictions for sexual offences have involved a perpetrator aged less than 21 (Home Office 1995), and Horne, Glasgow, Cox and Calam (1991) reported that 36 per cent of child molesters were under 18. Similarly, Bourgon *et al.* (1999) cite figures of 33 per cent being less than 21 years, 21 per cent being aged between 12 and 19. Prentky *et al.* (2000) quote estimated figures of 20 per cent of all rapes and 30 to 50 per cent of all child molestations are committed by adolescent males. Such high rates of conviction naturally give rise to concern which is exacerbated by retrospective studies of adult sex offenders suggesting that approximately 50 per cent have disclosed some form of sexually deviant behaviour in adolescence. Having dismissed earlier myths that 'boys will be boys', clinicians have swung to the position of believing adolescent sex offenders to pose a high risk of sexual recidivism.

The limited – albeit methodologically flawed – literature does not support this belief. Most adolescent recidivism studies have found a sexual reconviction rate of between 4 and 14 per cent. For example, Sipe, Jensen and Everett (1998) followed up 170 juvenile sex offenders as adults, for an average of six years, and found a sexual reconviction rate of 9.7 per cent and a reconviction rate for property offences of 16 per cent; this was compared to a group of non-sexual juvenile offenders who were reconvicted at rates of 3 per cent and 33 per cent for sexual and property offences respectively. Smith and Monastersky (1986) studied 112 juvenile sex offenders completing a community treatment programme, who were at risk for an average of 28 months; 14.3 per cent reoffended sexually and 34.8 per cent were convicted for non-sexual offences. Alexander's (1999) meta-analytic review included 1,025 juvenile sex offenders with a variable time at risk. She found that the overall sexual recidivism rate was 7.1 per cent, with 5.8 per cent of rapists reoffending and 2.1 per cent of child molesters reoffending. A few studies cite higher recidivism figures, but these are largely thought to be due to sampling bias. Hagan and Gust-Brey (2000) followed up 50 juvenile rapists for ten years, all of whom had participated in an eight-month inpatient treatment programme, and found that 16 per cent sexually reoffended. Rubenstein, Yeager, Goodstein and Lewis (1993), in an eight-year prospective study of 19 violent juvenile sex offenders found that 37 per cent sexually reoffended and 89 per cent reoffended generally.

### Female sex offenders

Having clearly outlined the definitional and methodological limitations of the work on female sex offenders (see Chapter 1), there is a growing consistency in the literature regarding the descriptive profile of female sex offenders. Key recent references include Grayston and De Luca's (1999) general review paper, Atkinson's (2000) work on Canadian incarcerated female sex offenders, Nathan and Ward's (2002) study of convicted women in Victoria, Australia and Saradjian and Hanks' (1996) work with both convicted and unconvicted female perpetrators in Britain. All these papers refer to the work of Matthews (1987) – amended by Matthews, Mathews and Speltz (1989) – which lays out a suggested typology for female sex offenders.

It is thought that Finkelhor and Russell's (1984) work provides the most accurate estimate to date of the prevalence of female sex offending: they tentatively suggest that females may account for up to 13 per cent of the abuse of females and 24 per cent of the abuse of males; they estimate that approximately 6 per cent of sexual abuse against females and 14 per cent of sexual abuse against males is thought to be perpetrated by females acting alone. In terms of convicted female sex offenders, researchers agree that just 2 to 5 per cent of all sex offenders are women. Official statistics for England and Wales would suggest that less than 1 per cent of all sex offences are committed by women; of the 1,031 allegations or suspicions of child abuse in Greater Manchester in 1992 (Rogers & Roberts 1995), only 3.5 per cent of perpetrators were female.

Risk is only directly mentioned by Saradjian and Hanks (1996), but without reference to any empirical evidence which might under-pin it. There would appear to be no reference to base rates for sexual recidivism in this group of women, indeed there is almost no refer-ence even to previous conviction histories. The absence of this data might well reflect a reality, which is that female sex offenders have no prior criminal convictions and rarely – if ever – reoffend sexually. However, this cannot be assumed. An alternative assumption might be that the profile of risk and recidivism in women mirrors that found in male sex offenders. This also has some appeal as a starting point for assessment, but may be misleading as an approach. Nevertheless, Saradjian and Hanks (1996) outline a model for risk assessment which overlaps considerably with good practice for risk assessment with men. They suggest attention should be paid to four areas:

1   The offender's history of severe developmental trauma and disturbed attachment experiences.
2   Evidence for the offender's poor socio-affective functioning, including an abusive relationship history.
3   Attitudinal issues relating to the offender's beliefs about children as characterised by emotional congruence, sexualisation and hostility.
4   Offending characteristics, including distortions, disinhibitors, victim empathy, multiple victims and motivation to change.

There are no actuarially based tools for risk prediction in female sex offenders. Of the instruments which are detailed below, only the Psychopathy Checklist (PCL-R, Hare 1991) has been used on female offenders, but not specifically female sex offenders.

## Actuarial risk prediction tools

In selecting prediction tools which are both meaningful and accurate, there are a number of factors to be considered. First, the sampling procedure needs to be scrutinised to ensure that the sample is suf-ficiently large and fairly representative of the population in question. Second, as described above, the base rate for sexual recidivism needs to be taken into account, as any tool is likely to be more accurate the larger the base rate. Third, the length of follow up should be long enough to capture most of the recidivists; this may be referred to as 'time at risk' – that is, the time the individual has spent in the community since the index conviction. Fourth, the tool must be clear about what it is predicting – sexual, violent or general recidivism, arrests or convictions. Fifth, the tool should have good inter-rater reliability – that is, that any two independent raters should arrive at the same, or nearly always the same, score. Finally, but most importantly, the tool should be able to be replicated across independent samples with comparable results.

When interpreting the statistical components of any prediction tool, the results may be presented as a correlation coefficient, r. For example, the average correlation between prior sex offences and sex offence recidivism is .19 (Hanson & Bussiere, 1998). Any prediction tool would need to improve upon this minimum standard. Researchers may analyse the data using the area under the Receiver Operating Characteristic (ROC) curve, which plots the hits (true positives) and the false alarms (false positives) at each level of the risk scale. The area under the ROC curve can range from .50 (prediction no better than chance) to 1.0 (perfect prediction). Thus the ROC area can be interpreted as the probability that a randomly selected recidivist would have a more deviant score than a randomly selected non-recidivist. Furthermore, prediction tools may identify false positive and false negative rates for differing cut-off points of the scale. Since recidivism rates are highly influenced by the length of the follow up period, survival analysis may be used. This calculates the probability of recidivating for each time period given that the offender has not yet reoffended. Survival analysis has the advantage of being able to estimate recidivism rates year by year even when the follow up periods vary across offenders (Hanson & Thornton 2000).

The following sexual recidivism tools are outlined in detail. They have been chosen either for their robust psychometric properties, ease of administration and/or predictive accuracy. Theoretically, all the information for these tools can be drawn from files. Save for the Psychopathy Checklist, the tools are itemised in full in the Appendix.

## Minnesota Sex Offender Screening Tool – Revised

The origins of the Minnesota Sex Offender Screening Tool (revised) (MnSOST-R) (Epperson, Huot & Kaul 1999) lay in a response to the Minnesota Department of Corrections in 1991 which called for a more formal and uniform process to identify predatory and violent sex offenders. The initial sample for the development of the tool comprised three groups of adult, male sex offenders: a) all 221 sex offenders released in 1988; b) a stratified random sample of 150 sex offenders released in 1990; and c) any other sex-offender (16) who had committed another sex offence upon release prior to May 1994, regardless of year of release. This sampling procedure resulted in 123 sex recidivists and a random sample of 120 recidivists (but non-sexual) and a random sample of 144 non-recidivists (those who did not reoffend at all). Sex offenders who had committed only intra-familial offences that did not involve penetration or high degrees of physical force were excluded from later analyses. Complete data was available for 256 of 274 sex offenders (152 rapists and 122 extra-familial child abusers) through six years at risk. Six-year recidivism rates were selected because preliminary analyses indicated that recidivism rates had clearly declined by the sixth year, and prediction rates were relatively stable from year three through to year eight. Arrests, rather than convictions, were used as the index of recidivism.

The baseline sexual recidivism rate was 35 per cent for the whole sample. The inter-rater reliability coefficient was .80, indicating that the ratings of individual raters were quite reliable. The correlation of MnSOST-R scores with recidivism status was .45 (ROC .77) and there was a large effect size (greater than one standard deviation) differentiating the average score for recidivists from the average score for non-recidivists. The effectiveness of the MnSOST-R in pre-dicting six-year sexual recidivism was approximately equivalent for rapists (r = .47) and extrafamilial sex offenders (r = .41)

When compared to other prediction tools, the MnSOST-R per-formed considerably better. For example, the Psychopathy Checklist – shortened version (Hart, Cox & Hare 1995) in this study was essentially unrelated to recidivism status (r = .04).

The MnSOST-R is intended for use on adult, male, incarcerated sex offenders, excluding incest offenders. It may not be accurate for offenders receiving community sentences (probation). The tool comprises 16 variables, of which 12 are historical/static and four are institutional/dynamic. An individual can score between a minimum of −14 through to a maximum of 31. In fact, in the research sample no offender scored lower than −5 or higher than 17. The authors recommended risk level cut scores are detailed in the Appendix and in Table 2.2.

*Table 2.2* Recommended risk level cut-off scores (MnSOST-R)

| Risk level | MnSOST-R score | Recidivism rate (%) (base rate 35%) |
|---|---|---|
| 1 (low) | 3 and below | 16 |
| 2 (moderate) | 4 to 7 | 45 |
| 3 (high) | 8 and above | 70 |
| Refer for commitment* | 13 and above | 88 |

*The commitment group is a subset of the high risk group.

Which cut-off score is used is likely to depend on the purpose of the assessment and the possible consequences for the offender and society. For example, with a cut-off score of 8, the recidivism rate of 70 per cent captures 44 per cent of all recidivists; with a cut-off score of 13, the recidivism rate of 88 per cent captures 15 per cent of recidivists.

The MnSOST-R has recently been cross-validated (Epperson, Kaul, Huot, Alexander & Goldman 2000) on a sample of all rapists and extrafamilial child molesters released in 1992. The total sample was 220, with a base rate sexual recidivism (contact offences) rate of 20 per cent. Full data for six years at risk was available for 170 of the 220, with a base rate for sexual recidivism of 26 per cent. The MnSOST-R correlated with sexual recidivism (r = .46, ROC .78) but to a slightly lesser extent than the original study. The outcome was slightly better for rapists (r = .51, ROC .83) than for child molesters (r = .41, ROC .76).

Information regarding the MnSOST-R can be downloaded from the website http:www.//psych-server.iastate.edu/faculty/epperson/mnsost_download.htm

## Static 99

The Static 99 (Hanson & Thornton 1999) is an amalgamation of two earlier risk prediction tools: the Structured Anchored Clinical Judgement Scale (SACJ-min, Grubin 1998) and the RRASOR (Hanson 1997). The development of the tool was based on four samples:

1   Institut Philippe Pinel (Proulx, Pellerin, McKibben, Aubut & Ouimet 1997), a maximum secure psychiatric facility in Canada. This study followed up 344 sex offenders treated at

the institution between 1978 and 1993 and recidivism data was collected in 1994. The average length of follow up was four years, with a sexual recidivism base rate of 15 per cent.

2   Millbrook (Hanson, Steffy & Gauthier 1993), a maximum security correctional facility in Canada. This study followed up 191 child molesters released between 1958 and 1974 at risk for an average of 23 years. The sexual recidivism base rate was 35 per cent.

3   Oak Ridge Division of the Penetanguishene Mental Health Centre (Rice & Harris 1996), a Canadian maximum security mental health centre. This study followed up 142 sex offenders referred between 1972 and 1993, for an average of 10 years at risk. The sexual recidivism base rate was 35 per cent.

4   Her Majesty's Prison Service (UK) (Thornton 1997). This study followed up 531 sex offenders released from prison in England and Wales in 1979 for a period of 16 years at risk. The sexual recidivism base rate was 25 per cent. Very few of the offenders in this sample would have received specialised sexual offender treatment.

The predictive accuracy of the scales was relatively consistent across the samples, the variability being no greater than would be expected by chance. The results for the combined sample (n = 1,208), for whom the Static 99, RRASOR and SACJ-min were administered, were as follows. The Static 99 performed best – its correlation with sexual recidivism status was .33 (ROC .71) and this was comparable for rapists and child molesters. The Static 99 also performed quite well in predicting violent recidivism (r = .32, ROC .69) with comparable results for rapists and child molesters. Survival analyses allowed for differential recidivism rates to be calculated for 5, 10 and 15 years and are outlined in the Appendix.

The Static 99 is intended for use with adult, male, convicted sex offenders. It comprises ten static/fixed variables which can be derived from file information. An individual's score can range from 0 to a maximum of 12. As with the MnSOST-R, the interpretation of risk levels must vary according to individual circumstances. The recommended risk level categorisation is listed in the Appendix and below in Table 2.3. The tool may also be useful for predicting violence recidivism, although the PCL-R (Hare 1991) – outlined below – and the Violence Risk Appraisal Guide (VRAG, Quinsey, Harris, Rice & Cormier 1998) may be superior tools.

*Table 2.3* Recidivism rates for Static 99 risk levels

| Static 99 score | Sample size (%) | Violent recidivism (%) | | | Sexual recidivism (%) | | | Risk category |
|---|---|---|---|---|---|---|---|---|
| | | 5 years | 10 years | 15 years | 5 years | 10 years | 15 years | |
| 0 | 107 (10) | 6 | 12 | 15 | 5 | 11 | 13 | Low |
| 1 | 150 (14) | 11 | 17 | 18 | 6 | 7 | 7 | |
| 2 | 204 (19) | 17 | 25 | 30 | 9 | 13 | 16 | Medium-low |
| 3 | 206 (19) | 22 | 27 | 34 | 12 | 14 | 19 | |
| 4 | 190 (18) | 36 | 44 | 52 | 26 | 31 | 36 | Medium-high |
| 5 | 100 (9) | 42 | 48 | 52 | 33 | 38 | 40 | |
| 6+ | 129 (12) | 44 | 51 | 59 | 39 | 45 | 52 | High |
| Average 3.2 | 1086 (100) | 22 | 32 | 37 | 18 | 22 | 26 | |

Beech, Friendship, Erikson and Hanson (2002) used the Static 99 to assess sexual reconviction rates after six years at risk in a group of 53 convicted sex offenders treated in probation sex offender treatment programmes (Beckett, Beech, Fisher & Fordham 1994). The sexual recidivism base rate was 15 per cent (8 out of 53 men). The Static 99 was a good predictor of risk, with high or medium-high risk men (33 per cent) being over six times more likely to be convicted of a serious sexual assault than low or medium-low risk men (5 per cent).

Information regarding the Static 99 can be obtained from the Solicitor General of Canada website: http://www.sgc.gc.ca/epub/corr/e199902/e199902.htm

## Risk Matrix 2000

The Risk Matrix 2000 (Thornton *et al.*, in submission) is an improved and updated version of the Structured Anchored Clinical Judgement Scale – min (Grubin 1998) that has been widely used in the UK. The revised system contains a section – Risk Matrix 2000/S – that is concerned with sexual reconviction, and a second dimension – Risk Matrix 2000/V – that is designed to predict future non-sexual violent reconviction by sex offenders. The development and cross-validation of the tool was based on two samples:

1   Sample 1 consisted of 647 male sex offenders identified from a central database as having participated during the early 1990s

in the national sex offender treatment programme operating in prisons in England and Wales, and having been subsequently released and at risk for at least two years.

2    Sample 2 comprised all male offenders discharged from prisons in England and Wales in 1979 following a sentence imposed for a sex offence. The follow up period was between 16 and 19 years, and included 429 cases.

Although Sample 1 was older, contained more child molesters and had a shorter follow up period, the results for the two samples were remarkably similar. The four Risk Matrix/S risk categories show a monotonic trend with sexual reconviction rates rising in the expected way. The results are shown in the Appendix and in Table 2.4. The area under the ROC curve was .77 for Sample 1 and .75 for Sample 2. Thornton does not provide comparable rates for child molesters and rapists. However, the results compare favourably with the Static 99.

Risk Matrix 2000/V was designed as a simple predictor of violent reconviction and has been cross-validated on three samples. Only the sex offender sample results are presented in the Appendix. This sample is derived from the same source as Sample 2 described above and comprised 423 sexual offenders. It should be noted that

*Table 2.4* Sexual and violence recidivism rates for Risk Matrix 2000 risk levels

| Risk Matrix/S | | Sexual recidivism rate (n) | | |
|---|---|---|---|---|
| Score | Category | 2-year follow up | 19-year follow up | |
| 0 | I (low) | 0.9% (215) | 8.0%  (87) | |
| 1, 2 | II (medium) | 1.3% (298) | 18.1% (166) | |
| 3, 4 | III (high) | 5.7% (105) | 40.5% (121) | |
| 5 or more | IV (very high) | 17.2%  (29) | 60.0%  (55) | |

| Risk Matrix/V | | | | Violent recidivism rate (n) 19-year follow up |
|---|---|---|---|---|
| Score | Category | | | |
| 0, 1 | I (low) | | | 5% (151) |
| 2, 3 | II (medium) | | | 19% (130) |
| 4, 5 | III (high) | | | 41%  (96) |
| 6 or more | IV (very high) | | | 63%  (46) |

this scale was designed to predict non-sexual violence only. Again, a monotonic trend was apparent with higher rates of violent reconviction being observed for higher risk categories. The area under the ROC curve was .80. This compares favourably with the results of the VRAG and it may be that the Risk Matrix 2000/V is the tool of choice for violence risk prediction with sex offenders.

The Risk Matrix 2000 is intended for use with adult, male, convicted sex offenders. It has not been validated on child, juvenile or female sex offenders. It comprises three steps and all the data can be derived from file information: Step 1 consists of three static variables which result in an individual score ranging from 0 to 6, and an associated risk category. Step 2 relates to four aggravating factors – if two are present, the risk category is raised one level; if all four are present, the risk category is raised two levels. The final category denotes the risk of sexual reconviction. Step 3 relates to the prediction of non-sexual violence: it comprises three static variables which result in an individual score ranging from 0 to 8, and an associated risk category. This category denotes the risk of future violent reconviction.

## Psychopathy Checklist – Revised

The Psychopathy Checklist (Revised) (PCL-R) is subject to copyright and published by Multi-Health Systems Inc (Hare 1991). Although the PLC-R is one of the most rigorously validated and most widely used actuarial instruments, the construct of psychopathy has been widely misrepresented and inaccurately used. It is frequently confused with antisocial or dissocial personality disorder and the category of 'Psychopathic Disorder' as defined in the Mental Health Act (1983) of England and Wales. Rather than assessing personality deviation generally, the PCL-R relates to a specific form of personality disorder. Psychopathy has an early onset, is characteristic of the individual's long-term functioning and results in social dysfunction. Symptoms are usually evident by middle to late childhood and the disorder persists well into adulthood. Psychopathy can be differentiated from other personality disorders on the basis of its characteristic pattern of interpersonal, affective and behavioural symptoms:

> Interpersonally, psychopaths are grandiose, egocentric, manipulative, dominant, forceful and cold-hearted. Affectively, they

display shallow and labile emotions, are unable to form long-lasting bonds to people, principles, or goals, and are lacking in empathy, anxiety, and genuine guilt and remorse. Behaviorally, psychopaths are impulsive and sensation-seeking, and they readily violate social norms. The most obvious expressions of these predispositions involve criminality, substance abuse, and a failure to fulfill social obligations and responsibilities.

(Hare 1991: 3)

There is a range of studies establishing the psychometric properties of the PCL-R, too numerous to report. Essentially, indices of internal consistency (.80), inter-rater reliability (.80–.90) and all aspects of validity are high. Although it measures a unitary construct, it has a stable two-factor structure. Factor 1 consists of items to do with the affective/interpersonal features of psychopaths: egocentricity, manipulativeness, callousness and lack of remorse. Factor 2 reflects features associated with an impulsive, antisocial and unstable life-style. It is Factor 2 which is most strongly correlated with antisocial personality disorder and substance misuse. Factor 1 items are most likely to occur at high levels of the construct (high psychopathy scores) and are most likely to differentiate psychopaths from non-psychopaths. As one might expect, research suggests that scores on Factor 2 decrease sharply with age, while scores on Factor 1 appear to remain stable with age.

The PCL-R is a 20-item clinical construct rating scale, completed on the basis of an interview and detailed collateral or file information. Each item is scored on a three point scale: 0 = the item does not apply; 1 = the item applies to a certain extent or there is uncertainty that it applies; 2 = the item definitely applies. The 20 items can therefore produce a score ranging from 0 to 40. In North America, average PCL-R scores in male and female offender populations typically range from 22 to 24 and in forensic psychiatric populations are slightly lower at around 20. The recommended cut-off point for researchers identifying psychopathy is a score of 30. However, cross-cultural research in Scotland (Cooke 1998) suggests that there is a lower prevalence of psychopathy in the UK. For example, a PCL-R score of 25 in Scotland is metrically equivalent to the diagnostic cut-off score of 30 in North America. Even utilising this lower cut-off, only 8 per cent of offenders within Scottish prisons were found to be psychopathic compared to approximately 29 per cent in North American samples.

There is increasing evidence for the reliability and validity of the PCL-R with female offenders and psychiatric patients. With slight modifications, it can also be useful with adolescents (PCL – Youth Version: Forth, Kosson & Hare 2003).

The PCL-R is potentially cumbersome to rate as it requires hours, rather than minutes, to complete. Ratings cannot be made on the basis of interview alone and adequate collateral information is a prerequisite. Indeed, if there are discrepancies between the interview and the file information, greater weight is given to information from the source most suggestive of psychopathology. Furthermore, items are rated on the basis of the person's lifetime functioning and not on the basis of the individual's present state; that is, across the life span and across domains of functioning. For example, a sex offender may demonstrate a lack of responsibility, empathy and remorse in interview, in relation to the index offence, but may not have displayed these characteristics over the period of their adult life.

Some PCL-R items are quantifiable, such as 'many short-term marital relationships' or 'juvenile delinquency'. However, the majority require a clinical appraisal in line with the extensive PCL-R manual guidelines. For example, in rating 'impulsivity', the item describes:

> an individual whose behavior is generally impulsive, unpremeditated, and lacking in reflection or forethought. He usually does things on the 'spur of the moment' because he 'feels like it' or because an opportunity presents itself. He is unlikely to spend much time weighing the pros and cons of a course of action, or in considering the possible consequences of a course of action, or in considering the possible consequences of his actions to himself or others. He will often break off relationships, quit jobs, change plans suddenly, or move from place to place, on little more than a whim and without bothering to inform others.
>
> (Hare 1991: 25)

Given the importance of the PCL-R in predicting violent recidivism and its potential role in detaining offenders within restricted settings, the potential for harm is considerable if it is not used correctly. Hare recommends that the assessor should be a registered psychologist or psychiatrist, should have experience with forensic populations, should limit their use of the PCL-R to those populations in which it has been fully validated and should ensure that they have adequate training and experienced in its use. Specifically, he recommends that the scores of two independent raters should be averaged so as to increase the reliability of the assessment, and that five to ten practice assessments should be completed in order to ensure acceptable levels of inter-rater reliability.

There is a screening version available (PCL:SV) which is less onerous to complete and can be used for screening psychopathy in forensic populations. It has the same factor structure as the PLC-R and comprises 12 items, scores ranging from 0 to 24. A cut-off score of 18 is considered equivalent to a score of 30 on the PCL-R.

In terms of sex offenders, the prevalence of psychopathy (a score of 30 plus) appears to be relatively high among convicted rapists and those identified as sexually dangerous. Forth and Kroner (1995) found that 26.1 per cent of incarcerated rapists, 18.3 per cent of mixed rapist/child molester offenders and 5.4 per cent of incest offenders were psychopaths. Of those rapists who were serial offenders or killed their victims, 35 per cent were psychopaths. These findings were supported by the work of Porter, Fairweather, Drugge, Herve, Birt and Boer (2000) who found that 39 per cent of their 95 psychopathic sex offenders had raped only adult victims, 17 per cent had offended against both children and adults, 4 per cent had committed only incest, 3 per cent had molested children outside the family and 1 per cent had molested children both in and out of the family. Porter *et al.* suggested that psychopathy may add little to the prediction of sexual recidivism in child molesters, given that psychopathy is considerably less common in molesters than in the general prison population. However, those that crossed over from child to adult victims were nearly all psychopaths and also had the highest Factor 1 scores, indicating a ruthless and callous personality.

Quinsey, Rice and Harris (1995) followed up treated rapists and child molesters and found that within six years of release more than 80 per cent of psychopaths but only about 20 per cent of non-psychopaths violently recidivated. Rice and Harris (1997) reported that sexual recidivism was strongly predicted by a combination of a high PCL-R score and phallometric evidence of deviant sexual arousal (see SORAG, below).

## Sex Offender Risk Appraisal Guide (SORAG)

The Sex Offender Risk Appraisal Guide (SORAG) (Quinsey *et al.*
1998) has been developed as an extension of the work on the Violence
Risk Appraisal Guide (VRAG), with the specific aim of identifying
recidivism risk in sex offenders. It aims to predict violent – including
sexual – recidivism, as well as purely sexual recidivism. The
researchers have published extensively on the subject of risk, much of
which can be found in their book, *Violent Offenders* (1998). Data
related to the SORAG, as well as the VRAG, is outlined below. The
samples used for the development of the instrument were all derived
from one institution – Oak Ridge, a high secure psychiatric facility
in Canada, comprising assessment beds and inpatient treatment
facilities for mentally disordered offenders. Although the admission
population resembles that of a prison, the cross-sectional population
comprises a more severely mentally disordered group. The treatment
programmes include a behavioural regime and a therapeutic community regime. The sex offender samples are described in four pub-
lications, Quinsey *et al.* (1995), Rice and Harris (1997), Rice,
Harris and Quinsey (1990, 1991). The subjects included both adult
rapists and child molesters, but excluded any non-contact sexual
offenders. A validation sample comprised of a total of 288 sex
offenders (142 child molesters, 88 rapists and 58 who met both sets
of criteria). Twenty-five subjects (9 per cent) in the sample had a
diagnosis of schizophrenia, a significantly greater number being in
the mixed victim type group. Furthermore, approximately one third
received more than five years of treatment in the maximum security
psychiatric facility. The mean opportunity to reoffend was almost
ten years. Overall the base rate of violent recidivism was high: 58 per
cent of the subjects committed another violent (including sexual)
offence; 35 per cent committed a new sexual offence.

The correlation of the VRAG with violent recidivism was .47
(ROC .77) in the validation sample; and the correlation with sexual
recidivism was .20 (ROC .62). Victim injury – inversely related to
violent recidivism in a study of non-sex offenders – was positively
related to sexual recidivism and unrelated to violent failure in
this study. Being a rapist or a child molester with male victims, or
multiple types of victim, was associated with sexual and violent
recidivism. These items were incorporated into the SORAG.

There was a marked interaction between psychopathy (as defined
by a cut-off score of 25+) and sexual deviance (an absolute preference

*Table 2.5* SORAG categories and the probability of violent recidivism over 7 and 10 years

| SORAG category | SORAG score | 7 years | SORAG score | 10 years |
|---|---|---|---|---|
| 1 | <-9 | 0.07 | >-10 | 0.09 |
| 2 | -9 to -4 | 0.15 | -10 to -5 | 0.12 |
| 3 | -3 to +2 | 0.23 | -4 to +1 | 0.39 |
| 4 | +3 to +8 | 0.35 | +2 to +7 | 0.59 |
| 5 | +9 to +14 | 0.45 | +8 to +13 | 0.59 |
| 6 | +15 to +19 | 0.58 | +14 to +19 | 0.76 |
| 7 | +20 to +24 | 0.58 | +20 to +25 | 0.89 |
| 8 | +25 to +30 | 0.75 | +26 to +31 | 0.89 |
| 9 | +31 and higher | 1.00 | +31 and higher | 1.00 |

for deviant stimuli on phallometric assessment) in the survival analyses for sexual recidivism but not for violent recidivism. The authors hypothesise that, for a non-psychopath, concern for the victim and lack of selfishness and callousness would help an individual with deviant preferences to restrain his sexual behaviour. A psychopath with deviant preferences would act on them. Conversely, a psychopath without deviant sexual preferences is likely to commit further violence, but that violence is not especially likely to be sexual. As before, those sex offenders whose victims come from all categories – adult, child, male, female – are the most dangerous of all: they are generally psychopathic offenders whose thrill-seeking and impulsive propensities include a sexual component; in the absence of empathy or remorse, they can victimise different types of victim when the opportunity arises or when they grow bored (Porter *et al.* 2000).

The SORAG comprises 14 variables and an individual can score between a minimum of −23 and a maximum of +47. There are nine possible SORAG categories, each with its estimated probability of violent recidivism over a seven- and ten-year period. See the Appendix and Table 2.5 for the cut-off scores.

## JJPI Juvenile Sex Offender Risk Assessment Schedule

Prentky *et al.* (2000) developed the JJPI as an actuarially based procedure for assessing risk with juvenile sex offenders. They were concerned that the most comprehensive collection of literature on adolescent sex offenders made little or no mention of risk assessment, and pointed out that mention of 'high risk' factors related to identified treatment needs, rather than robust evidence for a relationship between identified problems and their relationship to recidivism. The items for the JJPI scale were drawn from the known clinical and academic expertise in the area as well as the risk literature on adult sex offenders. Twenty-three items fell into four factors, the first two comprising static variables and the second two comprising dynamic variables:

- Factor I: Sexual drive/sexual preoccupation
- Factor II: Impulsive/antisocial behaviour
- Factor III: Clinical/treatment
- Factor IV: Community adjustment

Outcome variables were comprehensive and included type of re-offending (from court records and interviews with carers), removal from the community to a residential facility or prison and the reason for placement (poor adjustment, high risk, reoffended).

The sample consisted of 96 juvenile sexual offenders (ranging from 9 to 20 years) referred for assessment and treatment at an inner-city establishment, two thirds of whom had been convicted. The subtypes of offender were carefully defined and included child molesters, rapists and non-contact sexual offenders. Victims ranged in age from 2 to 35 years, and their relationship to the offender was largely family (55 per cent) and acquaintance (41 per cent). The scale was completed as part of a comprehensive intake battery – coded from archival documents and data obtained by clinicians at assessment – and readministered at the time of discharge, on average two years later. Follow up data was obtained for 75 of the 96 subjects, 12 months after discharge, and included court record information and follow up assessment information.

Inter-rater reliability was good for all but one item (averaging .83) and internal consistency was adequate for Factors II, III and IV (alphas from .68 to .73). However, the only item in Factor I with a reasonably high correlation with the total score was 'prior charged sex offences'.

The base rate for sexual recidivism was extremely low – 4 per cent – and precluded any meaningful statistical analysis. The overall recidivism rate of 11 per cent included three sexual offences, four non-sexual victim-involved offences and one non-sexual victimless offence. Clearly the relatively small sample, the short follow up period and the probable prevention of offences by removing some offenders back into a residential setting will all have contributed to the low base rate. A descriptive analysis of the outcome data found that Factor I was unsatisfactory because although it predicted removal from the community it was not associated with sexual reoffending. There was support for the role of Factors II, III and IV as well as the total risk score which was associated with the range of community failures.

Clearly, the JJPI tool needs to be developed and more widely validated if it is to provide a robust prediction of sexual recidivism in adolescents. Although in its infancy it is nevertheless one of the few actuarially based approaches to assessing risk in adolescents and preliminary findings are promising. The tool and its scoring system are detailed in the Appendix. While practitioners should feel confident that the items are likely to be the most relevant to risk, *extreme caution should be applied in utilising the scoring system* until further research has established its validity.

## Case studies

Table 2.6 details the risk prediction scores for *Stephen, Anthony, James, Peter* and *Martin*, using the schedules given above. One can immediately identify striking differences between the tools for the same offender, both in terms of categorisation and in terms of estimated probability of a sexual reconviction.

*Stephen* is generally rated as a low risk offender with a less than 20 per cent chance of reconviction, yet the Risk Matrix 2000 labels him as medium risk, albeit with a chance of reconviction of between 1–18 per cent depending on years at risk. The discrepancy for *Anthony* is highest between the MnSOST-R and the SORAG, which assess his likelihood of reconviction as 16 per cent and 76 per cent respectively. Both *Peter* and *Martin* are consistently viewed as very high risk for sexual offending.

The extent to which these preliminary actuarial assessments – based largely on fixed or historical factors – are relevant to the community management plans and accurate in terms of the outcomes for the five cases will become evident throughout the rest of the

*Table 2.6* Actuarial risk assessment results for the case studies

|  | *Stephen* | *Anthony* | *James* | *Peter* | *Martin* |
|---|---|---|---|---|---|
| *Likelihood of reoffending* |  |  |  |  |  |
| Static 99 (10 years) | Score = 0 Low 11% | Score = 5 Med-high 38% | Score = 6 High 45% | Score = 6 High 45% | Score = 7 High 45% |
| Risk Matrix 2000 S/V | Medium-S Medium-V | High-S High-V | High-S Low-V | V.high-S medium-V | V.high-S Low-V |
| MnSOST-R (6 years) | Score = –7 Low 16% | Score = 3 Low 16% | Score = 2 Low 16% | Score = 8 High 70% | Score = 12 High 70% |
| SORAG (10 years) | Category 1 9% | Category 6 76% | Category 3 39% | Category 5 59% | Category 7 80% |
| PCL-R | <4 | 15–24 | 10–14 | 5–9 | 15–24 |
| **Seriousness of impact** | Potentially high | Variable | Very high | Variable | Variable |
| **Public interest** | Low | Low | High | Medium | High |

book. The somewhat discrepant results in Table 2.6 highlight three important points. First, actuarial tools are best understood in terms of relative results; that is, one offender is higher risk or lower risk than another offender. Second, the label 'low' or 'high' in different tools refers to different probabilities of sexual recidivism, so it is important to remember the underlying reconviction rates in relation to the relevant time at risk in the community. Finally, whenever there is controversy or disagreement over the risk that a sex offender may pose, it is helpful to compare the results of at least two actuarial tools.

As emphasised in Chapter 1, consideration of the likelihood of reoffending should be made separately from the seriousness of impact or the public interest should reoffending occur. Table 2.6 also contains a crude attempt to estimate these factors in relation to each offender.

For example, while *Stephen*, as an incest offender, might cause the most profound emotional harm to a child in his care if offending went undetected over time, reconviction is unlikely to stir up public interest. In contrast, it is difficult to estimate the degree to which *Martin* might cause enduring harm to a child if he reoffended (depending on a range of indeterminate variables), although public interest and unrest in response to his release from prison must form a central consideration in his risk management plan. Should *James* reoffend, it is common sense to assume that his offence might be potentially fatal to a future victim, with serious consequences for the agencies involved; in such cases, any actuarial assessment which places him as low risk would have to be markedly adjusted to take account of these factors.

# Chapter 3

# Fixed and dynamic variables associated with risk

## Introduction

Having endorsed the role of actuarial assessment tools in predicting risk, with modest enthusiasm, this chapter aims to introduce a rather cautionary note. So much emphasis over the past few years has been placed on persuading professionals to anchor their clinical judgement with actuarial assessments that there is a danger that we can lose sight of the meaning behind risk factors (Grubin & Wingate 1996). Sex offenders are more than a handful of historical variables; they have complex behavioural and emotional difficulties which, admittedly, the actuarial tools may represent in summarised form. Risk, based on a percentage likelihood of reoffending over the long term, tells us little about the subgroup of offenders to whom the percentage applies, nor when or why they might reoffend.

This chapter examines the main characteristics of sex offenders which are relevant to a risk assessment. It is neither exhaustive nor is it a substitute for a broad-ranging clinical assessment (see Craissati 1998 for details on assessing child molesters). It is not limited to those characteristics which have been consistently proven to be related to risk; indeed, it specifically identifies a range of variables – often dynamic – which are positively *unrelated* to risk, but commonly believed to be important. Where studies have compared child molesters and rapists a detailed breakdown is given; otherwise, the discussion is general to all sex offenders.

## Fixed variables

Fixed variables are sometimes referred to as 'static' or 'historical'. The term refers to characteristics of the offender which cannot be changed. The cluster of fixed variables which are important in sex offender risk prediction are found in the common actuarial tools (see Chapter 2) and are largely overlapping between tools. The variables fall into two main categories: offending history and personal history.

## Offending history

### Previous sexual charges/convictions

The salience of this variable is, perhaps, obvious; and there is no risk assessment which does not give it key importance. It represents those sex offenders who are prepared to put their urges into practice. It may suggest a compelling drive to offend or a disregard for personal and social rules. Critics will immediately point out that a large number of sex offenders remain undetected or are only caught for a small proportion of their crimes. This view is based on the assumption – as yet unproven – that convicted sex offenders are no different from their unconvicted counterparts. On the contrary, there is likely to be something different about offenders who offend sufficiently often, perhaps against victims more likely to disclose, with sufficient recklessness, that they are eventually caught and convicted. They may be impervious to feelings of apprehension about being caught again, or life inside prison may not be the terrifying prospect that it would be to other sex offenders.

### Previous violent or general convictions

Some caution needs to be applied in considering this variable, not least because it may be of differential importance in rapists as compared to child molesters. Arguably, these two variables are capturing the essence of the dynamic variable, antisocial personality disorder; that is, a propensity for aggressive behaviour, anti-authoritarian attitudes and general criminality which may be associated with substance misuse problems or a poor employment record. Research generally suggests that child molesters have lower levels of prior violent or general convictions than rapists (Quinsey *et al.* 1995), but nevertheless the variables contribute to sexual recidivism in both subgroups.

*Victim variables: gender and relationship to perpetrator*

All research identifies male victims as a key risk variable for child molesters. It is not clear to what extent this applies to rapists as, historically, convictions of sexual assault by men on men are extremely rare. The evidence suggests that a male victim is much more likely to represent a fixed and enduring deviant sexual interest (see sexual arousal in the dynamic factors section, p. 60); this is particularly the case if the offender also has previous sexual convictions (Hanson *et al.* 1993). Clinically, this group of sex offenders may present with more 'perverse' psychosexual functioning, a tendency to relate to their victim as an extension of their internal world (Glasser 1988).

Risk also rises the less close the pre-existing relationship between offender and victim is – from relative, to aquaintance, to stranger (Hanson & Harris 2000), and this applies to both rapists and child molesters. Clinical judgement may differ as to the explanation for this. It may be 'practical' considerations which apply; that is, offenders who seek victims who are close to them, wish to minimise the chances of apprehension and take pains to seduce the child carefully over time; they may have difficulty in selecting future victims because of these considerations. Clinical experience would suggest that intimacy deficits and attachment problems may be more profound in those offenders who select stranger victims, and they may be more able to dehumanise their victim and be more impervious to victim distress and fear. Further evidence of a link between victim gender and victim-perpetrator relationship is the assertion (Abel *et al.* 1987) that fathers rarely sexually abuse their sons, comprising less than 8 per cent of all child molestation cases. A caveat needs to be that boys have traditionally been thought to be less likely to disclose sexual abuse (Watkins & Bentovim 1992).

A contentious issue, and one that is highly pertinent to risk, is the potential for crossover in offending, either in terms of victim gender or offence type. As with other relatively rare characteristics, actuarial tools based on large sample sizes do not find gender crossover to be predictive of risk. Individual studies have found variable results: child molesters who have offence victims of both sexes do not usually pose a greater risk than those with male only victims (Firestone, Bradford, McCoy, Greenberg, Curry & Larose 2000a; Hanson *et al.* 1993). Approximately 10 per cent (see Grubin 1998) of child molesters have victims of both sexes. Thornton and Hanson

(1996) found that only those child molesters with male child victims
(<13 years) were at risk for reoffending against females (14 per cent);
less than 3 per cent of offenders with female child or adolescent
victims reoffended against males; there were almost no rapists who
crossed over gender when reoffending.

Similarly, the question is often raised regarding the likelihood
of crossover between child molestation and rape. Craissati, Falla,
McClurg and Beech (2002) found that 4 per cent of their child
molesters had previous sexual convictions against adult women;
Quinsey *et al.* (1995) found that 5 per cent of their child molesters
reoffended against adults and none of their rapists reoffended
against children. However, as the research on actuarial tools highlights, those offenders with mixed victim types – child and adult – are
more likely to be psychopathic, more prone to recidivate at a faster
rate and most likely to sexually reoffend. As previously discussed,
this is likely to reflect callous, sensation-seeking individuals who
opportunistically offend, often as an antidote to 'boredom'.

### Prior non-contact offences

Two of the five risk prediction tools outlined in Chapter 2 rate prior
non-contact offences as a significant variable. This issue must be
considered quite separately from the question of risk in those
offenders who have *only* committed non-contact sex offences. Risk
prediction, in this book, is focused on contact sex offenders. There
are probably two main behaviours to consider: indecent exposure or
exhibitionism and illegal pornography, including that available on
the internet.

Although now rather out of date, Gayford (1981) reviewed the
literature on indecent exposure. He found that indecent exposers
were most commonly in the younger age group (mid-20s); 20 per cent
had a history of other sexual offences and an overlapping 20 per
cent had a history of other criminal offences; 80 per cent of those
who appear in court are first offenders and the assumption is that
the majority do not reoffend, the court case itself acting as a major
deterrent.

In a study, much criticised for its confused presentation of results
and its biased sampling procedure (Craissati 1998; Fisher &
Thornton 1993), Abel *et al.* (1987) attempted to assess self-reported
sexual behaviours in a specially recruited group of sex offenders.
They found that 11 per cent of rapists and between 6 to 18 per cent

of child molesters had a secondary diagnosis of exhibitionism. Bard, Carter, Cerce, Knight, Rosenberg and Schneider (1987) found that rapists and child molesters had equal rates of prior offences for indecent exposure and voyeurism (30–31 per cent).

Essentially, this is a question of *escalation*. It is a commonly held belief among both professionals and the public that sex offenders escalate their behaviour over time. Clearly a small proportion of indecent exposers go on to commit contact offences. But within an offence type there is little evidence for escalation – if anything, child molesters are reconvicted for less violent or intrusive offending over time (McClurg & Craissati 1999).

Pornography as a clearly identifiable risk factor is usually taken to mean prior arrests or convictions for the possession of, or intent to supply, illegal pornography. It must be said that pornography, in some ways, is in the eye of the beholder. Child molesters have long been noted to identify apparently harmless films, such as *Oliver!*, or children's television, mail order catalogues and so on as a source of sexual fantasy and stimulation. The same is true of rapists who may feed on mainstream violent imagery or legal 'soft' pornography to fuel sexually aggressive impulses. The use of explicit child pornography is probably uncommon (Howitt 1995) and Elliott, Browne and Kilcoyne (1995) found that only one fifth of their sample of child molesters said they knew where to obtain child prostitutes and illegal child pornography. This figure is supported by Bauserman's (1996) review of pornography and sexual offending. As a risk factor, illegal pornography is likely to reflect the extent to which the offender is driven to seek explicit sexual imagery and is thus preoccupied with his deviant sexual impulses.

There is no published research on the link between involvement in the child pornography industry and risk for contact sexual offences. This is particularly the case for recent cases involving pornography available on the internet, about 10 per cent of which is thought to relate to children (Grubin 1998). Bauserman (1996) found that rapists and child molesters tended to be exposed to sexual materials at a later age and reported less use in adolescence than non-sex offenders. There is clearer evidence that a proportion of sex offenders – ranging from 16 to 38 per cent in different studies – report pornography played a role in their offending, either as preparation for the offence or as part of the act itself. However, only a small proportion of this pornographic material would have been illegal.

Bauserman suggests that it is the unusual sexual fantasies of rapists and child molesters which perpetuate their arousal patterns, and sexually explicit materials are simply integrated into those patterns rather than shaping them. There is no evidence that use of pornography is related to key aspects of the offending behaviour, such as the number of victims or the degree of violence used. It is worth noting that many sex offenders have been reported as stating that pornography provided a 'safety valve' for antisocial impulses, relieving them of the desire to commit an offence. However, there does not appear to be empirical research to corroborate this assertion.

## Use of force in the index offence

The use of excessive force in the index sexual offence is directly assessed by the MnSOST-R and is alluded to in Static 99 in terms of an additional index conviction for violence. Many professionals find it difficult to distinguish between the aggressive components of any sexual assault, particularly rape, which are likely to be more or less implicit, and the requirement for some element of additional or excessive violence. Force may relate to severe attachment deficits (see below) or the effects of serious alcohol or drug intoxication; in rare cases it may reflect a degree of rage in the offender which is very near the surface and potentially life threatening. The degree of physical harm inflicted on the victim has not been shown to be reliably related to risk unless there has been clear evidence of an escalation in the degree of violence over time (see the section on homicide, p. 46). With rapists, one of the greatest pitfalls in assessing the likelihood of future offending, is to place too much emphasis on the degree of terror or humiliation experienced by the victim, unless there is clear evidence of sadistic sexual interests.

## Penetration in the offence

Penetration – vaginal or anal – in the offences of either child molesters or rapists has *not* been shown to be related to future risk. Ironically, many child molesters will choose to admit to fondling, masturbation and oral sex with the victim, but adamantly deny an allegation of penile penetration as though this represented a markedly more serious level of behaviour. Clinically, it becomes clear that most penetration by child molesters is perpetrated by intrafamilial offenders with female victims, and that their implicit aim is to mimic adult heterosexual activity. The high risk child molesters, those who offend against boys and strangers, are much more likely to report preoccupations with fondling and masturbating, and less drive and/or opportunity to strive for penile penetration.

## Homicide

In Britain, the number of sexually motivated homicides is thought to be tiny. Despite increased media attention the official figures suggest that the incidence of stranger killings of women in England and Wales remains steady, around 30 per annum, 10 to 15 per cent of all female homicides (Home Office 1995). Nevertheless, practitioners are occasionally faced with two important risk considerations: First, determining whether a worrying, high risk sex offender is likely to escalate his offending to homicide. Second, whether an offender serving mandatory or discretionary life for a sexually motivated homicide could be considered for release.

There are considerable methodological problems in determining whether (or how) sexually motivated homicide contributes to risk. The limited research available is largely derived from small samples studied in the USA. Many such studies are concerned with serial sexual homicide; that is, men who have murdered more than once before being apprehended and incarcerated. This comprises a tiny proportion of all homicides and only a subsection of sexually motivated homicides. Furthermore, the published material is particularly horrific in its detailing of unusual and abhorrent crimes, which is likely to provoke in the reader a sense of uncomfortable voyeurism and intense anxiety. Of course, incarcerated sexual homicide offenders are rarely released from custody, given the potential for devastating harm should they reoffend. This is likely to represent a large number of false positive predictions of risk, and does not assist us greatly in establishing the important factors predictive of success upon release.

Keppel and Walter (1999) have detailed a typology of sexual murder which comprises four categories (the descriptions of which are quoted from the article). The *power-assertive rape-murder* is a series of acts in which the rape is planned, whereas the murder is an unplanned response of increasing aggression to ensure control of the victim. When the perpetrator senses a challenge to his control and masculine image – or a revelation of his internal weaknesses – he may become even more violent. The *power-reassurance rape-murderer* has no intent to harm or degrade the victim, but the failure of the rape-assault and the rejection from the victim panics him into a homicide overkill. Believing that he can act sexual fantasy in reality, he prepares a scenario designed to seduce the victim into validating his sexual competence. When the victim does not follow his plan, he feels threatened. The *anger-retaliatory rape-murderer* plans the rape and the murder involves overkill. It is an anger-venting act that expresses symbolic revenge on a female victim. Nettled by poor relationships with women, the aggressor distills his anguish and contempt into an explosive revenge on the victim. Although the assault is not predicated on a fantasy system it is often precipitated by a criticism or scolding from a woman with power over the subject. Regardless of whether the victim is alive or dead, the assault continues until the subject is emotionally satisfied. The *anger-excitation rape-murderer* selects the victim and escalates violence through various acquired and learned incremental levels of ritualistic carnage. Unlike other murderers, the luxury of sadism is found in the art and process of killing, not the death. In some instances the actual death may be anticlimactic. However, excitement is hightened by the realisation of a rehearsed scenario of eroticised anger and power that has been building in the subject's fantasy life.

Canadian statistics suggest that only 3 per cent of homicides in Canada between 1985 and 1995 were sexually related (Firestone, Bradford, Greenberg & Larose 1998), and that these offenders comprise a subset of serial sex offenders against strangers, most frequently victimising women and children. Langevin, Ben-Aaron, Wright, Marchese and Handy (1988) compared a small number of sex offence killers, non-sex offence killers and non-homicidal sexually aggressive men; they found that the three groups were more similar than different, although the sex offence killers victimised strangers more frequently and were more likely to have a diagnosis of antisocial personality disorder and a higher incidence of sexual sadism. Firestone *et al.* (1998) found that in comparison to incest offenders, sexual homicide offenders reported themselves as functioning better in terms of sexuality and psychological well-being. Significantly, they also scored much higher on the PCL-R (psychopathy), with particularly raised levels on Factor I. As might be expected, the sexual homicide group demonstrated much greater levels of paraphilia – non-contact behaviours such as exhibitionism, cross-dressing and voyeurism – and this has been observed in other studies.

Burglary may be an important variable in the consideration of potential homicide risk, although studies are hampered by being retrospective rather than prospective. Schlesinger and Revitch (1999) studied 52 sexual murderers and found that 42 per cent had a history of burglary. None of these individuals had simply committed burglaries for financial gain: 32 per cent were defined as committing 'fetish' burglaries with overt sexual dynamics and 68 per cent were classified as committing 'voyeuristic' burglaries. Almost all the victims were adult women, 68 per cent of whom were killed by voyeuristic burglars. Where a woman was killed in her own residence, there was a 77 per cent chance that the offender had a history of sexual burglary.

Firestone *et al.* (2000b) went on to compare homicidal child molesters with non-homicidal child molesters and non-offenders. Approximately half of both the child molester groups exhibited a significant sexual interest in children, as measured by phallometry, but significantly more of the homicidal group demonstrated sexual arousal to coercive/aggressive scenes with children (63 per cent). However, it should be noted that 37 per cent of the homicidal group did not show arousal to coercive scenes, and in fact 40 per cent of the non-homicidal child molesters were significantly aroused by coercive scenes. This would appear to suggest that although deviant sexual interest is an important factor (see below), there is considerable variability within the group of sexually motivated murderers.

### Personal history

#### Age

Strictly speaking, age is a dynamic factor, but since it is not amenable to intervention it falls best among the fixed factors. The actuarial tools clearly demonstrate the importance of age in determining risk. Unlike general offenders, whose propensity to act out diminishes with age in a linear fashion, adolescent sex offenders and sex offenders over 30 are thought to pose a lower risk than those in their twenties. A recent review of recidivism and age (Hanson 2002) established that it is important to differentiate between types of offender: rapists tended to be younger than child molesters and their recidivism rate steadily decreased with age; extrafamilial child molesters showed relatively little reduction in recidivism until after the age of 50; incest offenders were older and the recidivism rate was – as expected – low. Hanson hypothesised that developmental changes in key variables – sexual drive, self-control/impulsivity and opportunities to offend – underpinned these findings.

*Intelligence*

There is a common understanding that sexual offending is committed by individuals of all levels of social and educational standing. However, clinical impressions may suggest that offenders tend to have below average levels of intelligence. This could relate to a differential propensity to be caught, or a less sophisticated defence strategy which is more likely to result in a conviction. The empirical support for intelligence (IQ) as a significant risk variable is unclear. Certainly, Hanson, Steffy and Gauthier (1993) did find that low IQ was associated with recidivism, but examination of the mean scores showed that both recidivists and non-recidivists were scoring within the average range of cognitive functioning.

There has been some work looking at sex offending and recidivism in those sex offenders who have an identified learning/intellectual disability. However, research is limited to very small sample sizes and sampling bias, and to date has not made reference to known risk predictors in the general sex offending population. For example, almost no reference is made to the victim-perpetrator relationship, victim age or gender. Indeed, a recent review on offenders with intellectual disabilities (Lindsay 2002) concludes that the extent to which there is an association between such individuals and sexual offending remains unclear. What evidence there is suggests that between 21 and 50 per cent of offenders with intellectual disabilities have committed a sexual crime (Gross 1985; Sundram 1990) and mentally impaired offenders committed under a hospital order for sexual offences comprise 30 per cent of this population (Walker & McCabe 1968). Sexual recidivism rates are difficult to determine: Lindsay, Smith, Law, Quinn, Anderson, Smith, Overend and Allan (2002) report on 48 clients followed up for between one and four years, 4 per cent of whom had reoffended at one year, 21 per cent having reoffended at four years. An Australian study (Klimecki, Jenkinson & Wilson 1994) reported on offenders with a mild intellectual impairment, followed up for three years, and found that

32 per cent of the sex offenders reoffended; a substantial proportion of recidivists had a history of psychiatric disorder and substance misuse. These high recidivism figures may reflect the well-documented distortions in the criminal justice process which render intellectually disabled offenders more vulnerable than the general population (Murphy & Mason 1999). A report on the follow up of 391 patients in 1994, discharged from hospital having been detained on restricted hospital orders between 1987 and 1990, found that 5 per cent were reconvicted of serious offences (including sexual and violent); 10 per cent of this sample were detained under the category of mental impairment (see Chapter 6) (Street 1998).

## Attachment

There are three main variables discussed in the research literature which relate broadly to attachment issues. These are a negative relationship with mother as a child (Craissati, McClurg & Browne 2002b; Hanson & Bussiere 1998); single status as an adult or never having had a live-in lover for two or more years (Hanson & Thornton 2000; Quinsey *et al.* 1995); and being sexually abused as a child (Craissati, McClurg & Browne 2002a).

In recent years, attachment experiences in sex offenders have begun to be studied (Hudson & Ward 1997; Marshall, Hudson & Hodkinson 1993), usually underpinned by Griffin and Bartholomew's (1994) model of four attachment types. The premise is that erratic and rejecting parenting behaviours, which alienate children from the possibility of forming secure attachment bonds, distinguish the family context in which sex offenders grow up (Marshall 1989). Support for this was identified by Hanson and Bussiere (1998) who found that a negative relationship with mother was the sole developmental history variable related to sexual offence recidivism. Further research by Ward, Hudson and Marshall (1996) has found rapists to be more likely to be dismissive and child molesters fearful/preoccupied in their attachment styles. Smallbone and Dadds (1998) found that sex offenders only differed from property offenders in their maternal attachments which were less secure; specifically, they found intrafamilial child molesters to be more likely to regard their mothers as unloving, inconsistent and abusive, while rapists were more likely to regard their fathers as uncaring and abusive to them. Craissati *et al.* (2002b) found that low levels of maternal care were linked to verbal threats to the offence victim for both child molesters and rapists, and there was a link between poor maternal care in child molesters and a history of previous sexual or violent offending.

Strictly speaking, the variable of single status/never having lived with a lover for two or more years could be considered a dynamic factor, for sex offenders may, over the years, develop lasting adult relationships. However, it is so often considered a static variable it is discussed here. Much of the discussion on intimacy deficits, in the dynamic section below, is very relevant. For this variable – so strongly related to risk – to have some clinical validity there needs to be an understanding of its meaning for individual sex offenders. Being single, of course, may well reflect a primary lack of interest in forming relationships with adults, and would therefore be considered an indicator of deviant sexual interest. However, it may reflect a deficit in an individual's capacity for empathy or marked avoidance of potentially threatening – albeit desirable – adult intimacy. Looked at from the opposite point of view, being married may have a protective effect (Grubin & Wingate 1996): offenders no longer need to seek out partners or the emotional support of a partner may decrease loneliness or feelings of inadequacy.

Strictly speaking, sexual abuse as a child has not been shown to be a strong predictor of risk. However, it is clinically important and may well have an indirect relationship to recidivism. Despite variability in findings, due to sampling effects and research design, one can be confident in saying that sex offenders are more likely than other offenders – and of course the general population – to have been sexually abused in childhood (Craissati et al. 2002a; Weeks & Widom 1998) and that this finding is usually stronger for child molesters than rapists (Bard et al. 1987; Weeks & Widom 1998). Craissati et al. (2002a) found that sexually abused child molesters were significantly more likely to have male victims, to have engaged in sex play with male peers in childhood, to have homosexual contacts in adulthood and to be more honest in reporting offence-related cognitions and sexual preoccupations. In other words, childhood sexual victimisation is likely to make an important contribution to the development of psychosexual disturbance.

## Dynamic variables

In comparison to fixed variables, there has been some difficulty in establishing empirical evidence to support the relevance of many dynamic factors to risk prediction in sex offenders. Until recently, work was largely focused on the role of deviant sexual interests, including the physiological measurement of arousal. More recently, work in Canada (Hanson & Harris 1998, 2000) and in England and Wales (Beckett *et al.* 1994; Beech 1998; Thornton 2002) has begun to establish meaningful relationships between a cluster of dynamic variables and sex offender recidivism.

Dynamic variables are those characteristics of sex offenders which are capable of changing. The most useful, of course, are those that are amenable to deliberate intervention. Hanson and Harris (1998) suggest that dynamic variables can be further subdivided into *stable* risk factors, which would be expected to persist for months or years, and *acute* risk factors, which may last for days or only minutes.

### Stable dynamic variables

Hanson and Harris' work relates to both child molesters and rapists, although they have excluded incest offenders from their analysis. They identified groups of recidivists and non-recidivists, matched on key static variables, and then interviewed their supervising officers in the community using a structured interview schedule and examined the offenders' files. The defining characteristics of this design lay in its emphasis on *observable dynamic variables*, although this method could also lead to problems with reliability if other researchers try to replicate the work. The best three stable predictor variables from the officer interviews strongly differentiated the recidivists from the non-recidivists: these were 'sees self as no risk', 'poor social influences' and 'sexual entitlement'. It should be noted that the differences were generally much stronger for rapists and child molesters with male victims, and not so strong for child molesters with girl victims. From this, the Sex Offender Need Assessment Rating (SONAR) was developed in an attempt to find a standardised method for measuring change in risk levels over time. The SONAR was based on the five dynamic categories outlined in Table 3.1, with the addition of four acute factors. Scores can range from 0 to 14. Overall the scale showed adequate internal consistency and moderate ability to differentiate between recidivists and non-recidivists ($r = .43$; ROC area of .74), even when well-established static risk indicators were controlled for.

Revisions to the SONAR model are ongoing, and up-to-date information – including an expanded and detailed scoring system – can be obtained from Hanson and Harris (email dsp-psd@sgc.gc.ca).

Table 3.1 Dynamic factors related to risk

| Hanson and Harris (1998 & 2000) | Beech (1998) | Thornton (2002) |
|---|---|---|
| **Intimacy deficits**<br>• Grave difficulty in establishing meaningful relationships with adult women<br>• Poor empathy<br>• Numerous, uncommitted relationships | **Social competency**<br>• Self-esteem<br>• Emotional loneliness<br>• Under-assertiveness<br>• Personal distress (general empathy)<br>• Locus of control | **Socio-affective functioning**<br>• Self-esteem<br>• Emotional loneliness<br>• Emotional congruence<br>• Rehearsal of negative emotions<br>• Rumination of anger |
| **Social influences**<br>• Negative peer associates<br>• Peers supporting denial<br>• Peers facilitating victim access<br>• Peers with antisocial attitudes | | |
| **Attitudes**<br>• Little remorse or victim empathy<br>• Sexualisation of children<br>• Sexual entitlement<br>• Antisocial attitudes | **Pro-offending attitudes**<br>• Cognitive distortions<br>• Victim empathy distortions<br>• Emotional identification with child | **Distorted attitudes**<br>• Rape myths<br>• Justifications for sex with children |
| **Sexual self-regulation**<br>• Strong sexual urges to be gratified<br>• Sexual activity increases social status<br>• Sexual activity mitigates life stress<br>• Negative affect leads to sexual imagery | | **Sexual interests** |
| **General self-regulation**<br>• Impulsivity<br>• Lifestyle instability, substances<br>• Non-compliance with supervision<br>• Self as low risk, no avoidance of high risk situations | | **Self-management**<br>• Benign control<br>• Aggression control |

Reproduced from Craissati, J. & Beech, A. (2003) A review of dynamic variables and their relationship to risk prediction in sex offenders, *Journal of Sexual Aggression*, 9: 41–55. www.tandf.co.uk

In England and Wales the development of sex offender treatment programmes has been underpinned by systematic evaluation over the past eight years by the Sex Offender Treatment Evaluation Project (STEP) team evaluation (Beckett *et al.* 1994; Beech 1998; Beech, Fisher & Beckett 1999). This work has focused on child molesters who have engaged in community probation treatment programmes, residential programmes and prison programmes for sex offenders. The STEP team established that child molesters could be divided into 'high deviancy' and 'low deviancy' groups on the basis of their deviation on psychometric measures from non-offending norms. The psychometrics were selected in order to assess pro-offending attitudes and levels of social competency. Specifically, high deviancy means that the dynamic risk factors underlying offending are relatively intense and pervasive. Such offenders perceive children as sexually sophisticated, sexually proactive with adults, unharmed by such contact and able to consent to it; they have a variety of problems dealing with adults and initiating or maintaining intimate relationships with other adults; they are generally underassertive, with low levels of self-esteem; they cannot cope with stressful interpersonal situations and see themselves as having little control over their lives. Low deviancy refers to dynamic risk factors that are relatively weak in intensity and circumscribed in their effect. These offenders do not have globalised cognitive distortions about children or high levels of social incompetence. Beech (1998) determined the deviancy level from psychometric measures using cluster analysis techniques (see Table 3.1 for dynamic domains). As might be expected, Beech found that high deviancy men were typically sexual recidivists who had either committed extrafamilial offences against boys or crossed over between male and female victims or between victims in intra- and extrafamilial situations. In a six-year follow up study of sex offenders receiving community treatment, Beech *et al.* (2002) found that pre-treatment deviancy levels increased the predictive power of Static 99 by between 25 and 86 per cent in terms of reconviction rates (see Table 3.2). Pre-treatment deviancy levels were also crucial in determining the number of treatment hours required to produce treatment change: 78 per cent of low deviancy men showed significant improvements in pro-offending attitudes when given more than 80 hours of group treatment compared to only 20 per cent of high deviancy men. Twice as many hours of treatment (160 plus) were necessary to effect change in pro-offending attitudes for high deviancy men, 60 per cent of whom demonstrated a treatment effect.

Table 3.2 Six-year follow up reconviction rates by Static 99 and pre-treatment deviancy level (Beech et al. 2002)

|  | High deviance | Low deviance | Total sample |
|---|---|---|---|
| **Total sample** | 7/23 (31%) | 1/30 (3%) | 8/53 (15%) |
| **High static** | 2/4 (50%) | 0/1 (0%) | 2/5 (40%) |
| **Medium-high static** | 4/9 (44%) | 0/4 (0%) | 4/13 (31%) |
| **Medium-low static** | 0/2 (0%) | 0/6 (0%) | 0/8 (0%) |
| **Low static** | 1/8 (13%) | 1/19 (5%) | 2/27 (7%) |

Although the sample size is relatively small, the results would suggest in particular that identifying high deviancy sex offenders who would otherwise be considered low or medium risk on static tools would greatly assist risk assessment. The strength of this approach is the use of standardised measures which can easily be replicated. However, psychometrics require a level of training and knowledge that may not be accessible to all practitioners in the field. To this end, the STEP researchers provide regular training in the UK for the psychometric evaluation of sex offenders. There is now an algorithm, based on the results of the measures, with a cumulative scoring procedure which allocates individual offenders to a high or low deviancy category: emotional congruence with children, cognitive distortions regarding children and underassertiveness are the three most heavily weighted variables.

Thornton's (2002) work on an Initial Deviance Assessment (IDA) contains four domains of dynamic variables, as shown in Table 3.1, which overlap with the approach adopted by Hanson and Harris (2000) and Beech (1998). Thornton defines deviancy in terms of the extent to which the offender's functioning is dominated by the psychological factors that contribute to his offending, by means of psychometric measures (akin to Beech 1998). He postulates that the main dynamic risk factors fall into four domains:

- sexual interests;
- distorted attitudes;
- socio-affective functioning;
- self-management.

The IDA has three deviancy levels: high, moderate and low. High deviance is defined as an individual showing problems within at least two domains; moderate deviance is when marked dynamic risk factors are present in just one domain; and low deviance is when no marked dynamic risk factors are apparent. The IDA model was tested on a group of 158 child molesters currently serving a prison sentence and undergoing assessment. The sample was broken into two groups: first-time sexual offenders and recidivist sexual offenders. The repeaters' group tended to score in a more dysfunctional way on all five indicators of social-affective functioning, to demonstrate worse self-management on both indications and to score higher on all measures of distorted attitudes. The IDA was subsequently cross-validated on a sample of 117 adult male sex offenders – including both child molesters and rapists – who were assessed in prison for the sex offender treatment programme, and who had been at risk in the community for an average of three years. Psychometric measures were available for all subjects across three of the four domains; no measures for the 'sexual interests' domain were available. The IDA showed reasonably good ability to differentiate between recidivists and non-recidivists (ROC 0.78). The Static 99 was also completed on the sample and was strongly related to sexual recidivism (ROC .92). Both Static 99 and IDA independently predicted sexual reconviction and combined led to an improved model (see Table 3.3).

## Dynamic domains

The cumulative evidence described above would lend weight to the consideration of five core dynamic domains which have a growing evidence base and which appear to contribute significantly to static risk assessment. The three models utilise different methodologies

*Table 3.3* Reconviction rates by Static 99 and Initial Deviance Assessment (Thornton 2002)*

|  | High deviancy | Medium deviancy | Low deviancy |
| --- | --- | --- | --- |
| **IDA alone** | 5 of 34 (15%) | 2 of 43 (5%) | 0 of 40 (0%) |
| **High static** | 4 of 6 (67%) | 1 of 5 (20%) | 0 of 2 (0%) |
| **Medium-high static** | 1 of 12 (8%) | 1 of 12 (8%) | 0 of 5 (0%) |
| **Medium-low static** | 0 | 0 | 0 |
| **Low static** | 0 | 0 | 0 |

*An average of three years at risk in the community

but there are no inherent contradictions. The domains are described more fully below.

## Intimacy deficits/social competencies

These variables are closely associated with the static variables of never having had a live-in lover, and the victim-perpetrator relationship (acquaintaince/stranger). The importance of intimacy deficits has been widely reported (Marshall 1993; Ward *et al.* 1996), and they are largely manifested by a) an avoidance of adult intimacy in child molesters who fear negative evaluations or b) rapists who lack empathy for women, have multiple uncommitted sexual encounters or experience difficulties in managing assertiveness (Overholser & Beck 1986).

Locus of control (Nowicki 1976) measures the extent to which an individual feels that events are contingent upon their own behaviour and the extent to which they feel that events are outside of their control. Child molesters with an external locus of control are less likely to respond to treatment, more likely to have previous sexual convictions and more likely to reoffend sexually (Fisher, Beech & Browne 1998). It is not clear how far locus of control is a relevant risk predictor for rapists. Low self-esteem has been found to distinguish child molesters from comparison groups. Emotional loneliness seems to distinguish sexual offenders more generally, and appears to be the only aspect of inadequacy which seems to distinguish rapists (Thornton 2002). Emotional identification with children should be distinguished from offence victim attitudes, and includes leisure/work activities as well as attitudes which suggest a child-oriented lifestyle.

Stable levels of negative affect – anxious, depressed or angry individuals – does not appear to predict sexual recidivism. Rather, it would appear that the experience of negative affect, especially that arising from interpersonal conflict (humiliation and resentment) seems to precipitate offence-related fantasies; child molesters may be especially prone to avoidance-focused coping strategies and sex may be used as a way of coping with loneliness (Thornton 2002).

## Social influences

Although the number of criminal companions is one of the strongest predictors of recidivism among the general criminal population, there is limited research on its importance for sex offenders (Hanson & Harris 2000). There is understandable concern when sex offenders associate with other sex offenders, yet sometimes this is likely to be a response to the ostracisation they otherwise encounter. Nevertheless, Hanson and Harris (2000) found it to contribute significantly to a model of dynamic risk prediction. They suggest identifying all those within an offender's network who are not paid to be with him, and then making a judgement as to whether each person is a positive, neutral or negative influence in the offender's life.

### Pro-offending attitudes

The relationship between sexual attitudes supportive of sexual assault – attitudes or values that excuse, permit or condone sexual offending – and sexual offence recidivism seems to be significant, but only to a limited extent (Hanson & Bussiere 1998). An assessment of pro-offending attitudes by means of clinical interview will be heavily influenced by the circumstances in which the offender is being assessed, the degree of shame – rather than distorted belief – that they experience, and the motivational interviewing skills of the assessor (Craissati 1998). Psychometric measures, as utilised by Beckett et al. (1994) assist in standardising responses. It can be surmised that those who readily endorse obviously distorted views may well pose a high risk of recidivism; it is less likely that those who deny pro-offending attitudes can be reliably classified as recidivists or non-recidivists. Generally, pro-offending attitudes are best viewed as a treatment target, psychometric measurement providing an essential pre- and post-treatment comparison (see Chapter 6).

There is likely to be some difficulty in differentiating between child molesters and rapists in terms of pro-offending attitudes. Hanson and Harris (1998) found that there was no significant difference between the two groups in the extent to which they endorsed rape myths or held attitudes which sexualised children. However, they also found that justification for the sex crimes, sexualising children and feeling entitled to express their strong sexual drive were all significant in differentiating between recidivists and non-recidivists generally.

There is also a lack of clarity as to whether empathy deficits are general (as measured by the Interpersonal Reactivity Index, Davis 1980) or specific to a class of potential victims or actual victims, as measured by the Rape Myths Scale (Burt 1980), or victim empathy distortions (Beckett & Fisher 1994). Thornton (2002) found that recidivist child molesters showed more distorted attitudes to sex with children and rape myths, suggestive of a more general tendency to distorted attitudes rather than minimisation of a specific kind of offending. Beech *et al.* (1999), in contrast, found that child molesters did not demonstrate general problems in empathy deficits, although cognitive distortions in relation to their own offence victims contributed to a model of high deviancy.

Finally, it should be noted that *denial of offending behaviour*, whether partial or total, has *never* been shown in the research literature to be significantly associated with future sexual reoffending. This is perhaps the most commonly held myth by professionals in the field, and the area of work which is most likely to result in a position of confrontation and stand-off between an offender and the agency/professional.

### Sexual self-regulation

There is strong evidence to support the view that sex offenders who present with a poorly controlled expression of sexual impulses are at a higher risk of reoffending. In assessing sexual preoccupation, it is important to differentiate between the direction (see deviant sexual interests, below) and the strength of sexual interests; for example, how frequently the offender engages in sexual activity (not necessarily illegal) such as masturbation, consenting intercourse and frequenting prostitutes. Sexual thoughts/activity may be perceived as intrusive by the offender or interfere with other pro-social goals. High risk sex offenders are more likely to respond sexually to stress or negative affect, or feel deprived/frustrated if they are unable to quickly satisfy their sexual urges (Hanson & Harris 2000). Clinically, this is often referred to as 'sexualisation', that is, a preoccupation with sex as a necessary and persistent regulator of self-esteem (Rosen 1979), which comforts the individual in the face of anxiety-provoking internal conflicts. The degree to which this mechanism pervades the life of an offender contributes to risk (Glasser 1988).

### General self-regulation

General self-regulation concerns the offender's ability to self-monitor and inhibit antisocial thoughts and behaviours. This cluster of variables – also related to the static variables of violent and general previous offending – incorporates many of the elements of personality disorder (see Chapter 6) and Factor 2 within Hare's concept of psychopathy (see Chapter 2 on the PCL-R). Lifestyle impulsivity is not referring primarily to a lack of planning in the index offence, but to a disorganised, irresponsible lifestyle and poor impulse control established prior to adolescence, likely to result in negative consequences. It refers to an individual's ability to plan, problem-solve and regulate impulses so as to better achieve long-term goals. An individual's ability to accurately identify problems generate potential solutions to problems, and weigh the advantages and disadvantages of important decisions contributes to their ability to achieve long-term goals, or anticipate the consequences of their actions.

Cooperation with supervision – or compliance – warrants separate consideration. Compliance can be interpreted in several ways:

- poor attendance at supervision or treatment;
- disengagement from or manipulation of supervision/treatment;
- being excluded from treatment or dropping out (for whatever reason);
- failure on conditional release;
- adjudications for a range of behaviours whilst incarcerated.

It is worth paying particular attention to attrition in treatment programmes (Craissati & Beech 2001), as non-compliance has regularly been shown to be related to high recidivism rates (Cook, Fox, Weaver & Rooth 1991; Marques 1999). Failure to complete treatment is *not* the same as failing to meet the treatment goals; a compliant sex offender is one who attends and cooperates with the structure of treatment, regardless of whether that offender has made any demonstrable progress in improving their offence attitudes or social competencies. A difficulty with complying with statutory expectations is likely to relate to psychological difficulties, or personality factors, particularly impulsivity and hostile attitudes.

### Deviant sexual interest

Deviant sexual interest can be defined as a distortion in aim (e.g. children as victims) or in means (e.g. coercion in the 'courtship disorders' of rape). It does *not* refer to sexual arousal during the course of the offending episode, but should be based on an assessment of *persistent* erotic interests over time.

Hanson and Bussiere (1998) concluded that deviant sexual interest as measured by the penile plethysmograph (PPG) was the single most important dynamic factor in predicting sex offender recidivism. Yet the area is not without controversy and inconsistency.

There is research available to support the view that men without sexual convictions may hold deviant sexual fantasies and endorse pro-offending attitudes (Dean & Malamuth 1997). Laboratory experiments using phallometry also found non-offending men to be sexually aroused by depictions of rape (see Murphy, Haynes & Worley 1991 for a broader review of the literature). It may be that the low reporting and detection rate for sexual offences distorts the link between fantasies and offending, or it may be that deviant sexual arousal alone is insufficient to reduce normal inhibitions to sexual offending. Dean and Malamuth (1997), in their study of students, found that all those who were assessed as high risk for sexual violence against women were likely to imagine aggressing sexually. However, it was only those high risk individuals who were relatively self-centred/dominant (versus those sensitive to others' feelings/ nurturant) who were more likely to actually be sexually aggressive. Similarly, Malamuth, Heavy and Linz (1993) found empathy to be a moderator between phallometric assessment of deviant sexual arousal and actual aggression towards women. When empathy was high, there was no relationship between deviant arousal and aggression.

When considering sex offender samples, it has generally been found that only a proportion of offenders demonstrate deviant sexual arousal. These were generally child molesters with male victims. Marshall (1997) suggests that around 25 to 40 per cent of child molesters fall into this category. Firestone *et al.* (2000a) found that recidivist child molesters showed higher sexual arousal to child assault stimuli (involving coercion) than non-recidivists, as measured by phallometry. However, this was also a significant predictor of general recidivism. Quinsey *et al.* (1995) also found that deviant sexual interest, as measured by phallometry, was associated with sexual recidivism for both child molesters and rapists, along with previous criminal history and psychopathy.

There is no evidence that the absence of deviant sexual activity reliably predicts non-sexual recidivists. With apparently low or medium risk individuals, other factors seem to be more salient, such as pro-offending attitudes, social competencies and lifestyle impulsivity.

How can deviant sexual interest be measured? The simplest means of assessing this variable, and one often underrated, is encouraging the offender to self-report deviant sexual interest. Many offenders with a previous history of sexual convictions will respond to sensitive exploration of their sexuality, and will acknowledge persistent or sporadic deviant sexual interests. It is, of course, more difficult to ascertain change over time, as the offender is likely to want to reassure the interviewer that his potential risk has reduced. In the absence of self-report, deviant sexual interest in child molesters could be deduced – probably fairly accurately – from static factors, such as victims who are male, or of both sexes, previous sexual convictions and single status (Hanson *et al.* 1993). The situation is less clear for rapists with a persistent interest in coercive sexual activity. Common sense would dictate that those with previous convictions, probably against strangers, and/or elements of sadism within the offence (see below) are likely to hold persistent deviant interests. Additional elements of any static risk assessment could usefully include personal and social activities of offenders – for example, child molesters who coach children's football teams, or rapists who work in night clubs or as minicab drivers.

The third most prevalent means of ascertaining deviant sexual arousal is the use of phallometry. The PPG is a laboratory-based technique for directly measuring penile tumescence in response to a range of auditory and visual stimuli. These may include a range of subjects, both male and female, from children to mature adults, and may portray varying degrees of coercion, threat and seduction. The perpetrator's sexual response is then compared to his reaction to consenting sex between adults. Despite its clinical and research value the PPG has never been as widely used in Britain as in the USA. The equipment is expensive and requires skilled administration and considerable expertise in interpreting the results.

Langevin (1988) elaborated on some of the problems associated with interpreting PPG results, including questions regarding the validity of the stimuli, the influence of anxiety and/or prolonged sexual abstinence on arousal and attempts at conscious repression or distortion of arousal. Fisher and Thornton (1993) suggest that the PPG might best be used for determining treatment need and perhaps in establishing changes in deviant sexual arousal over time, as a consequence of treatment.

## Sadism

Sadism as a sexual interest represents a subgroup of all those sex offenders with persistent deviant sexual arousal. It warrants specific attention because of its link with risk, particularly serious harm, to the victim. To some extent the literature on sadism overlaps with the discussion on homicide in sex offenders, and this section should be read in conjunction with the review of homicide on pages 46–8.

Establishing the prevalence of sadistic sexual interests in offenders is problematic, as it appears to be dependent upon the definition used (see Marshall & Kennedy 2001 for a summary of the area). MacCulloch, Snowden, Wood and Mills (1983) defined sexual sadism as 'the repeated practice of behavior and fantasy which is characterized by a wish to control another person by domination, denigration or inflicting pain for the purpose of producing mental pleasure and sexual arousal (whether or not accompanied by orgasm) in the sadist'. A slightly more restricted definition is found in the *Diagnostic and Statistical Manual of Mental Disorders* (DSM-IV, American Psychiatric Association 1994) which requires evidence for the presence of 'recurrent, intense, sexual urges and sexually arousing fantasies, of at least six months' duration, involving acts (real, not simulated) in which the psychological or physical suffering (including humiliation) of the victim is sexually exciting. The person has acted on these urges, or is markedly distressed by them' (p. 287).

A number of studies (e.g. Fedora, Reddon, Morrison, Fedora, Pascoe & Yeudall 1992) have found that 45 per cent of sexually aggressive offenders fulfilled this criteria for sadism. Studies which rely on police descriptions of damage or mutilation to the victim, or offender self-report, tend to estimate sadism in 5 to 10 per cent of rapists. This is not greatly different from studies examining sadistic sexual interests in non-offender populations (Freund, Chan & Coulthard 1979).

Common features found in sexual sadists which differentiate them from non-sadistic sexual offenders include a significant history of physical abuse, known cross-dressing, obscene telephone calls and indecent exposure. Their offence characteristics include careful planning of the offence, victim taken to a preselected location, intentional torture, victim beaten, forced anal sex and fellatio. Furthermore, there may be organic features associated with extremely poor impulse control, around half in one study having abnormal neurological findings (Gratzer & Bradford 1995). Some studies suggest that sadists may suffer from sexual impotence, while others have found that sexual sadists are skilled at seducing women into complying with their core fantasies within the context of a relationship.

Sadistic sexual killers have been characterised by the long-standing nature of their violent fantasies, usually with an onset in adolescence and containing a ritualised, repetitive core that is highly arousing to the sexual sadist (Warren, Hazelwood & Dietz 1996). They are highly likely to keep collections on a violent theme, such as videotapes, pictures, bondage material, weaponry, sexually sadistic pornography or detective magazines (Warren *et al.* 1996). A surprising number may have had no arrest record prior to the murder. The victims tend to be strangers and the means of killing is usually asphyxiation or stabbing – the greater 'intimacy' of the weapon being indicative of the sexual component.

MacCullough *et al.* (1983) commented that sadistic fantasies tend to be progressive in nature, the sadistic context increasing and fantasy material being based on previous behavioural 'try-outs' of the main fantasy sequence. They suggest that a history of sadistic sexual fantasies, previous try-outs (not necessarily resulting in arrest) and a demonstrable pattern of progression of offending and fantasy are highly indicative of a probable progression to killing.

## Acute risk factors

Acute risk factors are regularly addressed in treatment programmes, particularly those with an emphasis on relapse prevention. However, their evidence base is much less developed than the work on stable dynamic factors. Acute risk factors are not primarily related to long-term risk potential – that is, *whether* an individual will reoffend. Their importance lies in predicting *when* an offender might be likely to reoffend sexually. Therefore, in assessing acute risk factors, the practitioner is interested in deviations from the baseline level of the behaviour for a particular offender, rather than the baseline itself. For example, an offender may be feeling low in mood, but not out of proportion to his current situation; he may hold a generally hostile attitude towards women, but a positive acute risk factor score would relate to an identifiable increase in anger and hostility. Hanson and Bussiere (1998) found four acute variables which were linked, to some extent, with recidivism and their utility was reinforced by their contribution to the SONAR (Hanson & Harris 2000). These are:

- substance abuse;
- negative mood (depression or anxiety);
- anger/hostility;
- opportunities for victim access.

Hanson and Harris (2000) rated these acute factors for the month prior to the assessment, on the basis of no change, improvement or deterioration. Substance misuse problems were defined as interfering in normal daily activities or causing health problems. Negative mood included depressed or anxious feelings, frustration, loneliness or suicidal thoughts. Anger/hostility included volatility, anger towards women and aggressive or threatening behaviour. Victim access included general opportunities, creating opportunities, computer use and relevant hobbies. All four factors significantly differentiated between recidivists and non-recidivists, although the effect was weakest for negative mood. More recent revisions to the acute risk factor ratings have added the following components:

- collapse of social supports;
- an increase in sexual preoccupations;
- an increased propensity to reject supervision.

Clearly there may be links between the acute and stable risk factors. Increased substance misuse may relate both to a dysfunctional coping mechanism for managing low mood or anger and a deliberate attempt to overcome inhibitions to offending. The relevance of mood supports the premise that these offenders sexualise their behaviour in response to uncontained feelings. Opportunities for victim access were not chance events but a tendency for the offenders to expose themselves to high risk situations, to minimise their relapse potential just prior to reoffending.

## Adolescent sex offenders

While a range of variables have been found to be associated with juvenile offending in general – maltreatment in childhood, early onset of criminal/aggressive behaviour, family instability, substance misuse – the evidence for factors specific to sexual offending has been inconsistent (Righthand & Welch 2001). Much of the research on incarcerated – and therefore higher risk – juvenile sex offenders would suggest that their offending is likely to be but one expression of antisocial, violent behaviour (Jacobs, Kennedy & Meyer 1997).

Prentky *et al.*'s (2000) work on an actuarial tool for risk prediction in juvenile sex offenders (detailed in Chapter 2 and the Appendix) provides a framework for considering the fixed and dynamic variables identified by the research. It may be that the factors contained in the JJPI can be mapped onto the adult sex offender domains identified by Hanson and Harris (2000) and others.

Factor I (sexual drive/sexual preoccupation) relates to high levels of sexual pathology, including poor sexual boundaries, uncontrollable sexual urges, deviant sexual fantasies and non-contact sexual behaviours. Prentky *et al.* (2000) refer to this factor as static, although evidence of sexual preoccupations and deviant sexual interests would appear to be dynamic variables, akin to the sexual self-regulation domain identified in adult offenders. This factor was the least satisfactory in terms of the predictive accuracy of the tool, and the equivocal findings are supported by the evidence. That is, self-reported deviant sexual fantasy and behaviour appear to be unrelated to risk (Prentky & Knight 1993), although there is limited support for physiological measures of deviant sexual arousal being linked to recidivism in sexual offenders. Hunter, Goodwin and Becker (1994) point out that deviant arousal is most likely to be found among those juveniles who commit offences against children, and that there is greater fluidity in the offence patterns of juvenile offenders, and less correspondence between measured arousal and offence histories than for adults. Prior sexual offences do appear to predict risk, although the young age of the adolescent, a short history relative to an adult and the low base rates for sexual offending create a restriction in range which might reduce the magnitude of the statistical relationship (Bourgon *et al.* 1999).

Factor II (impulsive/antisocial behaviour) captures the range of general delinquency, antisocial behaviour and lack of impulse control which are typically found in juvenile sex offenders. Examples are arrest prior to age 16, fighting, a diagnosis of conduct disorder, problems in primary school, school suspensions, alcohol abuse, parental alcohol abuse, non-living with natural parents until the age of 16 and 'criminal versatility' (multiple types of offences). Clearly there are similarities in this cluster of variables to the general self-regulation domain in adult sex offenders. One might anticipate that such adolescents may be at risk for developing pervasive personality problems in adulthood, particularly attracting a diagnosis of antisocial personality disorder or concerns regarding the level of psychopathy. Poor peer relationships and substance abuse are generally treatment targets in services for adolescent sex offenders, although the relationship between changes in such dynamic factors and reduced sexual reoffending has not been established (Bourgon *et al.* 1999).

Factor III (clinical/treatment) focuses not only on compliance with treatment but on the attainment of treatment goals, such as taking responsibility for sexual offences, motivation to change, understanding the sexual assault cycle, evidence for empathy and the absence of cognitive distortions. These variables correspond to the pro-offending attitudes domain in adult offenders.

Factor IV (community stability/adjustment) relates to the stability of the adolescent's social and interpersonal situation over the past six months, including his management of anger, chaotic lifestyle, attendance and behaviour at school, peer influences and pro-social network. To some extent, this factor would appear to tap into similar concerns as the acute factors described in the SONAR. Lowered risk should be linked to settled behaviour in the community with strong social integration and positive interpersonal influences.

It has been repeatedly documented that juvenile sexual offenders have significant deficits in social competence, including inadequate social skills, poor peer relationships and social isolation (Righthand & Welch 2001). However, no research has established a link between these treatment goals and recidivism risk, in contrast to the work on adult sex offenders where intimacy deficits have been identified as a dynamic risk domain.

In summary, the evidence-based work on adolescents thus far would suggest that some of the established research on adult sex offenders is relevant to adolescents. Consideration needs to be given to the developmental tasks of the adolescent stage of life, as a period of fluidity and transition. Specifically, extreme caution needs to be applied in considering emerging deviant sexual interests and fantasies, as the research evidence does not support this dynamic factor as a central risk concern for adolescents.

## Female sex offenders

The literature suggests that female sex offenders share some characteristics with their male counterparts. They tend to be young, with low socioeconomic status, high levels of unemployment and poor education; they may deny or minimise their behaviour and have substance misuse problems. However, they are less likely than men to use force against their victims and more likely to express feelings of considerable remorse, viewing their behaviour as inappropriate. They usually victimise female children who are known to them, often in a babysitting situation, and male victims and adult victims are less common. They report higher rates of sexual victimisation in their own childhood, and these experiences are typically more severe or prolonged than in male sex offenders. Although the rates of severe mental illness are low (less than 10 per cent), high rates of general psychiatric disturbance are generally reported, including diagnoses of borderline personality, post-traumatic stress disorder and depression. Self-destructive acts are common, including substance abuse, eating disorders and self-harm. In terms of deviant sexual arousal, the research evidence is limited and diagnoses of paedophilia are rarely found. However, some female perpetrators report sexual arousal and victim-related fantasies during the offences and limited evidence for persistent deviant sexual arousal and sexual preoccupation has been reported (including the use of the vaginal photoplethysmograph – equivalent to the PPG for men). More commonly, motivation for offending has been ascribed to excessive dependency on male partners/co-offenders, fear of rejection and feelings of hostility and revenge (Grayston & De Luca 1999; Nathan & Ward 2002).

The most commonly cited typology for female sex offenders was proposed by Mathews (1987) and subsequently amended by Matthews *et al.* (1989). More recent support for this classificatory model has been reported by Atkinson (2000) and Nathan and Ward (2002). Three main types of female sex offender are proposed: teacher/lover; predisposed; and male coerced/male accompanied.

### Teacher/lover

The teacher/lover type is an adult woman who acts as the initiator of the sexual abuse of an adolescent, usually a male. The position of power obtained through either age or status is masked by the offender's belief that she is seeking a loving sexual expression in her interactions with the victim which are reciprocated; as such she tends to be defensive and deny the reality of her actions or their potential negative impact on the victim. Such offenders are likely to have experienced extrafamilial abuse as an adolescent and may have ongoing substance misuse problems. Atkinson (2000) suggests that such offenders pose a low risk of recidivism, although no data is provided to substantiate this.

## Predisposed

Predisposed female sex offenders usually victimise their own children, without male accomplices. Their victims are likely to be younger, perhaps aged less than 6, and may have been physically abused and neglected by the offender. These women may be motivated by anger and compulsive sexual urges, revealing sadistic fantasies which they find difficult to control. They are likely to have been extensively sexually victimised in childhood and, having extricated themselves in adolescence from their abusive family, they tend to become involved with abusive male partners. They may present with extensive psychopathology, including chronic suicidal feelings and self-harming behaviour. It would seem likely that this group contains a number of women with persistent deviant sexual interests, as found in paedophilic male offenders.

## Male coerced/male accompanied

More than half of all convicted female sex offenders have abused children in conjunction with a male accomplice. A male coerced offender is influenced by a male to participate in sexual abuse, often joining in sexual abuse which their partner has previously committed alone. The victim is likely to be the offender's daughter. These women tend to fear their partners and feel powerless in interpersonal relationships. They are desperate to maintain the relationship and may even initiate sexual abuse to please a male partner. Male-accompanied offenders usually participate more actively in sexual abuse and may be motivated by anger and sexual gratification. The women reveal a wide range of attitudes towards their victim, from remorse and a wish to repair the relationship to overt hostility towards the victim who is perceived as the focus of attention and responsible for the abuse. Nathan and Ward (2002) caution against succumbing to the temptation to assume that the majority of female sex offenders with male accomplices are coerced. They found that examining the motivation of these women in detail revealed a range of motivations, including jealousy, feeling rejected, being coerced, wanting to placate a male partner and attempting to establish a personal sense of power and control. They suggest an amendment to the male-accompanied category to include a subgroup of male accompanied: the rejected/revengeful.

Nathan and Ward (2002) suggest that practitioners should remain open to different offence pathways for different female sex offenders. It may be that a small group are predominantly motivated by sexually deviant preferences, and that future research will establish this group as posing a higher recidivism risk. A second group will be characterised by an inability to establish an independent identity effectively (akin to the intimacy deficits domain highlighted in research on male dynamic factors associated with risk – see Hanson & Harris 2000). A third group may manifest a primary difficulty with effectively regulating their aversive emotional states, which leads them to view sex as a coping strategy (the sexual self-regulation domain).

## Case studies

### Stephen

#### Background

Stephen's personal and family history was as follows. He described himself as a rather unhappy child who had a distant relationship with his mother. His father had left when he was a baby and his mother's bitterness about the failed relationship manifested itself in repeated derogatory comments about men and a clearly stated regret that she had not had a daughter. Although Stephen was quiet and withdrawn at home, he enjoyed school and managed to achieve academically and to integrate socially. His mother did not encourage him to mix with other boys outside of school hours, and he could not recall an occasion when school friends came back to the house. He did, however, forge an intense friendship with the girl next door, who was his age. He perceived her as being immersed in a very loving family atmosphere and was often round at her house, receiving the interest and warmth which was lacking at home. He was distraught when she and her family moved away from the area when they were aged 12, and after initial attempts to remain in contact the children drifted apart. In retrospect, Stephen described their relationship as his 'first love'.

Stephen left school at 16 with qualifications and, after a period of apprenticeship, worked as an electrical engineer. After a period of five years, he became self-employed. There was a period of financial stress in the year leading up to the index offence, when business was slack; he kept this hidden from his partner at that time, but nevertheless resented her spending money freely on the house and herself. More recently his business was maintained on a stable financial footing.

Stephen met his first partner when he was 17, and she was his first sexual relationship. Prior to that, he had felt anxious about dating women, often comparing girls unfavourably to his 'first love'. His partner quickly fell pregnant, and although unplanned, Stephen had felt that this new family would bring him the security he so craved. However, the relationship floundered; Stephen felt that his partner lost interest in him, sexually and emotionally, after their baby – Natalie – was born, and he resented her casual reliance on his finances. He suspected that she was having an affair, although he never dared to confront her about this. Stephen met his current wife – Jane – three years later. She was slightly older than him, with a daughter – Penny – from a previous relationship. He said he was attracted to her because of her warmth and 'motherliness', her easy nature and sense of fun. He felt they were equal partners in the relationship; she worked as well as him, and they shared care of Penny. She was a demonstrative woman, physically affectionate, and he said they had a good sexual relationship.

Stephen drank socially but had never had a difficulty with excessive use of alcohol. He had never used illicit drugs and had no psychiatric history.

## Offending behaviour

Stephen had no previous arrests, cautions or convictions prior to the allegations of sexual abuse against his biological daughter, Natalie. Natalie disclosed the abuse to her friend's mother when she was aged 8, and the matter was immediately brought to social services' attention. Natalie said that Stephen had been coming to her bedroom in the mornings before she went to school. Initially he had wanted cuddles and affection which she had been happy to give because she felt that they were very close and she loved him. Gradually he began to make her feel uncomfortable, touching her breasts and genitalia, repeatedly asking her if she loved him and reassuring her that physical contact between people who loved each other was normal. The abuse occurred on a fortnightly basis over the period of about one year, and progressed to digital penetration and her masturbating him to the point of ejaculation. She said that she was never coerced by her father, but wanted the abuse to stop, although she still cared for him.

Stephen initially denied abusing Natalie, but when challenged more recently by social services he admitted that she had told the truth. He felt that the abuse occurred within the context of rejection by his partner and financial stress, together with a growing feeling of closeness to Natalie; that in some ways they sought refuge in each other against his partner. He was deeply regretful about his behaviour, but was confident that it would never reoccur, that Penny would never be at risk.

### Formulation

Stephen grew up without a strong sense of himself as lovable and worthy, acutely conscious of his mother's rejection of him. In his closeness to the girl next door he was able to seek out and vicariously experience the comfort and love she received. The intensity of their relationship appeared to be rather idealised, suggesting that he had never resolved his feelings of loss when she left. Although anxious about intimacy in adulthood, he did have relationships: both appeared to be characterised by an emotional neediness which was certainly unmet in the first relationship. The sexual abuse of his daughter, Natalie, could be understood within the context of perceived rejection by his partner, and a retreat into a non-threatening and loving relationship which mirrored his 'first love' and seemed in some ways an attempt to recapture the memory of it.

### Risk

The static assessment tools generally viewed Stephen as posing a low risk in general terms. A review of possible risk variables suggested that there were some intimacy deficits in terms of his low feelings of self-esteem and insecurity in relationships. He was clearly emotionally identified with his victim, but there was no suggestion of this being the case with other children. The main risk factor appeared to be that he viewed himself as low risk but was in fact living in a potentially high risk situation.

## Anthony

### Background

Anthony was the youngest of three boys. He described his mother as 'very loving', a soft-hearted woman who found it difficult to exert control over her children – particularly Anthony's overactive behaviour – or to protect them from her husband's fury and harsh discipline. His father was a cold and rather distant presence in the household; he worked long hours, but when at home was viewed by Anthony as excessively strict, domineering and, ultimately, physically abusive. Both Anthony's older brothers had been in trouble at school and with the police (for relatively minor matters), as adolescents and Anthony felt that his father was all the more determined to beat him into submissiveness. Their relationship was one based on fear, anger and contempt, on Anthony's part, while he believed his father viewed him as worthless.

At school, Anthony was considered to be a bright, charming and quick-witted boy. However, from primary-school years, he was restless, easily distracted and disruptive in the classroom. He found it difficult to concentrate and was impulsive and reckless in his behaviour. He allied himself with other behaviourally disturbed boys and was often the centre of a disruptive group. In secondary school, he began to truant regularly with other boys. Occasionally he was embroiled in playground fights, but aggression was never noted to be a particular feature of his behaviour. After two suspensions, he eventually dropped out altogether at the age of 14, and obtained no qualifications.

In adolescence, the situation at home deteriorated as Anthony increasingly rebelled against his father's aggressive discipline to the point where his parents threw him out of the home. An aunt offered to take him in, but he ran away. For approximately two years Anthony stayed with friends, sometimes sleeping rough and always involved in a group of peers with whom he had a strong bond. He was a streetwise adolescent, popular, with a confident attitude and strong interpersonal skills. From early adolescence, he began dating girls of his

age and had a number of both fleeting and sustained relationships. There was no suggestion of violence within the relationships;
although affectionate towards his longer-term girlfriends, he found
it difficult to sustain any commitment and was repeatedly unfaithful.
However, he had cohabited for the first time for one year prior to the
index offence and had a baby boy from this relationship.

Anthony had never had stable employment. He found it easy to
pick up casual jobs, and had worked as a nightclub bouncer and
minicab driver on occasions. He supplemented his state benefit with
some earnings from limited drug dealing.

Anthony had been misusing illicit substances for many years. He
was introduced to cannabis while living on the street in adolescence
and had experimented with a range of Class A drugs. Although his
use of cannabis was heavy – several joints daily – he maintained that
he only used cocaine or ecstasy in socially appropriate settings,
with others – for example, when out in a nightclub. He drank alcohol
socially and sometimes to excess, although his use of alcohol had
diminished in recent years. There was no evidence of alcohol
dependency. He had no previous psychiatric history.

### Offending behaviour

Anthony had four previous convictions, none of which were for
sexual matters. At the age of 15 he was convicted of theft and at the
ages of 15 and 17 he was convicted of burglary – receiving a six-
month custodial sentence on the latter occasion. All these offences
were committed with others and all were motivated by financial
need, particularly in the light of his homelessness and drug use. At
the age of 20, Anthony was convicted of grievous bodily harm,
for which he received a two-year custodial sentence. This offence
related to a feud between two gangs in which Anthony became
embroiled; he believed himself to be at risk of serious harm from the
other gang and began to carry a knife around with him. When a fight
ensued, Anthony stabbed a young man in the shoulder. The judge's
comments at the time referred to Anthony's apparently sincere
expression of regret, which was reflected in the relatively short
sentence.

The index offence occurred one night when Anthony went out
with his friends to a nightclub. Although devoted to his girlfriend,
he had been feeling pressurised by the demands placed upon him as a
result of cohabiting and the birth of their son. This had culminated in

a row the evening of the offence. At the nightclub, the victim had 'come on to me', and Anthony responded, dancing with her and kissing her. They – and others – went back to his friend's flat, where more drinks and drugs were available. Anthony took the victim into a bedroom and they smoked cannabis together. He had been drinking and felt intoxicated but in control. He alleged that after kissing they had sexual intercourse with her full consent, whereupon they rejoined the others and had another drink. The victim maintained that she kissed Anthony but resisted his advances to have sex, whereupon he attempted to persuade her to change her mind; as she continued to resist, he became visibly angry and roughly forced himself upon her, bruising her genital area. She was frightened and did agree to have one further drink before leaving and reporting the matter to the police.

In prison, Anthony settled on the main wing and resisted all attempts to discuss his offence. However, he agreed to participate in a thinking skills course – a cognitive behavioural programme – which was not focused on the index offence. He also acknowledged that drugs and alcohol had played a part in his earlier difficulties and undertook a brief educational programme on this issue. He felt confident that he could abstain from Class A drugs and limit his use of cannabis and alcohol. He received good reports from both courses; furthermore there were no adjudications while in custody.

Anthony expressed regret that his current relationship was now over, and he clearly stated that he wished to maintain a close relationship with his son, with whom he apparently had a strong and loving bond. He was somewhat guarded in his relationship with the Probation Service, sensitive to any sign of them trying to control or dictate his future. He seemed to be most comfortable with his allocated officer when released, who was male and slightly older than him.

*Formulation*

Anthony's description of himself as a restless, easily distracted child, overactive at home and unable to concentrate at school, might possibly (in retrospect) have warranted a diagnosis of attention deficit hyperactivity disorder (ADHD). Although deeply cared for by his mother, one might speculate that his feelings towards her were somewhat ambivalent, given her failure to protect him. Rejection and contempt from his father was in stark contrast to his capacity to be liked, admired and effective in the outside world. His warmth of personality and quick-witted mind brought him a sense of control and freedom which was totally absent in the home, and seemed to provide a substitute for any primary attachment. As so often occurs, Anthony's failure to identify with the primary adult male role model led to an identification in adolescence with a delinquent peer group. However, prior to the index offence, there were signs that Anthony was seeking to make some meaningful attachment and to shed some of his shallow lifestyle. The index offence occurred within the context of his difficulty in facing up to the demands of intimacy and family life, his anger not only being the result of a sexual rebuff, but related to fears that he was being controlled and demeaned.

On actuarial tools, Anthony was predominantly scored as having a high risk of sexual recidivism. This was based on the number and range of previous convictions, as well as the victim being a stranger. In terms of dynamic factors, there are a number of areas of concern: despite recent attempts to engage in a sustained intimate relationship, there remain concerns about his capacity for commitment. This is closely related to issues of sexual entitlement and the central role that sex and dating play in maintaining his image to himself and his peers. All his offending – including his index offence – has been related to peer group influences, which are strongly implicated in the maintenance of his denial for the index offence. Although antisocial personality disorder was likely to have been the primary diagnostic possibility, recent evidence of maturation should lead to caution, although lifestyle instability and impulsivity remain a concern.

## James

### Background

James was the eldest of two children, his sister being three years younger than himself. He described his parents' relationship as 'cordial' and his own childhood as 'unremarkable'. His mother was a housewife and affectionate mother; his father was strict – but certainly not physically abusive – and set high standards for his son in terms of behaviour and scholastic achievement. James said he always felt that he let his father down and was regretful that they did not manage to be closer. His mother described him as jealous of his sister, from a young age, and the sibling relationship was persistently conflictual. He was a rather withdrawn and serious child, prone to occasional but intense temper tantrums, which his mother found difficult to manage.

James encountered no particular difficulties at school, although he did not appear to make friends. He was considered to underperform academically, leaving school at 16 with a few qualifications with low grades, despite an estimated IQ of above average. He subsequently worked as a clerk in a bank; again, he was considered to be reliable but unremarkable, often passed over for promotion. He stayed in this line of work until his index offence in his mid-thirties.

James was open in describing his developing sexuality: he could trace the beginning of his deviant sexual fantasies from approximately the age of 8. This appeared to coincide with an almost total cessation of aggressive outbursts. He could only ever recall being sexually excited by the thought of strangling women – both adolescent and adult. As he attained puberty, these fantasies developed to the point where he would imagine throttling a woman with his hands while intensely sexually aroused, to the point where she lost consciousness, whereupon he would ejaculate. His fantasy figures were both women he had met and also 'pin up' figures such as film stars. He never fantasised about being physically hurt himself, nor did he imagine killing the women. The important elements of the fantasy seemed to be the power he exerted over the women and their fear of him. In reality, he made attempts in adolescence and early adulthood to date women. These encounters never progressed beyond a few dates and were not sexual. He said that he was troubled by his sadistic fantasies towards his dates and preferred to avoid sexual intimacy. He was not so troubled by his fantasies when they were confined to imaginary or stranger figures. With time, James ceased to attempt to seek intimate relationships and spent almost all of his spare time in his room at home with his parents.

In the five years leading up to the index offence, James said that he used to drink quite heavily – four or five pints of beer – a few times a week. He never drank at home, but went to the pub, occasionally with work colleagues but largely alone. He had never used illicit drugs and had no previous psychiatric history.

## Offending behaviour

James had one previous conviction for indecent exposure which occurred when he was 20. He was returning from the pub one evening, having drunk five pints, and found himself walking behind a young woman whom he found attractive. He followed her for a few yards, feeling sexually excited, and then as she stopped at a bus stop, he took out his erect penis and stood beside her, masturbating. The woman immediately went to call the police and he was quickly arrested. He was extremely apologetic, blamed his intake of alcohol that evening, and when he went to court he was fined.

James described a build up of a few months prior to the index offence. Although there were no discernible changes in his personal circumstances, he was aware that he was becoming more determined to act out his fantasies. He found that alcohol disinhibited him so that it was easier for him to overcome any residual inhibitions to offending. He developed offending scenarios in which he would create opportunities to be alone with a woman, and would then strangle her while he obtained sexual satisfaction. Again, he denied any thought of causing lasting harm or killing a potential victim. On the night of the offence, he went to the pub with the express purpose of seeking out a suitable victim. He drank three pints and managed to strike up a relationship with an older woman (aged 45). She seemed to like him and invited him back to her flat for coffee. In the kitchen, he suddenly seized a knife and grabbed the woman, threatening to harm her if she did not cooperate. The victim, in an attempt to placate him, spoke soothingly to him, attempting to maintain a sense of calm. In retrospect, James described feeling disappointed and frustrated that she was not conforming to his rehearsed fantasy: she did not appear to be dominated and terrified. He felt very angry, put his hands round her neck and strangled her. He described a sense of losing control at this point and acknowledged that he continued to asphyxiate her well beyond her loss of consciousness. James 'came to' with a sense of numbed shock and sat by the woman's body for over two hours. Eventually he phoned the police, saying what he had done, and was arrested.

While on remand, psychiatric reports described James as 'chillingly' detached from his crime, apparently unconcerned about his future. He was thought to be psychopathic (although no formal assessment was undertaken), but no defence of diminished responsibility was put forward. After a few years, and following the death of his mother, James began to show an interest in seeking help for himself. Eventually he was transferred to a prison therapeutic community where he spent 18 months and made good progress. He went on to complete the extended prison sex offender treatment programme and the relapse prevention programme. Again, his progress was thought to be exemplary, probably genuinely so. During this period, James underwent a PPG assessment which yielded no significant deviant sexual interest (although James himself reported a very mild response to a slide depicting a woman being strangled). The turning point seemed to have hinged on James' decision to 'give up' his sadistic fantasies which had become abhorrent to him, and his ability to reflect on his sexual orientation. He felt more able to contemplate homosexuality, which he felt was his preferred orientation, and went on to develop two lasting relationships with other prisoners. There were no adjudications during his 20-year stay in prison, nor had there been any concerns regarding his sexual behaviour or his conduct within the relationships.

## Formulation

Although some difficulties from James' childhood could be identified, there seemed to be no obvious trauma or markedly disturbed attachment experiences which could account for such a striking development of deviant sexual interests. It may be that his temperament, interacting with his early environment, led to acute anxiety in managing his overwhelming aggressive impulses; an anxiety which was exacerbated by a fear that he would be rejected by his father to whom he wished to be close. The temporal link between the cessation of aggressive outbursts and the onset of sadistic fantasies might lend support to the premise that a withdrawal from overt violence into the realms of sadistic control within his internal world was an attempt to solve this emotional dilemma by means of the sexualisation of aggression (see Craissati 1998 and Glasser 1988 for an explanation of the 'core complex'). The index offence represented a breakdown in this precarious 'solution'; that is, fantasy was no longer sufficient to maintain the status quo, and – with the disinhibiting assistance of alcohol – James felt compelled to take the irrevocable step of putting fantasy into action. Some might feel that James never fully accepted his homicidal impulses, or even that he was deliberately denying such fantasies; however, it is also possible that the failure of the offence victim to 'play the part' triggered a loss of control and regression to raw, panic-stricken violence.

*Risk*

On actuarial tools, James mainly scored high, although not universally so, the main factor being a stranger victim. There had clearly been many changes over the years in terms of his personality and offending attitude. At the point of release, there was no suggestion of any problems with a capacity for intimacy, although this was untested in the community; he no longer held any pro-offending attitudes whatsoever, nor was there any evidence of significant deviant sexual interest either from self-report or PPG, although it was not clear whether this had dissipated or was lying dormant. He was well able to acknowledge a hypothetical risk for himself, although he felt fairly confident that he would not reoffend. His relapse prevention plan was detailed and appropriate. There was still the possibility of an acute risk factor – alcohol use – precipitating an offence, but this did not appear to be a long-term risk. The only remaining factor which was central to his risk appraisal was the long history of enduring sadistic sexual interests.

## Peter

*Background*

Peter was an only child and lived most of his childhood in the care of his father. He described his father as 'good', although it was not easy to assess the quality of the relationship. His father had met all his physical needs and had been generally caring, although he was an undemonstrative man and rather emotionally inexpressive. Peter had only vague memories of his mother, who had left the family home abruptly when he was 4. He had tried on one or two occasions to talk to his father about his mother, but soon stopped when it was clear that these conversations caused his father emotional pain. He simply knew that his mother's behaviour had been erratic and had caused his father embarrassment in the community; he thought she had probably been mentally ill. There were no photographs of his mother in the house and he felt there was an implicit code of silence surrounding her.

Peter found it difficult to cope with school. He had learning difficulties and failed academically. He was also bullied fairly per-sistently and only managed to make one or two friends during his education. He left aged 15 without qualifications, but nevertheless had managed to work consistently. He liked driving, and his most recent period of employment was as a long-distance lorry driver.

Peter described himself as an insecure and anxious adolescent, who was very preoccupied with his physical image, as he suffered from acne. He made no attempt to develop relationships with girls – although he would have liked to have a girlfriend – believing that he would be automatically rejected and humiliated. He was also worried at this time about his sexual orientation, as he had found himself sexually attracted to one or two boys of his own age. His first sexual experience was one of abuse: on one occasion, aged 15, he said that he had been befriended by an adult man who had bought him sweets and offered him a lift home in the car. The man then brutally raped him in the car, before dumping him in the street. He managed to tell his father, who told the police, and after giving a statement he thought that the perpetrator was caught and sentenced. However, he was vague about these details, not least because the matter was never again mentioned by him or his father. In late adolescence, Peter used to go to gay bars occasionally, and had two sexual encounters with adult men. He thought of himself as bisexual, but was not particularly comfortable with his homosexual inclinations.

Peter was hesitant to discuss any offence-related fantasies, but did eventually acknowledge that he was sexually attracted to adolescent boys, and that his offence victims had continued to form part of his fantasy life. However, he maintained that for at least '50 per cent' of the time he fantasised about adults.

Peter had never drunk alcohol, except for infrequent social occasions. He had never used illicit drugs and had no previous psychiatric history.

### Offending behaviour

Peter had two previous convictions for sexual assaults, when aged 18 and 20, in addition to his index offence (aged 23). He had received relatively short prison sentences on each occasion. On all three occasions the victims had been boys (aged 12, 14 and 15) with whom he had struck up a fleeting acquaintance. The offences had all occurred when he was not at work, and felt at something of a 'loose end'. He had frequented suitable places for potential victims – the seaside, the West End of London – and had engaged boys in conversation who were apparently 'hanging around'. Two of his victims were truanting from school and one – he claimed – was working as a rent boy. On each occasion he would offer the victims cigarettes, sweets or beer, and he clearly had a capacity to relate to them at their level. He would then invite the victim into his car, or home with him, and persuade him to allow himself to be fondled, or for Peter to perform oral sex on him, or to engage in mutual masturbation.

Peter was clear that he wanted to avoid future prison sentences, and that he wanted to be 'normal'. By this he meant that he felt ashamed of being attracted to underage boys and wanted a satisfactory adult relationship with either a man or a woman. However, he found it difficult to understand that the victims were anything other than entirely cooperative, and thought that the potential for harm was greatly exaggerated.

## Formulation

There appeared to be a constellation of difficulties underpinning Peter's offending behaviour. He experienced a certain amount of emotional deprivation in childhood, given the lack of maternal care and his father's emotional reticence. This was emphasised by the lack of tangible memories or mementoes of his mother which prevented him from developing an imagined relationship with her, leaving something of a void in his life. In adolescence, he was beset with anxieties about himself, others and his capacity to be valued in relationships. He avoided women but felt guilty about any sexual feelings towards men. Clearly the rape was a traumatic experience, although Peter played this down; it seemed likely – although he denied it – that he had been troubled by irrational feelings of guilt about the attack, somehow believing himself to be culpable by having made himself vulnerable. This hypothesis was partly based on Peter's evident hostility towards his own victims and his claims regarding their responsibility within his offences – as though he was symbolically attempting to replicate and reverse his own trauma. There was evidence that Peter was sexually attracted to pre-pubescent boys, but it seemed possible that his victim choice was predominantly related to emotional immaturity and an avoidance of adult intimacy.

## Risk

On actuarial tools, Peter scored very highly. This was largely related to his clear deviant sexual interest in boys and his choice of stranger victims. He struggled with a number of intimacy deficits in terms of avoidance of adult intimacy and low self-esteem. He also held strong victim empathy distortions and emotional identification with adolescent boys. There was some suggestion that deviant sexual activity served to mitigate life stresses and regulate his self-esteem. However, there were few antisocial features in either his background or current functioning. It was not clear that acute dynamic factors were implicated in his offending.

## Martin

### Background

Martin's early life was characterised, quite simply, by chaos. He was the middle child of five and both his parents were alcoholics. The children were sometimes poorly clothed and fed, often the butt of jokes by neighbourhood and school children. Martin's mother was prone to bouts of depression, at which time she would withdraw to her bed and rarely emerge. His father was often in trouble with the police and away from home. Martin described his mother as loving but unpredictable; his father was rather more consistently abusive, verbally and physically. The family were often evicted from their home and the children were occasionally separated and placed in care.

Martin changed school on several occasions. He found it difficult to keep up with the academic work and left at 15 unable to read or write properly. Repeatedly teased, even bullied, he learned to lash out in the playground and was sometimes suspended for fighting. He never managed to make friends, somehow losing these skills in all the moves. In late adolescence he managed to obtain a handful of short-term labouring jobs, but was usually sacked due to poor time-keeping. He had not worked – between prison sentences – for the past 15 years.

Martin's first sexual experience was one of abuse: between the ages of 8 and 12 he was sexually assaulted on a regular basis by an adult male neighbour. The abuse progressed from fondling to mutual masturbation and oral sex, culminating in an attempt at buggery, which Martin resisted. He was unclear why the abuse stopped, only that the neighbour no longer called round to invite him to his house. Martin never disclosed this abuse until his current sentence, although he was unable to explain why not. He denied that he was in any way traumatised by it, referring to the 'special attention' it afforded him and how he learnt to like it in due course, even to seek it out.

Martin described himself as exclusively heterosexual, his offence being something quite separate to his sexual orientation. He said that he had had girlfriends in adolescence and had been the lover of one of his mother's friends, in his twenties. On close questioning, it seemed that he had had sexual encounters with women, but there was no evidence of enduring affection or intimacy with his sexual partners. In terms of his fantasies, Martin was quite open in stating that 50 per cent of his fantasies were about pre-pubescent boys, 40 per cent were about adult women and 10 per cent were about adult men. At times he had talked, rather superficially, about his concerns that he might kill a child. He showed an interest in notorious killers (including child killers) and admitted to sexual excitement at thoughts of hurting children.

Martin drank alcohol socially, occasionally to excess. He was a habitual user of cannabis but not other illicit drugs. It was not clear how important a role cannabis use may have played in his offending, given that he used a regular amount daily. He had been admitted to psychiatric hospital on three previous occasions, each brief admission precipitated by an act of deliberate self-harm. Usually he cut his wrists or took a minor overdose; however, there was a record of him having attempted to hang himself while on remand on this occasion.

*Offending behaviour*

Martin had 18 previous convictions, commencing at the age of 14. They were nearly all for theft or minor driving offences. One was a burglary of industrial premises, but none were for violence. The thefts were often committed with peers, or on behalf of peers.

In terms of his sexual offending, Martin's first conviction was for the rape of a 10-year-old boy when he was aged 20, for which he received a six-year prison sentence. He was heavily intoxicated at the time and said that he felt sexually frustrated; he decided to pick a potential victim – a boy walking down the street – grabbed him and attempted to anally penetrate him, despite difficulty obtaining an erection. His second conviction was for indecent assault on a 6-year-old boy when he was aged 26, for which he received a four-year sentence. This offence involved Martin waiting outside a newsagents after school hours, offering to buy a boy sweets in exchange for touching his penis and then putting his hand down the boy's trousers. The index offence was relatively minor: Martin had been loitering in a park, watching young boys, when he decided to follow one boy as he walked home. Suddenly, in full view of passers-by, Martin impulsively ran up to the boy, smacked his bottom and asked him, 'Do you want to suck my cock?' He was subsequently assaulted by two men in the street and the police were called.

As he approached his parole date, Martin openly acknowledged that he had offended on further occasions. He also claimed that he had previously thrown acid into a social worker's face after she had been rude to him. He was willing to talk about his fantasies and readily explained that he felt he had the capacity to go 'completely crazy' and hurt someone. In the prison treatment programme, Martin had applied himself in a constructive manner and was thought to be sincere in his wish to change. However, his reports emphasised the worrying content of his fantasies, which tended to monopolise the group process. He was thought to have poor victim empathy but a well-developed relapse prevention plan. He had received two adjudications during this sentence, both for verbal outbursts to prison staff, threatening to harm them. On both occasions he felt he had been provoked by their disrespectful behaviour.

## Formulation

Martin was clearly emotionally damaged by his childhood experiences which had resulted in long-term psychological dysfunction. It seemed to be, predominantly, the absence of any consistent, nurturing bonds with adults or peers which lay at the root of his failure to establish any attachment behaviour. As is so often the case, he was drawn to his sexual abuser as the sole source of attention and feelings of self-worth: if he could not be loved for himself, he could be loved for his sexual attributes. In adulthood, the only consistent relationship Martin was able to develop was with his delinquent peer group and the criminal justice system, prison containing him emotionally as the community could not. Martin's self-image appeared to be built up around his capacity to excite and interest people, and the nearer he came to release the more he needed to impress with his capacity for violence. This was amplified in the agencies' anxious response to him. His sexual offending had a compulsive, reckless quality to it which seemed to suggest a persistent need to act sexually in order to keep his own emotional neediness at bay.

*Risk*

On actuarial tools, Martin scored high. As with Peter, this related to his repeated choice of stranger, male victims. There were clear attachment and intimacy problems, although he did not necessarily have insight into these. He was honest about marked pro-offending attitudes and emotional identification with children, as well as victim empathy distortions. There were problems with sexual self-regulation as he reported a preoccupation with sexual matters. He believed that sexual activity increased his social status and he was prone to strong sexual urges which he wished to gratify. In addition to dominant deviant sexual interests (and arousal to violence) there were marked antisocial features to his personality, not least a problematic level of impulsivity.

## Summary

The research on dynamic risk predictors is now sufficiently consistent to support a coherent framework for assessment. Three models have been described which, despite their different methodologies, are fairly consistent in emphasis. All three highlight two domains: pro-offending attitudes and intimacy deficits. The SONAR and IDA also address deviant sexual interests and general self-regulation, although the SONAR is probably the broadest in its scope. Further research and validation of the instruments will undoubtedly lead to adjustments and hopefully an established track record in enhanced risk prediction.

The question of whether one method is superior to others very much depends on the circumstances of the assessment and the setting. For example, for those who do not have access to psychometric measures, clinical interview and file data will provide the necessary information, as outlined by the SONAR. Scoring and algorithms provide a valid and reliable approach, allowing comparison pre and post interventions as well as across populations. However, a risk prediction framework may be less concerned with absolute scores than with guidance for good practice in risk management.

The risk management process could be considered to fall into four stages:

1    Initial classification according to static factors.

2    Adjustment of the risk classification with regard to the dynamic domains.
3    Reference to any unusual or offender-specific factors which have not already been considered (e.g. evidence of sadism or entry into a very high risk situation).
4    Identification and implementation of strategies to target high risk dynamic domains.

Clearly the case studies provide brief examples of working through Stages 1 to 3, although arguably Stage 4 poses the greatest challenge and is addressed to some extent in Chapters 5 and 6.

# Chapter 4

# Child protection: social services and the Children Act 1989

*Joanna Hall and Jackie Craissati*

## Introduction

Child protection in cases of alleged sexual abuse is beset with difficulty. In the last ten years or so, with growing public awareness about the prevalence of sexual abuse within families, professionals have been urged to intervene with more children and criticised when obvious causes for concern have been overlooked. At the same time there has been increasing public concern, fuelled by events such as those in Cleveland (Butler-Sloss 1988), that over-zealous professionals can themselves cause harm to children by incorrectly identifying sexual abuse. Allegations of child sexual abuse can be difficult to prove, particularly where the only evidence is from the child, and indeed there may be legitimate disagreement as to whether or not a particular act can be described as abusive. Without proof to a criminal or civil standard (beyond reasonable doubt or on the balance of probabilities) it can be extremely difficult to put any child protection procedures in place. Problems can also arise because of a conflict of roles between those involved in child protection – for example, between police anxious to convict a suspected child abuser and social workers anxious to protect the child from the potential emotional damage of giving evidence in a criminal trial. It would seem that only a minority of those children at risk of sexual abuse come to the attention of the appropriate authorities. Sadly, the ultimate goal of affording comprehensive protection to all children at risk may take a long time to achieve.

## Child protection through criminal proceedings

The Report of the National Commission of Inquiry into the Prevention of Child Abuse, published in 1996, estimated that up to 100,000 children each year have a potentially harmful sexual experience. (Department of Health 1996). The report also records the fact that in 1994 only 2,300 people were convicted of sexual offences involving children under 16 although a further 1,700 admitted guilt and were cautioned. From 1988/9 the number of successful prosecutions for sexual offences against children had been steadily declining (Department of Health 1996: 10, para. 2.4). These figures perhaps demonstrate that the criminal justice system's contribution to child protection is limited (see Chapter 1 for a discussion of rape convictions). It seems there is a twofold reason for the lack of successful prosecutions. First there are the evidential difficulties. Criminal allegations must be proved beyond reasonable doubt – a very high standard. Only direct, first-hand evidence of the alleged crime is admissible so that the jury will not hear important indirect and hearsay evidence that the child has been abused such as expert assessments of the child, evidence of the child's disturbed sexualised behaviour, evidence that the child's allegations have been consistently repeated and so on. Second, there is the fact that the principal prosecution witness is likely to be the child. It is now the position that a video of the child's interview with members of the child protection team, what is called a 'memorandum interview', will stand as evidence in chief and the child will be cross-examined via video link. Nonetheless, for some children giving evidence at all will be too traumatic. In other cases where the child has a close relationship with the alleged abuser, the child will not want to feel responsible for sending that person to prison. Where children do give evidence they are at a serious disadvantage when compared to adult victims of crime. Prior to a criminal trial, adult victims may well refresh their memories by reading statements made at the time of the alleged offence or will have discussed what happened with friends and/or therapists. Child victims do not view their videos again and are discouraged from talking about their experiences for fear that their evidence may become tainted. A child, particularly one traumatised by a sexual assault, may become confused and is likely to have difficulty remembering details of an event that happened months before. It is perhaps not surprising that in many cases of suspected child sexual abuse the CPS appear reluctant to prosecute.

The advantage of a criminal conviction in child protection terms is that it establishes beyond doubt that the convicted person poses a risk to children regardless of whether the offending behaviour is admitted or denied. In accordance with various circulars, a local authority may check with local police forces the possible criminal backgrounds of those who apply to work with children such as social services staff, volunteers, child-minders and foster parents. A person's criminal convictions, no matter how old, will always be admissible in proceedings under the Children Act 1989 even though those convictions would otherwise be 'spent' (Rehabilitation of Offenders Act 1974, Section 7(2) as amended by the Children Act 1989, Schedule 13, para. 35 and Schedule 15).

The disadvantage of a failed criminal prosecution is that it is invariably seen by the alleged abuser, and sometimes by the child's primary carer, as a vindication and proof of innocence. In cases where the prosecution has failed for reasons other than the defendant's innocence, it may be difficult, if not impossible, to engage that person in treatment or to put any child protection measures in place. This is well demonstrated in Stephen's case study (see below) where child protection measures can be put in place only because of Stephen's admissions and cooperation.

## Child protection and the Children Act 1989

The Children Act 1989 has been described as the most comprehensive enactment on children in our legislative history and was designed to achieve a unified system of civil law relating to children and their families. The philosophy underpinning the Act is that children are best brought up by their own parents or within their extended families. The Act imposes a duty on local authorities to investigate a child's circumstances where information suggests that a child is suffering, or may be likely to suffer, harm. Should those investigations suggest a cause for concern, the local authority's first duty is to work in partnership with parents and to provide a range of services to the family to enable the child to remain at home. Court proceedings will follow only where the authority considers that without an order its powers of protection are inadequate. Even where proceedings are commenced, the court must only make an order if it considers that to do so would be better for the child than making no order (Section 1(5)). The courts are thus encouraged to follow the least interventionist course. The philosophy of the Act has been endorsed and strengthened by Article 8 of the European Convention on Human Rights which provides that everyone has a right to respect for his (or her) private and family life. A public authority is not permitted to interfere with the exercise of that right except in accordance with the law for, *inter alia*, the protection of health or morals, or the rights and freedoms of others. Thus, although the Children Act provides a comprehensive framework for local authorities and others to seek the courts' assistance in protecting children, judicial intervention is not encouraged and the emphasis is on local authorities providing services in the community to enable vulnerable and abused children to remain safely at home. Inevitably, conflict may arise between the child's right to protection and the child's and parent's right to remain together as a family, particularly where actual or potential child abuse is strongly suspected but not supported by concrete evidence. Professionals working with families in such circumstances face the difficult choice of putting in place child protection measures which may be draconian and potentially damaging to the child's emotional health, or leaving things as they are and risking the possibility of continuing and future child sexual abuse. Not surprisingly there is a reluctance to make the child a 'double victim'.

## Identifying the need for protection

Section 47 of the Act imposes a duty to investigate on any local authority that has reasonable cause to suspect that a child within its area is suffering or is likely to suffer significant harm. The Act envisages that a Section 47 inquiry will be conducted where there is some urgency to the situation and the inquiry will usually form the start of a local authority's child protection process. *The Framework for the Assessment of Children in Need and their Families* (Department of Health 2000a) provides a structure for helping to collect and analyse information gathered during the inquiry. If the Section 47 inquiry raises cause for concern, subsequent procedures for protecting the child are set out in the *Working Together* handbook (Department of Health 1999). Though the primary responsibility for the care and protection of abused children rests with local authorities there should be a close working relationship between social services departments, the police, health professionals, voluntary agencies and other professionals involved with children. *Working Together* sets out ways in which the various agencies involved in child protection should cooperate for the benefit of the child.

Following a Section 47 inquiry it will be usual practice for the local authority to convene a child protection conference to which all relevant professionals will be invited. The purpose of the conference will be to assess risk, to devise a child protection plan and to decide whether the name of the child should be entered on the Child Protection Register (CPR). Every local authority should maintain a CPR that lists all children judged to be at continuing risk of significant harm and for whom there is a child protection plan. A child may be registered in one or more categories of actual or likely physical, emotional or sexual abuse, or neglect. Agencies and professionals may consult the CPR to establish whether a child is thought to be at risk.

In 2000, about 32,000 children were on a CPR at any one time and about 53,000 children were being looked after by local authorities (Department of Health 1998). These figures included children who had been subjected to, or were at risk of, emotional and physical abuse and/or neglect, as well as children who were beyond parental control or had been abandoned or orphaned. Only a proportion would have had sexually abusive experiences. Work by Browne and Hamilton (1999) and Hamilton and Browne (1999) on referrals to police child protection units found that 23 per cent and 30 per cent respectively of referrals were for sexual abuse concerns. The difficulty in identifying those children who are at risk of sexual abuse is compounded by the fact that most children who come to the attention of child protection agencies are working class and poor. Little is known about middle- and upper-class parents who mistreat their children (Department of Health 1995). There is no reliable evidence to suggest that the sexual abuse of children is linked to social standing and economic circumstances.

In some local authorities a second register is kept recording the names of alleged or known abusers. The purpose of this is to afford some protection to children with whom the alleged or known abuser may associate in the future. A local authority should, however, be very sure of its facts before entering a name on such a register. In a number of cases where a name has been entered on a register with little supporting evidence and without the alleged abuser being given notice or the opportunity to make representations, the alleged abuser has been successful in obtaining a court order to quash the local authority's decision. This highlights two difficulties: first of identifying genuine cases of sexual abuse and second of protecting children where professionals are convinced that a child has been abused but where hard evidence to establish this is lacking. It should be noted however that in a recent case the High Court held that what triggers a local authority's duty under Section 47 is a *reasonable cause to suspect* that a particular person poses a risk to children, and not a *reasonable cause to believe* that a particular child has or is likely to suffer harm. Thus in that particular case the court held that it was reasonable for two local authorities to take the view that allegations of child sexual abuse made some years earlier against the claimant were credible and to put in place an action plan to afford protection to the children with whom the claimant was now living. (*R (on the application of S)* v. *Swindon Borough Council and another* [2001] 3 FCR 702.)

Good practice dictates that an interdepartmental and inter-agency child protection investigation into an allegation of child abuse should proceed alongside a police investigation of whether a crime has been committed. In many cases the child will provide the best, and possibly the only, evidence that abuse has occurred. Therefore it is usual practice to begin an investigation by arranging for the child to be interviewed on video by a police officer and social worker in accordance with the *Memorandum of Good Practice* (Department of Health 1992). The *Memorandum* requires the interview to be acceptable in criminal proceedings. The interviewers are there to listen to what the child has to say, if anything, about the alleged abuse and the purpose of the interview is to establish whether there is evidence to support a criminal prosecution. Leading questions should not be asked and the interview should not have a therapeutic content. This style of interview was introduced after the Cleveland Inquiry (Butler-Sloss 1988) and following the condemnation by a number of High Court judges (see the seven cases reported in [1987] 1 FLR 269–346) of the practice of vulnerable children being led into 'disclosures' of sexual abuse following repeated interviews by professionals convinced from the outset that abuse had occurred. The extent to which children can be coaxed into making false allegations should not be underestimated. While many child care professionals adopt the view that children should always be believed, research suggests that children, while honest, are prone to suggestion and with a degree of encouragement will make up stories to fit in with what they believe their adult questioners want to hear. The most compelling research has been done by Stephen Ceci (see e.g. Ceci & Bruck 1993) and indeed a video presentation of his research is now routinely used for the purposes of judicial training. False allegations are thought to occur rarely (Goodwin, Sahd & Rada 1985), perhaps in less than 2 per cent of cases where the focus is on allegations made solely by children (Anthony & Watkeys 1991). Given that the purpose of the *Memorandum* interview is to establish whether there is evidence to justify a criminal prosecution or to put in place any other child protection measures, it is very important that those interviewing the child have the expertise to elicit the truth rather than what they, the interviewers, want to hear. There are undoubtedly some very skilled interviewers who, without leading the child, are able to draw out details of the child's abuse, but this is by no means the norm. Some children find the interview traumatic, particularly if video filming was involved in their own abuse. Many children have difficulty speaking fluently and openly about their abusive experiences and need skilled, professional help to describe what has happened to them. If a child is unable to speak about abusive experiences during a *Memorandum* interview, social workers may take the view that, whatever their suspicions, there is insufficient evidence to warrant child protection measures being put in place. Conversely if a *Memorandum* interview is badly conducted and an abused child is inadvertently led into making allegations, rather than being allowed to make them spontaneously, this may compromise further interviews and lead to the eventual conclusion that the evidence is too unreliable for the matter to be taken further.

## Protection through the civil courts

### Public law proceedings

Where a child protection investigation identifies causes for concern, the local authority's first duty is to address those concerns by the provision of services to the family. The types of services that should be provided are set out in Part III and Schedule II of the Act and include the power to provide alternative accommodation for an alleged abuser, thus enabling the child to remain within the family home. However, there will be cases where very serious concerns for the child's welfare arise and/or the local authority is not able to engage the family's cooperation. In those cases local authorities may seek to supplement their powers with orders of the court.

Where social workers are having difficulty obtaining a family's cooperation with a Section 47 investigation, an application may be made to the court for a child assessment order. Parents are required to produce the child and comply with directions relating to the assessment. If necessary the child can be kept away from home to enable the assessment to be completed.

In practice this order is rarely applied for. It is much more likely that care proceedings will be commenced and the local authority will seek to protect the child by obtaining a care or supervision order. A care order places the child in the care of a local authority which means that the local authority acquires parental responsibility for the child and can act, in almost every respect, as the child's parent. If necessary the authority can remove the child from home and place him or her in a permanent substitute family. A care order lasts until the child is 18 unless it is discharged at an earlier date by a court order. A supervision order does not confer any parental rights but obliges the local authority to supervise the child by advising, assisting and befriending him or her. A supervision order lasts for up to 12 months and can be renewed for a total period not exceeding three years.

In cases of suspected child sexual abuse it is not uncommon for local authorities to apply, when commencing care proceedings, for an emergency protection order. The application is usually made without notice being given to the child's parents and, if the order is granted, allows the local authority to remove the child from home. If necessary a warrant may be issued for the police to assist in the child's removal. In cases of suspected child sexual abuse, an emergency protection order reduces the risk of a child being 'silenced' prior to protective measures being put in place. A number of directions may be attached to the order that are likely to be par-ticularly helpful where child sexual abuse is suspected. The court may direct that the child is to be subject to a medical or psychiatric examination. An early medical examination may be crucial as many physical signs of abuse heal very quickly once the child is removed from the abusive environment. The court also has the power to exclude any person from the home in which the child is living and to regulate or prevent contact between the child and a particular person. Thus a suspected abuser may be excluded from the home, enabling the child to remain.

The grounds for making a care or supervision order are the same. The court must be satisfied that what are called the 'statutory threshold criteria' have been met; that is to say, that the child is suffering or is likely to suffer significant harm and that the harm or likelihood of harm is attributable to the care given to the child (or likely to be given to them if the order were not made) not being what would be reasonable to expect a parent to give.

Generally speaking, it is easier to obtain a finding that a child has been sexually abused in care proceedings than it is in criminal proceedings. This is due to a number of factors, in particular the lower standard of proof and the very wide range of evidence that the court is entitled to take into account. Allegations in care proceedings must be proved on a balance of probabilities; that is to say, the court must be satisfied that abuse is more likely than not to have occurred, or that a particular person is more likely than not to be an abuser. Any evidence that may assist the court in reaching a decision is admissible as is illustrated in the following passage from the judgment of Lord Nicholls in *Re H & R ( Child Sexual Abuse: Standard of Proof)* [1996] 1 FLR 80:

> The range of facts which may properly be taken into account are infinite. Facts include the history of members of the family, the state of relationships within a family, proposed changes within the membership of a family, parental attitudes and omissions which might not reasonably have been expected, just as much as actual physical assaults. They include threats and abnormal behaviour by a child, and unsatisfactory parental responses to complaints or allegations. And facts, which are minor or even trivial if considered in isolation, when taken together may suffice to satisfy the court of the likelihood of . . . harm.

While it is easier to obtain a finding of sexual abuse in care proceedings, local authorities may experience considerable difficulties in proving allegations to the requisite standard. The following case illustrates the numerous difficulties that all too often arise in establishing that sexual abuse has occurred as well as the difficulties faced by professionals who are convinced that a particular person poses a sexual risk to children but are unable to prove this to the requisite legal standard.

In *Re R (Care: Disclosure: Nature of Proceedings)* [2002] I FLR 755, the local authority sought care orders in respect of five children on the grounds that they had been neglected and also that the four boys had been sexually abused. The perpetrators were alleged to be the father, mother, maternal grandfather and maternal uncle and there were also allegations that the two eldest boys had abused their younger brothers. The children were initially removed from home because of serious concerns about neglect. The local authority's case was that the first allegation of sexual abuse had been made 'out of the blue' by one of the boys to the foster mother with whom he and two of his brothers had been placed. The foster mother gave written and oral evidence of this. At a later stage in the case, material on the local authority's file revealed that two of the boys had made earlier allegations of abuse which had been discussed with the foster mother. One of the boys had been interviewed three times by the police. At the first interview he made no allegations of abuse but did so at the second and third interviews when he had been accompanied by a friend of the foster mother with whom he may also have discussed his allegations. As a result of these evidential difficulties the local authority was obliged, on the thirteenth day of the case, to abandon the allegations of sexual abuse. In his judgement, Mr Justice Charles highlighted the need for allegations of sexual abuse to be properly investigated and for cases to be properly prepared. He detailed the necessity for there to be a proper examination of local authority files, for there to be detailed discussions with relevant witnesses and for factual details given by children in their interviews to be checked. In this particular case, there were no less than six expert assessments, all conducted on an incorrect factual basis as to when the first allegation of abuse arose. The extent to which those assessments could be relied upon was therefore limited. The police interviews with the boys were also of limited value as they too had been conducted on the same incorrect factual basis.

Further difficulties arose in relation to the disposal of the case as a result of the fact that the allegations of sexual abuse had been abandoned. At the conclusion of the case, care orders were made because of the level of neglect suffered by the children. However, the local authority's care plans assumed that sexual abuse had occurred as this was the belief of those professionals working with the children. Before making care orders the judge required the local authority to amend the care plans so as to delete any provision made for the children on the basis that they had been sexually abused themselves or posed a sexual risk to others. The judge highlighted the difficulties faced by local authorities, who must assess risk and take child protection decisions, but who cannot proceed on the basis that children are at risk of sexual abuse if the allegations are denied by the alleged abusers and have not been proved to the satisfaction of a court. For a child in care who has in fact been sexually abused, the absence of a finding to this effect may mean that he or she cannot be properly treated and that the potential risk posed by that young person to others cannot be properly assessed or reduced.

Unfortunately, many local authority social services departments are overworked and understaffed and all have finite resources. Thorough investigations of allegations of sexual abuse and/or proper case preparation may not be practically possible. If initial allegations of child sexual abuse are not adequately recorded or followed up, subsequent allegations may be rendered unreliable, no matter how plausible and genuine they seem. In this particular case, the local authority was able to ask the court to make orders affording protection to the children because of the allegations of long-standing neglect. However, had the only allegations been of sexual abuse, no orders would have been made and the children would have been returned to the care of their parents without there being any basis for the local authority to implement a child protection plan in the absence of cooperation from the parents.

Where findings are made, the court can ensure that the particular child involved in the proceedings is protected from further abuse, but cannot afford protection to children in general by directing that the abuser submits to a course of treatment. Even monitoring a known abuser in the community can be difficult as the following case example illustrates.

Mr Y was a seemingly respectable businessman with a keen interest in sailing. At the local yacht club he befriended many children, particular young girls, and took them out on his boat. He showed a particular interest in the 9-year-old twin daughters of a vulnerable single mother, Ms B. One of the twins, S, alleged to a teacher that, during a sailing trip, Mr Y had touched her in a sexual way. She repeated these allegations to her mother and a social worker. Mr Y was interviewed by the police and denied the allegations. However, a search of his home led to his being successfully prosecuted for offences relating to child pornographic material. He continued to keep in touch with Ms B and convinced her of his innocence. In care proceedings the court found that Mr Y had sexually abused S and posed a risk generally to girls of her age. The court made injunctions preventing Mr Y from going to Ms B's home or having any contact with the twins. Despite this, Mr Y's relationship with Ms B continued, the twins being looked after by relatives when Ms B visited Mr Y's home. The local authority suspected that the injunction was being breached but did not have the resources to police Ms B's home day and night. Consideration was given to seeking a care order so that the children could be removed from home, but the risks posed by Mr Y to the children had to be balanced against the emotional trauma they would suffer if removed from a mother to whom they were both devoted. At any time Mr Y may move to a different part of the country, where he would be difficult to trace and where he may begin to 'groom' another family.

A final difficulty in relation to care proceedings is that, unlike in criminal proceedings, the court does not have to determine any allegations, and has no power to compel the attendance at court of a suspected abuser. Thus an alleged abuser may choose to leave the family home and take no part in the subsequent care proceedings. If he is not a party to the proceedings, the court is unable to make a finding against him in his absence and if at some later stage he chooses either to return to the family or to form a new relationship, the local authority may be obliged to start proceedings again. The passage of time may then mean that the authority has evidential difficulties in proving its case.

A positive aspect of the Act is that some encouragement is given to alleged abusers to make admissions during care proceedings by giving them indemnity from prosecution for sexual offences. Section 98 provides that any statement or admission made by any person during care proceedings is not admissible as evidence against that person in proceedings for an offence other than perjury. From a child protection perspective, the best possible outcome for the child is that the alleged abuser admits what he has done. It is then possible for the court to direct a comprehensive risk assessment that may lead to the local authority agreeing to fund a treatment programme. Thus not only is the abused child protected but the future risk posed by the abuser to other children is reduced. It is clearly very difficult to assess and treat abusers who deny the allegations against them, even when they are proved to the satisfaction of the court. It is also much more difficult to obtain funding for the assessment and treatment of those who admit to child sexual abuse when there are no proceedings pending, particularly as admissions may lead to criminal proceedings. Unfortunately it remains the position in the UK that agreement to a treatment programme is not an alternative to prosecution, as it is in some parts of the USA.

### Private law proceedings

Generally speaking, private law proceedings arise where parents or other close family members dispute what is to happen regarding a child. The principal private law provisions are set out in Part II of the Act. The four principal orders made by the court are residence orders that specify with whom a child will reside, contact orders that specify who the child is to visit and in what circumstances, prohibited steps orders that prevent a named person or persons from exercising a particular aspect of parental responsibility and specific issue orders that resolve parental disputes such as where the child should go to school. The court may also make injunctions to support the making of any of those orders, for example by ordering that the child reside with the mother and making an injunction that the father is not to attempt to remove the child from the mother's care. It can be seen that these orders in combination might be used to protect a child from an alleged abuser – for example, by regulating or prohibiting that person's contact with the child. However, as in care proceedings, it may be difficult to prove that abuse has occurred or that a particular person is the perpetrator of that abuse.

In recent years it is the perception of many lawyers and judges that there has been an increase in the number of allegations of child sexual abuse arising where parents are separated, and difficulties occur in relation to the father's contact with the children. Some argue that this is hardly surprising given the increasing public awareness of the prevalence of child sexual abuse generally, while others argue that there has been an increasing awareness among mothers, reluctant to see their ex-partners enjoying contact with their children, that making allegations of sexual abuse usually brings contact to an end. Occasionally, estranged spouses have been thought to instigate allegations which are malicious or founded on fears rooted in their own abusive childhoods; or children have been victimised but have identified the wrong perpetrator. Robin Wilson (2002) from the University of South Carolina convincingly argues that divorce itself significantly elevates the risk of sexual abuse, though only for girls. While child sexual abuse occurs across all economic and racial backgrounds it is not distributed randomly but occurs more often after family breakdown when the sexual vulnerability of girls is much greater than that of boys.

Against that background it is unfortunate that when allegations of sexual abuse are made after marital breakdown they are rarely resolved to anyone's satisfaction and the following scenario is not uncommon. Mother reports that the child has returned from visiting father in a distressed state and has disclosed that father touched him or her in a sexual way. The report is often made to a local authority, whose attitude can be inadvertently unhelpful in that, if the mother is willing to ensure that the father no longer has contact with the child, there will be little or no social work investigation. The onus is then on the father to bring the matter to court. Contested cases may take months to come to trial by which time the relationship between the father and his child may have been irrevocably damaged. The 'innocent' father may take the view that there is no purpose to be served in asking the court to make a finding in relation to the allegations as contact will not be possible in any event. Conversely, an abusing father may simply use the breakdown in contact as an excuse to withdraw his application, abandon his child and move on to another family. If concerns then arise several years later it is very difficult to consider the earlier evidence. More disturbing still is the prospect that a child making allegations may have been abused, but not by the father. The actual abuser may then go undetected.

The following case example illustrates the difficulty.

The relationship between Mr and Mrs C has broken down. Mr C has contact with his 8-year-old daughter S but Mrs C alleges that S is unhappy after contact visits and reluctant to talk about what she and her father have been doing. Mrs C discovers that, years before, P, the daughter of a previous partner of Mr C complained that Mr C had sexually assaulted her. Mr C left the relationship and never saw P again. P, now an adult, agrees to give evidence for Mrs C in proceedings brought by Mr C for contact with S. P is a very plausible and convincing witness. The judge makes no criticism of her evidence but takes the view that because of the passage of time he cannot now find that it is probable that abuse occurred. Mr C continues to have unsupervised contact with S which eventually breaks down because of Mrs C's anxiety and S's distress. Mr C moves to a different area and forms another relationship. Whether or not he poses a sexual risk to children may never be determined.

## Children and young people

A particular area of difficulty exists where the alleged perpetrator of child sexual abuse is another child or young person. Calder (1997) highlights the fact that it may be difficult to differentiate between normal and abusive sexual behaviour in children and young people, and that professionals appear to have no clear and common approach about the identification and treatment of child sex offenders. It is clearly in the interests of child protection generally that sexually abusive behaviour by children and young people is quickly and reliably identified as treatment is likely to be much more successful when patterns of sexually deviant behaviour have not had time to become ingrained. However, our experience is that social work professionals and the courts have understandable difficulty in deciding whether a child should be treated as a victim or an abuser, and a consequent dilemma as to whether it is the abusing child or his victims who require to be protected. McClurg and Craissati's (1999) study of CPRs in two London boroughs identified that 9 per cent of perpetrators in one borough were children and associated with siblings placed on the register under the category of sexual abuse; the average age of these young perpetrators was 4.8 years, half had already been abused by someone else and their victims were almost always relatives. Interestingly the second borough had no registered young perpetrators. The following case example illustrates the problem.

Mr P has three sons whom he sexually abuses. He also obtains sexual satisfaction by instructing his sons to sexually abuse each other. His offending behaviour comes to the attention of the local authority and the three boys are moved to a residential unit. Once removed from home they do not demonstrate any sexually inappropriate behaviour and appear to be very distressed and ashamed of what has happened. A psychologist instructed to assess them recommends that they be placed in a specialist unit for adolescent sex offenders where they can address their offending behaviour and thus reduce their chances of offending again in the future. A social work assessment concludes that the boys should be placed in a specialist foster home where they can experience normal family life with non-abusing parents. The social worker's view is that the boys will be vulnerable to further abuse if placed in a sex offenders' unit. The child protection dilemma is obvious.

## Assessing unconvicted sex offenders

Very little has been researched regarding the risk assessment of unconvicted sex offenders. Yet the majority of child molesters – at least three quarters – sexually assault children they know (Grubin 1998) and up to 80 per cent of offences take place in either the home of the offender or the home of the victim (Bradford, Bloomberg & Bourget 1988). Obvious reasons include the difficulty in persuading such individuals to engage in assessment and in tracking them over time. McClurg and Craissati (1999) were able to obtain information on alleged offenders related to children placed on the CPR under the category of 'sexual abuse'. They found that 70 per cent of offenders were new cases with allegations made, not leading to a conviction, whilst 8 per cent were Schedule 1 offenders with new allegations. Only 21 per cent of the sample had previous sexual convictions. Of those with new allegations made against them, only 16 per cent accepted these, at least partially.

The assumption is usually made that unconvicted offenders are likely to resemble their convicted counterparts. This may be true, if failure to convict is largely related to police and prosecution procedures, responses in court or victim characteristics. However, it does not take into account possible offender variables, such as the quality of his relationship with the victim – whether hostile or enmeshed – or his willingness and capacity to lie fluently. Further-more, it seems likely that a successful prosecution will have a signifi-cantly aversive impact on many sex offenders, particularly those whose behaviour is not primarily driven by a deviant sexual interest, and that this may deter them from future temptation to offend.

Having sounded a note of caution, the recommendation would be to utilise well established risk assessment approaches in order to determine relative levels of risk posed by an unconvicted offender. This entails considering the credibility of the allegations carefully, and then treating them as though they led to conviction. Relevant variables (as detailed in Chapters 2 and 3) then need to be taken into account (*note*: the scoring systems of actuarially-based tools have not been validated on unconvicted sex offenders).

There are three additional factors to take into account. First, previous allegations made against the perpetrator are of relevance, as prior sexual convictions are important. For example, Craissati and Beech (2003) found that prior allegations against the offender were significantly associated with subsequent failure in the community (post conviction and sentence). However, previous allegations should relate to different victims in order to be significant, rather than repeated allegations from the same victim.

Second, there are understandable concerns regarding stepfathers, particularly men who have allegedly offended against previous step-children and enter new families. Clearly, one hypothesis to be held in mind is that these are individuals with a dominant sexual interest in children who consciously access victims by targeting single parent families. Alternative, and viable, hypotheses might conclude that such men have a primary difficulty in managing intimate relation-ships and seek out partners who are likely to be dependent upon them and thus less threatening to their precarious sense of self-esteem. Sometimes, having seriously failed in one relationship, an alleged offender may establish a strong and mutually satisfying relationship with a woman who has children. Such judgements can be finely balanced.

The third issue relates to the question of crossover, which was also discussed in Chapter 3. To reiterate, Thornton and Hanson (1996) found that only offenders with male child victims were at risk of subsequently offending against female children and adolescents (14 per cent); less than 3 per cent of child molesters with female victims crossed over to male victims. In Abel *et al.*'s (1987) oft-quoted study of a group of unusually disturbed child molesters, they found that sons were rarely targeted by their fathers (8 per cent) compared to 33 per cent who targeted daughters. Therefore, if an unconvicted offender has had a female victim the likelihood of a boy within the family becoming a victim is very low in relative terms, while an offender who has prior male victims, or victims of both sexes or previously unrelated to him may pose a higher risk to boys in the current family.

The alleged offender's denial of any sexually inappropriate behaviour in relation to a particular victim or allegation – as with convicted offenders – is *not likely to be closely related to increased risk*. This is probably the single most difficult myth to relinquish as it appears to be counter-intuitive. It provokes natural feelings of out-rage on behalf of the victim, and often influences the offender's partner in ways which render child protection procedures more difficult. The assumption that an alleged offender should 'confess' is based on the premise that it will be a constructive step forward. This may well be the case, particularly in validating the victim's experience and assisting recovery. However, the advantages for the alleged offender are minimal, and vastly outweighed by the likely consequences.

The Faithful Classification Scheme (FACS) (Friendship & Thornton 2002: 315–16) is based on the above principles and contains nine areas to guide risk assessment with unconvicted intrafamilial sex offenders where there is at least one credible allegation against them. It has been piloted but *not* formally validated. Any of the following should lead to raised risk concerns:

1   *3 + victims?* Are there credible allegations of sexual offences against at least three persons aged under 16 at the time they were first offended against?

2   *Young (18 to 30)?* The age offender will be when he next has the opportunity to offend (age now if in the community; age when offender is to be released if currently in prison or hospital).

3   *Extrafamilial victims?* Are there credible allegations of sexual offences against any child who is not a relative (count step-children as relatives if lived with the offender as a dependent child for at least two years before offending began; 'child' = under 16)?

4   *Criminal (non-sexual) offences?* Any convictions for non-sexual offences? Count only offences for which he could have been given a community rehabilitation order or a custodial sentence. Do not count offences for which he was only cautioned.

5   *Lack of stable adult relationships?* After the age of 18, has never lived with an adult sexual partner for at least two years.

6   *Violent offences?* Any credible allegations of non-sexual assaults sufficiently severe that if proved in court they could result in a criminal conviction for violence? Threatening behaviour short of physical violence does not count for this item.

7   *Distortions?* When assessed, does the offender express beliefs of the kind that might be used to 'give permission' for the sexual abuse of children? To count for this item these beliefs must be generalised (i.e. not be specificially limited to just one child). Typical examples of 'permission-giving' beliefs are: 'children are interested in sex with adults'; 'children are seductive to adults'; 'children can enjoy sex with adults so long as the adult is nice/gentle/kind'; 'men suffer when they are deprived of sex and are entitled to seek gratification where they can find it' etc.

8   *Impulsiveness?* Apart from the sexual offending itself, does the offender show evidence of any of the following:

- repeated poor problem-solving;
- repeatedly acting without thinking about the consequences of his behaviour;
- a lifestyle that is disorganised and chaotic;
- a general tendency to make irresponsible choices?

A lifestyle disrupted by serious alcohol abuse or drug problems would count as an example of 'disorganised lifestyle'.

9  *Sexual preference?* Is there evidence of a sexual interest in children below the age of 13? Score this item as present if there is a credible allegation of a sexual offence against any male under the age of 16. Score this item as present if there is a credible allegation of a sexual offence against three or more female children aged under 13. Also score it as present on the basis of finding child pornography, of specialist assessment, the finding of a diary recording fantasies or admissions by the offender.

## Mothers: the non-abusing parent

This section is predominantly focused on non-offending women, as female offenders are addressed elsewhere in the book. Practitioners whose core responsibilities lie with child protection may find it useful to turn to Calder's (2001) book on mothers of sexually abused children, written from a social services perspective or Furniss' (1991) work, written from a child mental health perspective, both of which are practically-based guides.

All too often, the focus of risk assessment remains preoccupied with the offender himself. In many ways, this is a reasonable back-lash to the way in which both mothers and child victims were previously viewed by clinicians. This is vividly illustrated by Salter (1988: 36–7) who cites quotes (mother 'keeps herself tired and worn out . . . a history of sexually rejecting and deprecating their husbands') which now shock us by their distorted and naïve perception of the way in which sexual abuse manifests itself in families. Nevertheless, a sex offender's risk cannot be viewed in isolation when he is linked to a family structure in which there are potential victims. Put simply, there is a child protection triangle (see Figure 4.1) which highlights three core elements: the offender's risk characteristics, the mother as non-abusing parent and the child as potential victim (also described by Calder 2001).

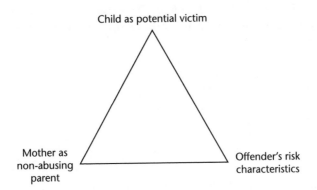

*Figure 4.1* The child protection triangle

Assessing potential child victims is beyond the remit of this book. In brief, it would be reasonable to consider potential child victims in terms of their identified vulnerabilities; that is, placing the child at an increased risk of victimisation. External vulnerabilities might be situational factors, such as the extent of time alone in the offender's care. Inherent vulnerabilities might include gender and age, given the offender's victim pool, significant learning difficulties, a history of prior sexual victimisation, poor integration with peers, concerning precocious or sexualised behaviour or a hostile/detached relationship with mother or other primary caregiver (such as grand-mother). Such variables have often been observed in the literature as being associated with raised risk of victimisation, although extreme care must be taken in determining whether these are the precursors to, or the consequences of, abuse (Calder 2001).

Mothers can find themselves in two positions in relation to child protection concerns with sex offenders: the mother's child discloses abuse perpetrated by the mother's partner, or a close family member; or the mother's new partner has previously sexually abused another child. Much of the literature fails to distinguish between these two situations, although it is reasonable to assume that the issues are largely similar. It is only when considering the extent or quality of the emotional impact that disclosure might have that there are likely to be differences: when a mother learns that another child was victimised by her partner in the past, the impact is likely to be diluted and she may well focus more intensely on the fact that he did not tell her, rather than other issues.

Both Salter (1988) and Calder (2001) put forward simple continuum models of a mother's role in sexual abuse. Salter (1988) suggests that mothers:

- did not know, but support the child;
- did not know, and deny it happened;
- did not know, but side with partner;
- knew, but did not stop it;
- set up or participate in the abuse.

Calder's (2001) model overlaps, but also includes mothers who seek help inappropriately and are therefore ineffective, and mothers who allow their children to dress and make-up in a way which is developmentally inappropriate and unsafe. Everson, Hunter, Runyon, Edelsohn and Coulter (1989) evaluated parental reactions on the basis of three ratings for:

- emotional support (ranging from commitment and support of child, to threats, hostility and psychological abandonment of child);
- belief of the child (ranging from a public statement of belief to denying that abuse occurred);
- action towards the perpetrator (ranging from actively demonstrating disapproval of the abusive behaviour to choosing them over the child).

Numerous studies have examined mothers' behaviour after a disclosure of abuse. Most have found that the majority of mothers take protective action (Mannarino & Cohen 1986; Peters 1976) in reporting the abuse to the authorities and are supportive when they learn of the disclosure (Berliner & Conte 1995). Peters (1976) found that only 17 per cent were angry with their child and 14 per cent were concerned about the effect it might have on their family, the others being predominantly concerned for the child's well-being. Wilson (1995) found that over 90 per cent of the mothers in her sample either believed the child and took steps to protect or were ambivalent but sided with the child. Lyon and Kouloumpos-Lenaris (1987) found that although 70 per cent of mothers believed their children had been sexually abused, only 50 per cent responded with protective action and emotional support. While none of the non-believing mothers provided a protective response, 58 per cent of the believing mothers were actively helpful (42 per cent, of course, being less actively helpful).

When faced with a disclosure of sexual abuse, most mothers will react with a variety of intense feelings – anger, shock, guilt and denial. As the allegations begin to be assimilated, most mothers – as described above – will be able to support the victim, place responsibility for what occurred on the perpetrator and take some form of protective action, usually expelling the perpetrator from the family home. However, sometimes denial persists and can often lead to a more ambivalent response. This is particularly striking when a mother is initially furious with the perpetrator but later appears to retract her acknowledgement of what has occurred, and deceives agencies in resuming a relationship with the perpetrator.

Denial in mothers – as with sex offenders themselves – is a coping strategy to defend against feelings of anxiety (Craissati 1998). It is likely to be a fluid state, which can be seriously aggravated by con-frontational or judgemental approaches by agencies which raise rather than reduce such anxieties. At its most benign, denial in mothers may well be at an emotional level, cognitively they believe the abuse occurred, but emotionally they cannot accept it (Johnson, 1992). At its most malignant, denial is maintained by mothers who are lying and who may have been present at the abuse or participated in it (Furniss 1991). In these rare cases, working with the mother and child will be counterproductive, often provoking increased hostility and scapegoating towards the abused child. More commonly, mothers may deny what has occurred for a range of reasons which are not necessarily indicative of a collusive relationship with the perpetrator, but rather of an intensely conflicting situation in which the wish to protect is opposed by other needs, loyalties and feelings (Heriot 1996). Such denial may be due to the following (Calder 2001):

- a fear of loss, in terms of financial and practical support, or in terms of a strong emotional attachment to the partner;
- a lack of social and family networks;
- a lack of information or understanding that the allegation of sexual abuse can really have been perpetrated by someone she knows and cares for;
- an overly dependent attachment on the partner, who is experienced as the source of all the mother's emotional needs;

- fear of a physically abusive partner;
- feelings of guilt at having failed to protect the child;
- difficulty in acknowledging her own experiences of victimisation as a child, which have been brought to the surface by this disclosure, and which lead to defensive reactions of hostility towards others;
- a strong rivalry between mother and child, suggestive of distorted mother/child boundaries.

Denial manifests itself in other ways. A mother might accept that sexual abuse occurred, but she takes the blame for this upon herself, or believes that it is she who will have to change in order to reduce risk. A proportion of mothers accept the abuse, but deny the need for any outside support for the child or the family. Some mothers who enter relationships with convicted or alleged sex offenders deny future risk to their children. It is not uncommon for a mother to agree that sex offenders, in general, reoffend all the time, but to state categorically that her partner will not reoffend. However, to what extent a mother must be able to envisage her partner as capable of sexually assaulting her children is unclear. Some would say that this precludes any possibility of a meaningful and happy relationship.

To a greater or lesser extent, many of the above issues can be addressed, particularly when due care is given to establishing an empathic, consistent and collaborative relationship between the mother and the child protection agency. However, there are features of a mother's early life and pattern of relationships which are a poor prognostic indicator in terms of future protection of the children. These include:

- a childhood history of severe and repeated sexual or physical abuse;
- a relationship with her own mother which was characterised by extreme rejection and emotional deprivation;
- a repetitive pattern of relationships with men in adulthood who are abusive, sexually or physically, to her or the children;
- prior concerns of neglect and abuse towards her own children;
- marked mental health difficulties, including personality disorder and substance misuse.

## Case study

### Stephen

Stephen was a 30-year-old man, referred by social services due to concerns regarding the potential risk he may pose to his step-daughter (Penny) who was currently aged 10. Four years ago, his 8-year-old biological daughter (Natalie) from a previous relationship alleged that he had sexually abused her while he was living at the family home. He was arrested and charged, but the case did not proceed as his daughter did not wish to give evidence against him. Three years later, he married a woman (Jane) with a young daughter, but the matter did not come to social services' attention for a year until a routine police check revealed his offending background.

Stephen initially denied abusing Natalie, but when challenged more recently by social services, admitted that she had told the truth. He felt that the abuse occurred within the context of rejection by his partner and financial stress, together with a growing feeling of close-ness to Natalie; that in some ways they sought refuge in each other, against his partner. He was deeply regretful about his behaviour, but was confident that it would never reoccur, that Penny would never be at risk.

The static assessment tools generally viewed Stephen as posing a low risk in general terms. A review of possible dynamic risk variables suggested that there were some intimacy deficits in terms of his low feelings of self-esteem and insecurity in relationships. He was clearly emotionally identified with his victim at the time of the offence, but there was no suggestion of this being the case with other children. The main risk factor appeared to be the absence of a detailed and realistic relapse prevention plan, in that he viewed himself as low risk but was in fact living in a potentially high risk situation.

A social services' assessment of Penny concluded that she was a cheerful, confident young girl who liked Stephen and had a strong and affectionate bond with her mother. Academically she was performing well at school and had a good circle of friends. The only risk factor – aside from her age and gender – was that she had no contact with her biological father and felt hurt by this; however, there was no evidence of an unhealthy attachment or dependence on Stephen as a substitute source of attention. She was consistently clear in stating to social services that she wished Stephen to return home with them.

Jane, Penny's mother, came from a happy and loving family background. She felt she had been spoiled as a child, and this was at the root of the failure of her first marriage. Her relationship with Penny's father was turbulent, largely because he was repeatedly unfaithful to Jane and drank heavily. Initially she was ashamed to admit to her family that a second relationship was failing, but eventually she accepted their support and left him. Having retrained and established herself as financially independent, she met and married Stephen. She felt he lacked confidence, but shared many of her interests and they had a strong relationship. When told about the previous allegation against Stephen, she was initially furious with him for not telling her, and told him to leave the family home. As Stephen admitted to the abuse, she was able to believe that fondling did occur, but felt that the victim may have exaggerated or been mistaken about some of the detail; she also felt it was situational, in that Stephen was in an unhappy relationship at the time, in which he was 'being used'. Three months after the initial disclosure, Jane made it clear to social services that she wished Stephen to be reintegrated into the family.

As no finding was ever made that Stephen had sexually abused his daughter, his move to another area was not monitored and no one alerted Jane to the potential risk he posed to her daughter. Child protection measures could be put in place only because Stephen admitted his offending behaviour and was prepared to cooperate with a risk assessment. If Stephen had chosen to disappear when the allegations came to light, the potential risk he posed to children would probably have gone undetected for many more years. Had he denied his offending behaviour, the local authority may have had difficulty, several years after the event, in proving that abuse occurred. When Stephen's background came to the attention of the local authority it is likely that consideration was given to whether care proceedings should be commenced. Had Stephen denied the allegations, the attitude taken by his wife would have been crucial. If she had taken the local authority's concerns on board and had agreed to Stephen's exclusion from the home, it is likely that proceedings would have been unnecessary. If she had accepted Stephen's denials the local authority would have had to consider, before commencing proceedings, whether they had the evidence to prove the allegations in court. Given that Stephen admitted the allegations, the local authority would have had no difficulty in proving their case and might have considered applying for a supervision order. However, given the 'no order' principle outlined above, the authority would have had to consider whether an order was necessary. The level of cooperation of Stephen and his wife would be the crucial factor in deciding whether or not to apply for a supervision order. Also, it is sometimes the case that local authorities have access to greater funding in, and are able to give priority to, those cases where there is a statutory order. Thus an application may be made for a supervision order where costly treatment is proposed.

The following were agreed as part of the management plan, written in a contract, and signed by all parties:

- Stephen would commence a community treatment programme.
- Jane would negotiate no night or weekend duties at work for the next six months.
- Jane would have six sessions with the social worker in order to understand the nature and level of risk, and to put in place an effective plan for monitoring and protecting Penny.
- If a positive report were received after the first module of treatment, Stephen would return home.
- Stephen would have no unsupervised contact with Penny, despite returning home, until reassessed after one year of treatment.

## Summary

It is extremely difficult to evaluate the effectiveness of current child protection measures in the long term. The sort of child protection measures outlined above can be very effective in protecting a particular child from a particular abuser and some therapeutic work with a child and his or her primary carer can be effective in reducing the child's sexual vulnerability. However, even if it were possible to identify all those children at risk of abuse it is totally unrealistic to suppose that child protection measures of the sort outlined above could be put in place in every case. The resources are not, and will never be, available. Outcome studies, specific to child sexual abuse and the efficacy of child protection measures, are not available. There is limited evidence for re-referral or reoccurrence of abuse. McClurg and Craissati (1999) found that there was evidence in 36 per cent of families registered (category of sexual abuse) that one or more of the children had previously been sexually abused by a different adult, and that physical abuse also occurred in such families. Hamilton and Browne (1999) found that sexual abuse cases were the least likely to be re-referred to police protection units (neglect and failure to thrive being the most likely); in total, four out of ten children in their sample were re-referred over a 27-month period, but only 4.6 per cent of sexual abuse cases were re-referred for repeat victimisation by the same perpetrator; 5.7 per cent were re-referred for revictimisation by another perpetrator. Child characteristics and the absence of the mother from the family home appeared to be linked to re-referral in sexual abuse cases. McClurg and Craissati (1999) concluded that there was an important sub-group of families which were characterised by: the victim choosing not to make the allegations of abuse to his/her mother; the adult parents remaining together following the allegations; a high incidence of physical violence within the family; and the victim subsequently being placed outside the family. Given resource limitations, it may be that child protection measures need to be graded in their intensity, targeting high risk, high pathology families where the risk of revictimisation is highest. Primary prevention – such as parental and child education – may need to play a far greater role in the longer term in managing risk.

Chapter 5

# Risk management: the probation and police perspective

*Geraldine Gavin and Jackie Craissati*

## Introduction

This chapter represents a shift in focus to criminal justice agencies, which have led the way in terms of risk management in the community. These developments will be addressed in terms of their legislative framework, and then via a more detailed examination of the Multi-Agency Public Protection Arrangements (MAPPA).

Those of us working in the criminal justice system have spend over a decade now learning to implement measures that prioritise the protection of the public. It could be argued that any work that aims to reduce an offender's criminal career is necessarily reducing the risk that further victims will be created. However, in reality there have been fundamental changes in legislation and policy which have changed the focus of the Probation Service's work. If historically Probation's mission statement was to 'advise assist and befriend', there is no doubt that it is now to 'enforce, rehabilitate and protect' (Her Majesty's Inspectorate of Probation 2001). These developments have been driven by a need to work in an effective way with offenders, and to concentrate our efforts on those who are assessed as posing the highest risk.

Some consideration of broader societal theory is essential to remind us that developments in the criminal justice system do not take place in a vacuum; we are subject to the same political climate as allied professions such as social work, mental health and others (Kemshall 2002). For example, Giddens (1990) identified an important feature of modern life as 'confidence in expert knowledge' – as citizens we tended to trust the architect who designed our home or the air traffic controller who guided our flight in. Giddens wondered if a period of 'late modernity' had arrived, whereby we have lost our faith in experts and have become cynical about their ability. In short, we are preoccupied with the perils in our world (and probably perceive them in an exaggerated way), but have lost faith in the powers of experts and science to deal with them. The position of professionals (whether it be in medicine, food science or the criminal justice system) becomes invidious: we do not trust experts to predict and control like we used to, but at the same time we cannot do without them because we want them to calculate risk for us.

Opinions differ in the academic criminology world (Garland 1991; Pratt 2000) as to whether developments in the risk industry signal a qualitative change in the criminal justice system. Pratt (2000) concludes that developments in the UK, USA, Australia, Canada and New Zealand hark back to principles of shaming and humiliation redolent of pre-modernism. Barbara Hudson (2001), however, cautions against the potential to disregard offenders' rights and liberties against the foreground of the victim, yet at the same time acknowledges the centrality that the criminal justice agencies work to measure and contain risk of harm. Feeley and Simon (1992) comment on the 'new penality' of the late modern era, noting a move away from the individual towards the management of risk as an insurance concept of crime control which includes the actuarial calculation of risk. It would be wrong to suggest that the Probation Service never thought about the chance that serious offenders might do something dangerous again, or equally that there might be media coverage and public anger when they did. Kemshall and Maguire (2001) describe an interesting case from the 1970s when Graham Young, a convicted murderer who completed his sentence in Broadmoor, was released on licence. Although he had killed by using poisons he was, soon after, able to take a job which gave him ready access to such substances and he murdered again. Then, as there would be now, there was a response from the public and the media. A debate followed, not dissimilar to those held in more recent years, questioning whether someone should be liable to detention in custody or in hospital when there were indications that a future offence would be committed. The significant difference between then and now was that any such move was then judged to be an invasion of the individual's civil rights – most importantly their right to be punished for what they had done, but not for what they might or might not do in the future. Yet, just over a decade later, the climate had changed sufficiently for a succession of measures that did just that.

## Recent legislation

Having charted the trends in the social and political climate, we now need to examine how this has been reflected in successive pieces of legislation.

The 1991 Criminal Justice Act was important in starting the shift. Although it had as a general theme of 'just desserts' it importantly allowed for disproportionate sentencing. Section 2 (2)b allows for sentences longer than the term commensurate with the seriousness of the offence to be available to the court when considering offences of a violent or sexual nature, where it is felt that the offender poses a risk of serious harm to the community (Home Office 1992). For the first time there was enshrined in law the possibility that an individual could get a longer sentence than the offence warranted on the basis that he or she might offend again. In practice this provision has not been used as regularly as intended, and when used has been vulnerable to appeals following sentence.

Also within the 1991 Act was the automatic conditional release licence (ACR). This meant that all prisoners serving a minimum of 12 months would automatically be released on licence to the Probation Service. For those serving four years plus, applications to be released on parole (now called discretionary conditional release) were considered from the halfway point of sentence, and if refused prisoners would still be released for a shorter period of licence. In effect this added a whole new group of offenders to the Probation Service's cases – those who had previously been refused any post-sentence licence because they denied committing their offences (and therefore would not have undertaken any of the treatment programmes being developed within the Prison Service) or had been disruptive and difficult to manage. Prior to the 1991 Act, for instance, convicted rapists would regularly be denied any parole, and the Probation Service might have no ongoing statutory involvement with this serious group of offenders.

The 1995 National Standards (Probation Directorate) were significant too in changing the focus of Probation Service work to the assessment and management of risk. These are effectively the rules imposed by the Home Office governing practice, which have been regularly reissued since 1991. In 1995 they required that all pre-sentence reports (PSRs) assess both the risk of reoffending and harm to the public – not just on sexual or violent offenders but on all offenders. Although familiar with the concept of harm to others by offending behaviour, this requirement to 'assess the risk' of each offender brought with it many more demands on the Probation Service which have continued to the present day. Since the first version, the National Standards have become increasingly prescriptive. Probation officers now need to adhere to these 'rules' and follow enforcement action (warnings and then a return to court) if the offender fails to attend appointments and engage with supervision.

In 1997 the Sex Offenders Act introduced the Sex Offenders Register. Sex offenders were required register their address and notify the police of any absences from it. The Act also held a requirement that the police (with the Probation Service) assess and manage the risk of sex offenders (usually interpreted by convening risk management panels). This is perhaps one of the clearest examples of legislation responding to the perception that sex offenders were a growing menace. Since its introduction the Sex Offenders Register has been constantly built upon. The police were clearly the custodians of this information although the Act did necessitate a significant cultural shift for Police Service and the Probation Service. Both agencies had to put some of their stereotypical myths about each other to one side and learn how to work closely together when trying to track and monitor the risks associated with sex offenders.

It is also worth mentioning another Act introduced in the same year. The Crimes (Sentences) Act 1997 introduced a mandatory life sentence for second serious violent or sexual offences. This was limited to the most serious convictions and in practice has been underused.

The Crime and Disorder Act (1998) introduced the sex offender order (SOO). This is applied for in court by the police when they have reason to believe that a convicted sexual offender is behaving in a way that previously seemed to be a precursor to offending. It is a civil order requiring the civil standard of proof and preventing a convicted sex offender from doing a specified activity or going to a specified place. Evidence has to be gathered to support a SOO application, both to show risky behaviour has taken place and to inform the development of suitable prohibitions. A breach, however, constitutes a criminal offence, triable either way, and attracting a maximum penalty of five years' imprisonment. Although still on the statute book these orders have failed to be used as much as the government envisaged. There have been criticisms on the grounds of erosion of civil liberties: for instance, an offender could end up with a criminal conviction for breaching a civil order sought on the grounds of suspicions that are not subject to the test of evidence applied in criminal trials. The police are also wary of having to state in open court the details of the offender and their concerns, when making the application.

Extended supervision periods of up to five years for a violent offence and ten years for sexual offences were other features of the Crime and Disorder Act 1998. In cases where it is invoked, the Probation Service now finds itself involved with these individual offenders for considerably longer periods than before.

The Criminal Justice and Court Services Act 2000 has continued the drive to frame the Probation Service as a law enforcement agency which exists primarily to protect the public. Section 69 of this Act made it a duty to consult victims of violent and sexual offences when the perpetrator had received 12 months custody or more. These victims' views are not influential in the decision making – whether or not an offender is to be granted home leave or release on licence – but are taken into account in deciding conditions which may be attached to the licence, concerning for instance place of residence and who the offender may or may not contact. There are now high expectations from this group of relatively new stakeholders for the Probation Service to deliver directly to them.

It was, however Sections 67 and 68 of the Criminal Justice and Court Services Act 2000 that put the multi-agency arrangements for public protection on their current statutory footing, and it is these measures which are described fully below. These sections make the police and the Probation Service jointly responsible for risk management. They share a duty to make joint arrangements for the assessment and management of the risks posed by sexual, violent and other potentially dangerous offenders.

## Multi-Agency Public Protection Arrangements (MAPPA)

Both the police and the Probation Service can now be held 'responsible' for virtually any offender who has the potential to cause harm to others. This has far-reaching consequences and is one of the legislative responses to the death of Sarah Payne, a young girl murdered by a convicted sex offender in the summer of 2000. Sections 67 and 68 of the Criminal Justice and Court Services Act

2000 extend the brief of the Probation Service beyond that of offenders currently in custody or on supervision or licence to include anyone in the community who poses a danger. This represents a considerable test to the organisation at a time when it has to target its resources very carefully.

There has been vigorous activity between the national Probation Service and the corresponding police areas. Each area has to have a panel meeting to discuss the highest risk offenders – the 'critical few'. There then need to be a host of supporting measures to ensure this statutory duty is fulfilled. Although as stated panels were to some extent already in existence in many areas prior to the Act they had previously only concentrated on sex offenders, and by including violent offenders this has expanded the scale of work and inevitably necessitated much more joint work from all agencies. The Act was clear in its expectations that the public are better protected from these types of offender by agencies acting on their behalf to manage these individuals and take action when necessary.

Other agencies were to be involved, although not on a statutory basis, and include social services, health, education, prison colleagues and housing. The involvement of these agencies has not been without some difficulties, and agencies inevitably vary in their practice and values. Initial guidance was issued and launched in March 2001 defining the seven minimum requirements that the responsible authorities had to make sure were up and running. Currently, MAPPA protocols are now in place in each area, endorsed by senior representatives of each agency. These protocols cover the terms of reference and, crucially, policy and procedure in relation to confidentiality and the disclosure of information.

MAPPA reports are published annually and state the number of registered sex offenders that the panels are dealing with. This information is now in the public domain for the first time and the media are inevitably focusing on how this work is carried out and to what degree it satisfies the public's demands to know more about sex offenders in their area. As an example, the MAPPA report for the Metropolitan Police area of London (2001–2) cites 1,847 registered sex offenders in the local community, 125 registered sex offenders cautioned or convicted for breaches of the requirement and one SOO applied for, one granted and five still in progress.

An evidence base for MAPPA is not yet established. However, Plotnikoff and Woolfson (2000) reported on some preliminary data on sex offender registration from the police perspective. In 1998, only

4 per cent of sex offenders released into the community and required to register were committing an offence by failing to register within 14 days. The compliance rate varied from 85–100 per cent across individual forces, averaging 95 per cent. Police forces reported a significant increase in their workload, but less than 50 per cent had provided additional manpower. There was a high level of police visits to offenders, used to record further details about the offender and his or her circumstances, or simply to verify the address. All forces had a community notification policy, but only five had invoked this in respect of a specific sex offender. Only a third of police forces thought that the monitoring activity had contributed to crime prevention, and a quarter reported using register intelligence in investigations.

Maguire, Kemshall, Noaks, Wincup and Sharpe (2001) reported on one of the few pieces of research to examine the workings and effectiveness of early public protection panels. The team observed 59 risk assessment/management panels and interviewed 147 practitioners ranging from senior managers to front-line staff (police, probation, social services, housing, psychiatrists and prison staff). McGuire *et al.* (2001) highlighted three areas which need attention:

- standardisation and consistency in the structure of panels, tighter gatekeeping in risk assessment and improved recording of decisions;
- resourcing should be more clearly designated, with dedicated coordinators to service preparatory work for panels;
- monitoring, managerial oversight and accountability of the public protection system.

Knock (2002) reported, from the police perspective, on the use of SOOs. Between December 1998 and March 2001, 92 had been awarded in England and Wales, nearly half of these being applied for by just six forces. Of these orders, 46 per cent had been prosecuted for a subsequent breach due to non-compliance, sentencing ranging from fairly lengthy custodial sentences to small fines. Fears that press coverage would be problematic were not founded, in that only 40 per cent of SOOs had received written press coverage, mostly in relation to the breach aspect. Only 14 per cent of articles gave precise details of where the offender lived.

## More recent MAPPA developments

New guidance has now been written which aims to standardise much of the current variety of MAPPA arrangements. Each area's strategic group overseeing the work are likely to expand the membership to providers from the electronic monitoring field. Various agencies will have a 'duty to cooperate', and although this falls short of the statutory obligations (which remain with the Police and Probation Services), all other agencies listed such as the Prison Service, social services and health will be expected to attend at a sufficient level of management oversight and authority.

Only the 'critical few' very high risk cases identified should go to the panel and a two-tier system is envisaged with the local risk management meetings concentrating on those of lesser risk. Several probation areas including London are moving to a more focused service delivery with community protection teams working as far as possible in jointly located police units.

Lay members are now being considered for membership of the strategic groups. Members are being recruited in five pilot areas and their training in the area of sexual abuse is being carefully planned. Again this is a response to the increasing demands for much more open access to the Sex Offenders Register and is seen as a step to try and better involve the communities where these offenders are predominantly based. Crucially, a serious offence case review (SOCR) is to be set up to examine MAPPA cases that reoffend.

There is some debate concerning the role of the chair. Currently, chairing is shared between the Police and Probation Services, but ideally the chair should be an independent person. The controversial matter of offender representation at MAPPA panels and/or legal representation remains to be addressed under the Human Rights Act. This is likely to be played out in the courtroom, as increasingly individuals expect to be party to discussions involving their management.

## Operating risk management principles

Risk assessment and information sharing appear to be relatively straightforward procedures, governed by protocols, research and a methodical examination of the 'facts'. On the contrary, risk management involves a great deal more individual judgement, negotiation and creativity if it is to walk a fine line between over- and under-control. Negotiation, specifically, needs to take place between professionals and agencies, and with the offender himself. Risk management plans involve an intelligent interpretation of the assessment, transforming static and dynamic concerns into a coherent and individualised strategy.

A risk management plan should involve consideration of four factors:

- *the offender's areas of strength* (e.g. motivation to change, feelings of shame, a compliant attitude, social skills);
- *the offender's areas of concern* (e.g. dominant dynamic domains, see Chapter 3);
- *the availability of relevant statutory obligations and restrictions* (e.g. conditions attached to probation supervision or conditional release on a restricted hospital order), and *over what time period*;
- *the resources available* (e.g. treatment, hospital admission, police surveillance, specialist work projects).

Clearly, risk management is more than the simple implementation of current legislation, policies and procedures. From a psychological perspective, the goal is to maximise the containment of the offender and thereby reduce the risk of sexual reoffending. Containment can be internally driven – notably in the form of the treatment interventions described in Chapter 6 – or externally driven. Treatment approaches need to maximise motivation, consider the individual's capacity for meaningful internal change and assist in the creation of appropriate boundaries for resisting impulses and avoiding high risk behaviours and situations. In this regard, the central role of supervision – the probation/offender relationship – can be underestimated or even undermined in the development of an offender's sense of responsibility for his own destiny.

In terms of external controls, the Probation and Police Services are central to the management plan for convicted sex offenders. Stringent reporting requirements, and conditions of treatment and residence attached to licences or community rehabilitation orders create firm boundaries for the offender with which he *must* comply. Conditions of residence at a probation hostel can provide necessary physical containment and additional curfew restrictions may help to manage high risk times of day, albeit perhaps restricting and isolating the offender in his room.

Police measures include regular visits, carried out informally and without antagonism. Perhaps more than any other recent development, this is the change which has had the most powerful impact on sex offenders' behaviour and attitudes. A curiously firm yet collaborative relationship can be forged, in which the offender is reminded of his risk, a 'paternal' eye is kept on him and in return he is protected from potential community retaliation. In contrast, police surveillance is used in cases of grave concern, where evidence is required for breach, recall proceedings or new charges to take place. The cost of surveillance is so prohibitive that an offence must be thought to be imminent, or an offender so impulsive and reckless that the necessary evidence will be obtained within a very few days.

The decision to disclose highly sensitive information to a third party has to be thoroughly justified and integral to an individualised risk management process. Unlike the American experience, England and Wales have almost no experience of community notification. A proposed public disclosure has to be authorised by a senior police officer. The Court of Appeal recently ruled (*R* v. *North Wales Police*) that disclosure of details of the identity and whereabouts of an offender can only be authorised when, after all the relevant factors have been considered, it is deemed necessary for the protection of the public. However, in reality, decisions about disclosure to specific individuals or to organisations (rather than the public) take place more frequently. For example, informing the learning disabled girl-friend of a rapist of his history; warning scouting or football associations of a particular offender who has recently assumed an alias in order to gain re-entry. Good practice dictates that disclosure should not just involve the passing on of information, but also pragmatic advice as to what course of action to take. For example, telling the head of a school that there is a dangerous paedophile in the vicinity is not particularly helpful; should that head inform parents, how much should he or she tell them, should the teachers simply be more vigilant, or is general education about offenders required? In many cases difficult decisions have to be made as to whether the offender is informed of the intention to disclose: transparency may trigger the offender to take action which avoids the need for disclosure, however there may be fears that he will be driven underground or otherwise seek to manipulate the situation.

These dilemmas are evident in a wide range of risk management decisions. For example:

- At what point should the Probation Service recall or breach an individual?
- When are friendships between sex offenders an inevitable result of their social exclusion and when are they networking to offend?
- At what point do risks in employment necessitate disclosure? Should child molesters never be lorry drivers, or rapists minicab drivers?
- Can a highly visible multi-agency agenda contaminate an individual professional's alliance with the offender to the extent that risk is raised rather than diminished?
- How does a multi-agency structure manage evident differences in their tolerance levels for managing an individual's risk?
- Can short-term goals of containment and return to custody undermine long-term aims of rehabilitation and management?

## The American experience

So far this chapter has outlined the legislative changes and associated developments in practice made in England and Wales over the last ten years or so. It is however worth pausing to compare such developments here with practice in North America, whose lead we have followed to some extent. In the USA, sex offender registration laws have been in place since the late 1980s to early 1990s (Bedarf 1995), based on the premise that there are high rates of recidivism among sex offenders and therefore they need to be kept under police surveillance. Registration requirements have been very similar to those currently in place in England and Wales. In 1990, Washington state was the first to take registration a step further, enacting a sex offender community notification law. A similar law was passed in New Jersey state in 1994, commonly known as 'Megan's Law'; this was prompted by public concern at the rape and murder of a 7-year-old girl by a violent sex offender living anonymously across the street from her (Zevitz & Farkas 2000a). Community notification statutes are currently in place in 50 states.

There are three basic types of notification statute (Finn 1997; Zevitz & Farkas 2000b):

- most identify an agency which is responsible for determining the level of risk an offender poses and then implementing a notification plan that reflects the level of risk;

- others provide for community groups and individuals to take the initiative to request information about whether a sex offender is living in their community, and to request details about the sex offender;
- one state uses a self-identification procedure which requires offenders themselves to notify – under close supervision – the neighbourhood where they live.

Many local jurisdictions have used a three-tier system of determining risk: low risk notification is likely to be limited to area law enforcement and correction officials; medium risk notification includes specific agencies or organisations which fall within the offender's identified pattern of behaviour; high risk notification may include additional procedures such as household visits, posting flyers, media releases or conducting community meetings (Zevitz & Farkas 2000b). For example, of all the flyers in Washington state which related to medium risk offenders, 49 per cent showed a photograph and 21 per cent gave the exact address of the offender; flyers in relation to high risk offenders had a photograph 86 per cent of the time, with 53 per cent detailing the exact address (Finn 1997).

It is unfortunate that, to date, the extensive North American experience has not been well researched. There appears to be a certain amount of anecdotal feedback and widespread support of the system, although the question of whether the laws succeed in their aim of effectively protecting the public is not established. It is clear that there are difficulties in maintaining compliance with sex offender registration, and California and Washington have published their compliance rates. Bedarf (1995) reports that compliance with registration in California and Washington was said to be around 70 per cent. However, limited police resources meant that they were unable to keep track of current offender information as they moved around. In terms of the key question of protecting the public, there has been one research study comparing the recidivism rates of sex offenders subject to notification with a matched group of sex offenders not subject to notification. The sexual recidivism rate was 19 per cent and 22 per cent respectively, with no statistical significance between the two groups (Schram & Milloy 1995). There has been concern that community notification would lead to vigilante attacks on the sex offenders. Commentators report that this has been surprisingly unproblematic: for example, less than 10 per cent of offenders in Oregon experienced some form of harassment.

Wisconsin, Washington, Oregon and New Jersey states all report that less than 1 per cent of their notification cases incurred physical assaults or property damage (Finn 1997; Zevitz & Farkas 2000a). Zevitz and Farkas (2000) have also explored the impact of neighbourhood meetings. They discovered that attendees almost always found the amount of information provided to be sufficient. However, a positive attitude to the meeting was related to the following: being alerted to the meeting by a public official; the meeting being well planned and organised; and the purpose of the meeting being clearly explained before and during the meeting. A large minority of attendees remained angry and resentful – they had hoped to be able to prevent the placement of a sex offender locally and they were more likely to leave the meeting feeling frightened and powerless.

Overall, commentators highlight the potential advantage of community notification as educating the public in general terms about sex offenders. This may assist with the rapid investigation of sex offences and seems to improve the criminal justice system's involvement in the community. The *threat* of notification is seen as a motivating factor in sex offenders who are resistant to supervision or treatment. All seem to agree that there is a problem with lack of resources to manage community notification, which is a burdensome process. Critics of the system point to the possible displacement effect when sex offenders move several times, often across states, and sometimes without re-registering. There is some evidence to suggest that social exclusion has increased as a result (Zevitz & Farkas 2000a), with sex offenders being sacked from their employment and refused housing, and their families and victims suffering as a result of the public exposure. Community notification may lead to a false sense of security, in so far as residents conclude that they know who the sex offenders are in their community, or alternatively, it may incite excessive community fear or anger. Bedarf (1995) speaks eloquently of community notification as shame punishment; a true shame punishment would aim to shape the offender's moral character – to shame him into conforming to the community's moral code. However, Bedarf points out that advocates of community notification reject the notion of rehabilitation for sex offenders, thus shaming becomes merely an outlet for the community's rage. The sexual recidivism rates are often lower than the recidivism rates for other serious crimes of violence, and community notification is likely to exacerbate the already large discrepancy between the public's estimate of risk and actual risk. If community notification is an effective method of public protection, why would the public not wish to know about murderers and violent individuals living close to them? Whether or not community notification is an effective method of public protection, this does appear to be a resource-intensive approach which receives a level of attention not supported by the evidence thus far.

## Case studies

### Stephen

As a low risk offender – and unconvicted – Stephen was not required to register with the police. His location in the borough was made known to the police but the case was not discussed further. His management is detailed in Chapter 4.

### Anthony

It was agreed to retain Anthony as a priority case for discussion. All agreed that he posed a high risk, although there were differing views on the role his denial of the offence played in this risk. Having identified risk concerns, Anthony's strengths were thought to be his level of intelligence, his interpersonal skills and warmth, his motivation to provide a good role model for his son and evidence of maturation in his personality. Given that his period on licence was brief – nine months – a desire to control his behaviour needed to be weighed against longer-term resettlement concerns. It was decided to focus on the latter goal, particularly given that risk issues were unlikely to be immediate, but were more likely to be medium term and situational. The strategy was to enhance and consolidate internal motivation to change, actively liaise with social services in order to support an appropriate level of contact with his son and to make assistance available, as required, for employment opportunities – recognising that adequate financial rewards needed to be in place in order to ensure that an illegal lifestyle was not unduly tempting. Licence conditions included a condition of psychological assessment (not treatment); residence at a probation hostel until appropriate independent accommodation could be found; and a condition to undertake a community drug team assessment, together with regular urine screening. Police intelligence would attempt to monitor any involvement with known local criminals, particularly those involved in drug dealing.

Anthony was compliant with the main conditions and responded well to the psychological assessment and probation supervision. However, he found the rules of the hostel difficult to tolerate and was aggravated by younger and more chaotic residents. Following a verbal and a written warning after returning late to the hostel on two occasions, he was finally breached and recalled to prison after going out to a nightclub, taking cocaine and sleeping overnight at a friend's flat. He had remained in the community five months. His attitude to recall was, in many ways, mature: he recognised his responsibility for what had occurred and accepted he had been overconfident and somewhat dismissive of others' concerns. When released at the end of his sentence, he was accepted on a voluntary basis back at the probation hostel. He subsequently moved in with his brother. Three years on, he had apparently not reoffended. He was living with his new girlfriend and contact with his son was regular and positive; he was engaged in a legitimate business with his brother which was not particularly financially successful but brought him satisfaction and allowed him to work independently; he said that he continued to smoke cannabis, but had not touched Class A drugs since his release from prison. At this point, it was agreed that he was no longer one of the 'critical few', that the risk for all forms of recidivism was reducing, in line with his increasing levels of maturity and self-control, and that Anthony would therefore be monitored on an intermittent basis.

## James

Initially, James was a high priority for discussion on a multi-agency basis. However, he had a number of strengths, despite the enormity of his offending behaviour. These included his mature, stable personality functioning and his capacity for reflective thought and emotional expression. Ironically, these were also the attributes most likely to be viewed suspiciously, as they could so easily mask underlying fantasies. James' relatively high profile upon release justified stringent risk management strategies. However, as an offender on life licence, the real challenge lay in pacing strategies across the long term; that is, sexual recidivism was possible over a very long time period, and risk might not be visible nor situationally triggered. All agencies agreed that the likelihood of a further offence was low, but the implications for any future victim, and for the professionals and agencies involved, were very high. The goal, therefore, was to maintain a balance between public protection and reintegration into the community for the foreseeable future. In practice, the Probation Service and forensic mental health service agreed to alternate sessions, sharing similar goals achieved by slightly different means. The file was reread regularly to hold in mind risk issues and records were maintained to an exemplary standard. Regular risk management meetings involved the police, although their concerns and involvement tailed off after three months, when James was clearly compliant and settled. It was agreed that a meaningful structure to his day was a crucial aspect of any plan, ensuring continuity from his stable prison life and as a primary source of self-esteem. Probation supported James in accessing employment opportunities, but they were also involved in ensuring that he developed an appropriate written disclosure regarding his offence, for prospective employers.

James made exemplary progress, given his long period of incarceration and the level of scrutiny to which he was subjected. This was despite repeated rejections from prospective employers who interviewed him, but were clearly frightened away by his disclosure letter. Eighteen months after his release – still resident in the hostel, but planning a move into independent accommodation – James requested permission to participate in an evening course in counselling at the local college, which would be relevant to the voluntary work with ex-offenders he had recently commenced. The forensic mental health agency was cautiously supportive of his approach in thinking through the issues, but concerned that he would become despondent in the face of yet more rejections. On balance, the risk management meeting – at which James was present – concluded that the evening course would be unwise, potentially risky and likely to be rejected by the Home Office (in terms of licence reporting). They emphasised his continuing high risk status. Four days later, James was remanded into custody on a charge of attempted murder: in the evening he had carried a knife and belt up to the city centre, followed a woman down a street and stabbed her twice in the neck from behind, subsequently stabbing himself in both his legs. When interviewed later, James said that he was 'quietly fuming' after the risk management meeting, and by the next day, was indulging in sadistic fantasies (without associated feelings of sexual arousal). He deliberately planned to attack a woman, thinking to himself 'if they still think I'm high risk, I'll prove it to them'. He purchased the knife two days later, rejecting thoughts of ringing his probation officer or psychologist. He sought out a prostitute the next day and, unable to find one he followed a woman at random and attacked her. Sentenced to a second life term, James is most unlikely ever to be released.

The aftermath for the professionals involved in such a major incident is considerable. The sense of disbelief at the rapidity of James' decline, his refusal to make use of support and skills easily at his disposal and close replication of the index offence all served to undermine the confidence of the multi-agency team. In organisational terms, the Probation Service led on the incident inquiry – although all files were scrutinised by senior managers in each service – but as this was internally driven there was no multi-agency responsibility for the conclusions and recommendations. The case was further scrutinised when James went to court. Although emotionally and professionally shaken, the inquiry did emphasise the high quality of care and professional communication involved, and there were no clear indicators that the new offence could have been prevented. In retrospect, there are perhaps two lessons to be learned. First, sadistic sex offenders – no matter how consistent their progress in treatment appears to be – pose a uniformly high risk of recidivism throughout their life. This does not necessarily lead to the conclusion that they feign improvement or change, but rather that powerful sadistic impulses merely lie dormant, re-emerging under stress or particular triggering circumstances. Second, there is a potential paradox in rigorous and stringent risk management strategies, which may in fact constrain and undermine a high risk offender to such an extent that they fear (and therefore wish to control) their failure in the community.

## Peter

Peter was subject to 11 months on licence, which contained conditions to attend treatment and to reside at the hostel, prior to a move to independent accommodation. Despite concerns about risk, the multi-agency teams felt reasonably confident he could be managed. His strengths lay in his likely compliance with expectations of him, his strong motivation to avoid a return to prison and strengthening feelings of shame with regard to his offending behaviour. There were two agreed goals to his management plan: first, containment – physical and emotional – and second, effecting internal change by means of group treatment. Residence at the hostel stopped Peter from managing his interpersonal anxieties by means of withdrawal and avoidance, as he was encouraged to relate to the staff; regular but informal police visits reinforced his internal anxieties about his capacity to reoffend, without him feeling unduly victimised. Their collaborative stance involved reassurance that he would be protected from exposure or vigilante attacks, which he feared. The leaders of the group treatment programme worked closely with the supervising probation officer to provide a containing framework for addressing issues.

Despite a formal probation warning (see Chapter 6), Peter was enabled to make good progress in the group and completed it on a voluntary basis. Although he refused the offer of ongoing support thereafter, he appeared to maintain his progress three years on. He settled in his own flat and became involved in an 18-month relationship with an adult male. While he continued to be on the Sex Offenders Register, and subject to police follow up, there appeared to be no evidence that he had engaged in further sexual offending.

## Martin

Martin's pending release was highly anxiety-provoking for those responsible for his care in the community, and he was discussed at length at the multi-agency meeting. His level of disturbance was such that there was little confidence in the potential for internal change being sufficient to contain his impulses to offend. Nevertheless, Martin knew that he was facing a life sentence should he reoffend, and was highly motivated to avoid this. He had well-developed relapse prevention skills and an interpersonal style – albeit highly dysfunctional – which was inclined to be dependent upon rather than avoidant of services. The primary purpose of the risk management plan was to focus on public prevention by means of reliance on external rather than internal controls. To achieve this, the agencies needed to coordinate their input and agree strategies. Martin was on an extended licence period of two years, with conditions of residence at the hostel, greatly extended curfew hours (particularly around key school hours), treatment, community drug team assessment and urine testing. He was forbidden from entering areas where he had offended in the past. The emphasis on external containment included a greater role for police intelligence and a crisis plan should public interest be aroused in his release. The role of forensic mental health services was to provide support for the hostel staff in terms of managing Martin's demands and the inevitable dynamics which would cause splits within the staff team. While the aim of treatment was to facilitate understanding and management at a psychological level, Martin's level of sexual preoccupation precluded any capacity for meaningful reflection. A referral to the prison medical staff initiated a course of anti-libidinal medication, commenced two weeks before his release. Subsequently agreeing a level of confidentiality in individual treatment aimed to allow him personal space to be viewed as an individual with psychological needs, not just a high risk offender.

For the first two months after release, the most striking feature was the chaos which occurred in Martin's presence. He had become acutely depressed when taking anti-libidinal medication, and this together with the stress of release triggered an incident of self-harm. Immediately there was a loss of confidence from the hostel and a request that mental health services take over full care of him – rigorously resisted by health services who insisted he was unsuitable for inpatient psychiatric care! Furthermore, Martin's propensity for disarming self-revelation regarding his deviant sexual fantasies was viewed by some agencies as evidence of honesty and engagement, but for others was evidence of the need to recall him to prison immediately. No sooner had matters settled somewhat, than Martin announced he had met an older woman (herself disordered and vulnerable) with whom he intended to live and forge an intimate relationship. Initially Martin was cautioned against this relationship, and this seemed to lead to a rift and loss of trust in agencies, in so far as he began to push boundaries and engage in conflict with professionals. The solution seemed to lie in involving his partner in the risk management plan, rather than trying to countermand her influence. With his permission and in his presence, she was informed of his offence history. During this period, Martin had ceased taking anti-libidinal medication, both because of his depressed mood and because he wished to be sexually active with his new partner. It seemed appropriate to consider relatively high dose anti-depressant medication, both for its effects in stabilising his mood and in an attempt to reduce his offence-related ruminations and fantasies.

Martin clearly struggled with urges to follow boys in the street, and began to acknowledge that in many ways this activity had superseded contact sex offending, in terms of the sense of excitement and control it afforded him. He decided to disclose this fantasy material to his probation officer and the hostel, knowing that this would be discussed at a risk management meeting. Meanwhile, attempts to find him daytime activity which would divert him from his inner world and provide meaningful structure were fruitless, given his background and the response of agencies. The risk management meeting was split: those who felt Martin was about to commit a further sexual offence and should be recalled, arguing against those who felt that his fantasies were a reflection of his personality functioning and should be stringently responded to and contained within the community. Police surveillance was instigated in order to obtain evidence for recall, and information was relayed to agencies, but was not for use in community containment strategies. Ultimately, Martin resolved the issue: he 'confessed' to his probation officer that he had touched a boy in the local park; his account was vague and contradictory, no corroborating details were found by the police and Martin subsequently retracted his 'confession'. Despite universal doubts that any offence had actually occurred, this was sufficient to tip the balance and he was recalled.

Martin will be released shortly, bound to register with the police, but not under any statutory supervision. He aims to cohabit with his partner and is requesting further treatment from the health service. Both of these factors are likely to provide stabilising influences. However, he is refusing contact with either Police or Probation Services, the latter, he says, having betrayed him. There seems little possibility of resolving the lack of daytime structure, and the police will need to carefully consider the possibility of a SOO, which could restrict his movements in terms of avoiding places and activities.

## Conclusion

Despite a really startling catalogue of changes in recent years, the debate regarding effectiveness has not really begun yet. Legislation, strategies, protocols and information exchange may be greatly improved, but does it make any difference to the prevention of future victims? The American experience might suggest that there will be significant optimism on the part of agencies, largely as a result of increased collaboration; the public may feel reassured – although a significant minority will remain deeply sceptical and resistant; and offenders may feel themselves to be scrutinised, and fear exposure. General improvements are likely to be overshadowed and undermined by 'unpredictable' and catastrophic offences which capture the public's attention. What are the useful measures that might indicate a substantive indication of success? Future evaluation might need to consider:

- Does the re-arrest and reconviction rate for sexual recidivism diminish over time?
- Does the social exclusion of sex offenders diminish or increase?
- Is the public better informed about the real risks posed by sex offenders, or made more fearful or more complacent?
- What are the outcomes of intensive surveillance?
- What are the effective components of containment?
- What should the relationship be between a treatment programme and the MAPPA?
- Does the offender learn to manipulate the system and the professionals?
- Is there a threshold beyond which increased external controls have a paradoxical effect, heightening risk rather than diminishing it?

# Chapter 6

# Forensic mental health services

## Introduction

It is probably fair to say that the role of mental health services in the assessment and management of sex offenders is often perceived as complex or even inconsistent. Practitioners from other agencies – the Probation or Police Services – may be frustrated and bewildered when faced with a mental health team's apparent stubborn refusal to admit chaotic and seemingly disturbed sex offenders to hospital beds. The implications of certain diagnoses for risk and treatability may not be explicit, and the role of the Mental Health Act (1983) may not be fully understood. This chapter attempts to clarify some of these issues in respect of mental health practice in England and Wales. Treatment options discussed later in the chapter have more universal applicability, not only across countries, but also across professional disciplines. For example, the majority of cognitive behavioural treatments are administered by non-health practitioners, usually probation officers, with or without the support of forensic and clinical psychologists.

## Current provision

Mental health provision includes outpatient/community services, although specialist forensic aftercare is not always consistently provided. Although psychiatric services to health care settings within prisons have been greatly developed over recent years, their role in relation to sex offenders has not been specifically developed. In terms of inpatient services, there are three types or levels of care: general mental health services are locally based, and manage hospital beds on 'open' wards where patients may be admitted voluntarily or under a section of the Mental Health Act. Such services also access intensive care beds or challenging behaviour beds which are locked but low secure facilities, designed to manage the severely mentally ill with acute symptoms and difficult behaviour that are difficult to manage. Forensic mental health services are usually based within medium secure facilities, located within each region of the country and serving a large catchment area. Although (rarely) specialist medium secure units exist for individuals with a primary diagnosis of personality disorder, the majority of units admit severely mentally ill patients who have committed serious offences, usually of a violent nature. Finally, there are three high secure hospitals in England and Wales – Broadmoor, Rampton and Ashworth – which admit offenders in need of mental health care and who pose a very serious or imminent risk of harm to others.

## Mental Health Act – England and Wales (1983)

In order to unravel the legal status of sex offenders resident in hospital settings, it is important to be clear about the categories of detention under the Mental Health Act (1983). These include:

- mental illness;
- psychopathic disorder;
- mental impairment (and severe mental impairment).

Sahota and Chesterman (1998) have reviewed the published litera-ture on sexual offending in the context of mental illness. They identified a number of studies which found that up to 10 per cent of all sex offenders are found to have a mental illness. The remaining majority either have no diagnosis or are labelled as personality disordered or paraphiliacs (see below). Home Office statistics demonstrate a rise in the number of restricted patients admitted to hospital for sexual offences between 1983 and 1995, from 23 to 105 patients. The 105 patients represented one fifth of admissions of restricted patients to hospital in that year, the rise being largely due to an increase in mentally ill admissions; over half of the 253 restricted patients detained in hospital in 1993 were under the category of mental illness. In terms of high secure hospital patients, it was estimated that the 'sexual element of offending behaviour may be present in 70 per cent of the patients on some of the wards of the hospital' (Lewis 1991). They were more likely to have adult female or pubescent victims. It is most unusual for mentally ill sex offenders to have child victims (Murray, Briggs & Davies 1992). Thus, although only a small minority of sex offenders are thought to be mentally ill, they comprise a large proportion of the medium and high secure hospital populations.

Personality disordered sex offenders are estimated to comprise 30–50 per cent of the sex offender population, depending on the sample. However, Home Office statistics show that there were eight restricted patients admitted to hospital in 1985 and seven admitted in 1994; this represented a proportional drop over the years from 24 per cent to 7 per cent of all restricted patients admitted. Psychopathically disordered sex offender patients in high security were more likely than other categories to have used violence in the offence, and to have pubescent or adult female victims (Murray *et al.* 1992). Personality disordered individuals are extremely difficult to manage on wards which also treat the mentally ill; they are reported to take up disproportionate amounts of staff time and often engage in bullying behaviours towards the mentally ill patients. The relatively greater numbers of personality disordered patients in high secure settings allows for specialisation between wards, and therefore a potentially more effective treatment and management approach.

In terms of mental impairment or severe mental impairment, Home Office statistics show that restricted admissions to hospital for sex offenders under these categories remained fairly stable over the years, at around 10 per cent of all admissions. Such offenders are more likely to have exclusively child victims and are less likely to have engaged in penile penetration of the victim (Murray *et al.* 1992) or serious sexual assaults (Day 1994).

### Recent developments

#### Dangerous and severe personality disorder (DSPD)

The government set out their proposals for the management of the risks posed by DSPD individuals in a joint Home Office and Department of Health paper (1999), which was circulated for consultation. The working definition of DSPD was designed to cover those individuals who:

• show significant disorder of personality;

- present a significant risk of causing serious physical or psychological harm from which the victim would find it difficult or impossible to recover (e.g. homicide, rape, arson);

and in whom

- the risk presented appears to be functionally linked to the personality disorder.

The proposals contained a variety of options, including amendments to the existing criminal justice legislation to allow for greater use of discretionary life sentences, and amendments to the Mental Health Act to remove the 'treatability criterion' for civil detainees. Suggestions are made to develop new powers in civil and criminal proceedings for the indeterminate detention of DSPD individuals, placing such individuals in a new service separately managed from mainstream prison and health services. Although most practitioners tended to agree that there was a small group of high risk individuals who were currently poorly managed, a number of concerns were raised regarding the absence of dedicated specialist services, inaccuracies in current risk assessment procedures and a lack of potential treatment success. The most controversial aspect of the paper related to the proposal that individuals should be detained in hospital on civil grounds, on the basis that they may pose a serious risk to others but had not offended.

### Reforming the Mental Health Act (Department of Health 2002)

The most significant proposed change to the Mental Health Act is a new definition of mental disorder, without any defined categories. Proposed powers in the new legislation will be based on the presence of a mental disorder covering 'any disability or disorder of mind or brain, whether permanent or temporary, which results in an impairment or disturbance of mental functioning'. The key effect of the change is the abolition of the 'treatability' criteria which formerly applied to the category of 'psychopathic disorder'.

Under the new proposals, care and treatment under formal powers will only be able to be continued after the first three days if clear criteria are met:

- The patient must be diagnosed as suffering from a mental disorder within the meaning of the new legislation.
- The mental disorder must be of a nature or degree as to warrant specialist care and treatment. This may be necessary in the best interests of the patient and/or because without care and treatment there is significant risk of serious harm to other people.
- A plan of care and treatment must be available to address the mental disorder. In cases where the use of compulsory powers arises, primarily in the patient's own best interests, that plan must be anticipated to be of direct therapeutic benefit to the individual concerned. In cases where compulsory powers are sought primarily because of the risk that the patient poses to others, the plan must be considered necessary either directly to treat the underlying mental disorder and/or to manage behaviours arising from the disorder.

These proposed changes, in principle, do not change the role of mental health services in the management of mentally ill sex offenders. However, there are strong potential implications for those sex offenders who present with significant levels of personality disorder and are considered to be high risk. The White Paper specifically identifies that in high risk cases, treatment will be designed both to manage the consequences of a mental disorder as well as to enable the individuals themselves to work towards successful reintegration into the community.

## Psychiatric diagnosis and its relationship with sexual offending

Psychiatric diagnoses are usually based on one of two classificatory systems: The ICD-10 classification of mental and behavioural disorders (World Health Organisation 1994); and DSM-IV, the *Diagnostic and Statistical Manual of Mental Disorders* (American Psychiatric Association 1994). In Europe, ICD-10 is normally utilised, although cross-reference to DSM-IV can be very useful, particularly in relation to personality disorder. This section aims to highlight the main diagnostic categories within which mentally disordered sex offenders may fall, and to discuss the potential relationship between the diagnosis and sexual offending. It is important to note that these guidelines should never be a substitute for the careful assessment of a sex offender by an appropriately trained and experienced mental health practitioner.

## Schizophrenia

Of the severe types of mental illness, schizophrenia is the most common diagnosis among sex offenders:

> The schizophrenic disorders are characterized in general by fundamental and characteristic distortions of thinking and perception, and by inappropriate or blunted affect ... The most intimate thoughts, feelings, and acts are often felt to be known to or shared by others, and explanatory delusions may develop, to the effect that natural or supernatural forces are at work to influence the afflicted individual's thoughts and actions in ways that are often bizarre ... Hallucinations, especially auditory, are common and may comment on the individual's behaviour or thoughts ... Perplexity is also common early on and frequently leads to a belief that everyday situations possess a special, usually sinister, meaning intended uniquely for the individual ... thinking becomes vague, elliptical, and obscure, and its expression in speech sometimes incomprehensible ... Mood is characteristically shallow, capricious, or incongruous ... The onset may be acute, with seriously disturbed behaviour, or insidious, with a gradual development of odd ideas and conduct.
>
> (World Health Organisation 1994: 86–7)

Sahota and Chesterman's (1998) review highlights the varied and inconclusive research on schizophrenic sex offenders. They rightly emphasise the need for careful appraisal of the role of symptoms in the offending behaviour, evaluated against more specific factors associated with sexual offending in the general population, as outlined in Chapter 3. First, a sexual assault may arise directly as a result of delusional beliefs or hallucinations; second, the assault may be related to less specific features of the illness, such as heightened feelings of arousal and irritability, or confused thought processes; third, the assault may be related to 'negative' symptoms of the illness – blunting of emotional responses, social withdrawal and lowered social performance – which are akin in some ways to the dynamic factors considered within the social competency domain (see Chapter 3). Finally, the assault may be largely unrelated to the schizophrenic illness and more closely related to underlying personality problems and/or fixed sexually deviant interests.

The following brief vignettes of sexual offending in patients with schizophrenia provide examples of the above points.

Patient A was experiencing auditory hallucinations of a male voice talking about his sexual inadequacies in the third person, then castigating him directly that 'you're a poof'. He decided to disprove the voices by going out and having sex with a prostitute. He followed a woman returning home from work, believed her to be a prostitute, and raped her.

Patient B had become noticeably more irritable and agitated as he stopped taking his anti-psychotic medication. He became increasingly preoccupied with feelings of sexual frustration and concern that he did not have a girlfriend. He followed a woman in a crowded area, and grabbed her breasts and genitals over her clothing, and said 'I want to have sex with you'. She struggled and passers-by came to her aid, as he ran off. Once arrested and held in custody, his behaviour clearly deteriorated; he became mute and smeared faeces on the cell walls.

Patient C was maintained on anti-psychotic medication and resided in a mental health hostel in the community. He was found in the bedroom of a fellow female resident and she complained to staff that he had forced her to have sexual intercourse. There were no signs of a relapse of his mental state, but he did have marked negative symptoms, including blunted affect and problems in managing to initiate and maintain relationships.

Patient D had a diagnosis of paranoid schizophrenia and had been admitted twice to hospital. When psychotic, his behaviour was characterised by intense anxiety and violence in response to persecutory, threatening beliefs. When stabilised, staff noted behaviour – such as bullying, substance misuse and sexual intimidation – indicative of an underlying personality disorder with psychopathic traits. He was reported to make opportunistic sexual advances and was transferred to high secure hospital after isolating and sexually assaulting a member of staff shortly prior to his discharge.

Deciding on the temporal relationship between the offending and the illness can be difficult, and often requires a retrospective evaluation involving information from key informants as well as the patient himself. Craissati and Hodes (1992), in their study of 11 mentally ill sex offenders, found that there was no evidence of mental illness contained within the prosecution evidence, particularly the transcript of the police interview. Yet the majority of the sample were found to be floridly psychotic when assessed shortly afterwards in prison. Retrospectively, it seemed likely that while three of the offences were committed in relation to hallucinations and delusional beliefs, the majority occurred within the context of deteriorating social behaviour and self care, heightened feelings of anxiety or depression and a degree of sexual preoccupation. This is sometimes referred to as the 'prodromal phase' of illness.

In terms of specific interventions for sex offenders with severe mental illness, the primary consideration must be for the potential role of anti-psychotic medication. For some patients, insight into their illness and compliance with medication may form the prime relapse prevention strategy which substantially reduces the risk of sexual recidivism. More usually, treatment involves a combination of medication, psychological and social therapies which aim to address a range of pro-offending attitudes, social competencies, personality factors and the symptoms of the illness.

### Depressive illness

Depressive episodes can encompass a wide range of diagnoses, reflecting the severity of the disorder. However, they usually include 'depressed mood, loss of interest and enjoyment, and reduced energy leading to increased fatiguability and diminished activity. Marked tiredness after only slight effort is common' (World Health Organisation 1994: 119). Severe depressive episodes may be characterised by psychotic symptoms in which there is a loss of touch with reality. The research literature does not discuss the relationship between a depressive illness and sexual offending in any detail, largely because the prevalence of such patients is very small. However, a small minority of depressed individuals may suffer from obsessional symptoms, including persistent and distressing ruminations. Individuals may present to services with anxieties regarding recurring thoughts or impulses to sexually offend, which may or may not have been associated with 'approach' behaviours, such as following women. Similarly, sex offenders may have sexually deviant preoccupations which mask an underlying depressive illness. As discussed in the section on pharmacological interventions (see p. 148), certain types of anti-depressant medication may play an important role in alleviating or even resolving such cognitions.

## Mental impairment

The classificatory systems refer to mental impairment as 'mental retardation'. It is defined, diagnostically, as 'a condition of arrested or incomplete development of the mind, which is especially characterized by impairment of skills manifested during the developmental period, which contribute to the overall level of intelligence, i.e. cognitive, language, motor, and social abilities' (World Health Organisation 1994: 226). ICD-10 recommends that standardised, individually administered intelligence tests should be used to determine IQ, and that for a definite diagnosis, 'there should be a reduced level of intellectual functioning resulting in diminished ability to adapt to the daily demands of the normal social environment' (World Health Organisation 1994: 227). The range of diagnoses reflect the severity of mental impairment, but it should not be confused with specific (rather than global) cognitive deficits which may also be referred to as 'learning difficulties'.

Determining the relationship between the mental impairment and the sexual offence can be complex. The choice of a child victim may reflect the emotional immaturity of the offender, who feels threatened by, or unable to access, peer relationships; the offender may have difficulties conceptualising the nature of consent, or lack the ability to establish whether consent has been given; there may simply be a skills deficit, in so far as the offender may be ignorant about sexual matters and the necessary skills involved in establishing sexual relationships. However, it is important to note that a diagnosis of mental retardation is often associated with other mental disorders, and the prevalence of other mental disorders is at least three to four times greater in this population than in the general population. Thus the sexual offending may be related more to personality disorder or an underlying fixed deviant sexual interest, than to the mental impairment itself.

## Personality disorder

ICD-10 introduces the section on personality disorders as follows:

These types of condition comprise deeply ingrained and enduring behaviour patterns, manifesting themselves as inflexible responses to a broad range of personal and social situations. They represent either extreme or significant deviations from the way the average individual in a given culture perceives, thinks, feels, and particularly relates to others. Such behaviour patterns tend to be stable and to encompass multiple domains of behaviour and psychological functioning. They are frequently, but not always, associated with various degrees of subjective distress and problems in social functioning and performance.

(World Health Organisation 1994: 200)

Personality disorder, in contrast to personality change, is a developmental condition which first appears in childhood or adolescence and which continues into adulthood. There are a number of specific personality disorders. However, there are two main types which are likely to pose particular problems when associated with sexual offending. *Dissocial – or antisocial – personality disorder* usually comes to attention because of a gross disparity between behaviour and the prevailing social norms. ICD-10 characterises it by:

- callous unconcern for the feelings of others;
- gross and persistent attitude of irresponsibility and disregard for social norms, rules and obligations;
- incapacity to maintain enduring relationships, though having no difficulty in establishing them;
- very low tolerance to frustration and a low threshold for discharge of aggression, including violence;
- incapacity to experience guilt or to profit from experience, particularly punishment;
- marked proneness to blame others, or to offer plausible rationalizations, for the behaviour that has brought the patient into conflict with society (p. 204).

Inevitably, there is a tendency to diagnose dissocial personality disorder in those individuals who repeatedly offend. It is important to note that the diagnosis cannot be made on the basis that a sex offender has repeatedly offended against children or adults.

The second important type of personality disorder is referred to as *emotionally unstable personality disorder* – borderline type in ICD-10, and simply borderline personality disorder in DSM-IV. It is characterised by a 'marked tendency to act impulsively without consideration of the consequences, together with affective instability' (World Health Organisation 1994: 204). Although the borderline type is described in ICD-10, it is more easily operationalised in DSM-IV (American Psychiatric Association 1994: 292–3) as follows:

A pervasive pattern of instability of interpersonal relationships, self-image, and affects, and marked impulsivity beginning by early adulthood and present in a variety of contexts, as indicated by five (or more) of the following:

1    Frantic efforts to avoid real or imagined abandonment. (Note: do not include suicidal or self-mutilating behavior covered in Criterion 5.)
2    A pattern of unstable and intense interpersonal relationships characterized by alternating between extremes of idealization and devaluation.
3    Identity disturbance: markedly and persistently unstable self-image or sense of self.
4    Impulsivity in at least two areas that are potentially self-damaging (e.g., spending, sex, substance abuse, reckless driving, binge eating). (Note: do not include suicidal or self-mutilating behavior covered in Criterion 5.)
5    Recurrent suicidal behavior, gestures, or threats, or self-mutilating behavior.
6    Affective instability due to a marked reactivity of mood (e.g., intense episodic dysphoria, irritability, or anxiety usually lasting a few hours and only rarely more than a few days).
7    Chronic feelings of emptiness.
8    Inappropriate, intense anger or difficulty controlling anger (e.g., frequent displays of temper, constant anger, recurrent physical fights).
9    Transient, stress-related paranoid ideation or severe dissociative symptoms.

The potential relationship between antisocial personality disorder and sex offending is perhaps self-evident, in so far as many of the features of fixed and dynamic variables associated with sexual recidivism are likely to be present, specifically, elevated scores on Factor 2 – chronic antisociality – of the PCL-R (Hare 1991), the number of prior court appearances, sexual entitlement or intimacy deficits and poor self-management, particularly impulsivity. While the risk of recidivism is raised, there are also problems with managing personality disordered offenders in treatment programmes. While antisocial personality disordered sex offenders may resist attempts to engage them in treatment, sex offenders with borderline features may seek treatment in a chaotic manner, characterised by intense distress and a raised propensity to self-harm as a result. For example, Craissati and Beech (2001) found that evidence of emotional and behavioural disturbance in childhood, as well as trauma, and contact with mental health services as an adult (excluding offenders with a diagnosis of mental illness) predicted both missed treatment sessions and attrition from treatment in a community programme for sex offenders. Offence-specific variables were not related to attrition and similar findings have been reported by previous researchers (e.g. Abel, Mittelman, Becker, Rathner & Rouleau 1988; Chaffin 1992).

Given the established link between treatment attrition and a high risk of sexual reoffending, there may need to be a much greater degree of structure and support underpinning treatment programmes for personality disordered sex offenders, including psychiatric back-up. Parallel treatment approaches to standard cognitive behavioural programmes should probably consider the role of medication for sex offenders manifesting very marked levels of emotional lability, as well as drawing on some of the treatment approaches developed for non-offending individuals with severe personality disorder, particularly borderline type. These approaches include schema-focused therapy (Young 1999) and dialectical behaviour therapy (Linehan 1993), both of which place emphasis on the importance of establishing a crisis management plan, addressing primary areas causing distress and developing self-management skills.

### Disorders of sexual preference – paedophilia

In contrast to the more generic term 'child molester', paedophilia is a diagnostic category within the section of disorders of sexual preference. It is defined as 'a sexual preference for children, usually of prepubertal or early pubertal age. Some paedophiles are attracted only to girls, others only to boys, and others again are interested in both sexes' (World Health Organisation 1994: 219).

ICD-10 goes on to state that a persistent or predominant tendency is required for the diagnosis, even though the diagnosis can include those men who retain a preference for adult sex partners but, because they are chronically frustrated in achieving appropriate contacts, habitually turn to children as substitutes. Clearly there is considerable overlap between a diagnosis of paedophilia and an assessment of deviant sexual interest, as described in Chapter 3.

It is perhaps interesting to compare this diagnosis to that outlined in DSM-IV (American Psychiatric Association 1994: 256–7), which states that there are three criteria to the diagnosis:

a) Over a period of at least 6 months, recurrent, intense sexually arousing fantasies, sexual urges, or behaviors involving sexual activity with a prepubescent child or children (generally age 13 years or younger).
b) The person has acted on these sexual urges, or the sexual urges or fantasies cause marked distress or interpersonal difficulty.
c) The person is at least age 16 years and at least 5 years older than the child or children in Criterion a).

There is no specific diagnostic category which encompasses sexual offending against adults. ICD-10 does contain reference to sadism, within the category of sadomasochism, and states 'Sexual sadism is sometimes difficult to distinguish from cruelty in sexual situations or anger unrelated to eroticism. Where violence is necessary for erotic arousal, the diagnosis can be clearly established' (p. 220). See Chapter 3 for a more detailed discussion on sadism.

## Offence-specific treatment

### Pharmacological treatments for deviant sexual interest

Pharamacological interventions to reduce sexual drive have been poorly researched, generally, but interested readers should read the useful reviews of Prentky (1997), Balon (1998) and a task force report of the American Psychiatric Association on *Dangerous Sex Offenders* (1999). The theoretical underpinnings of medical interventions are based on earlier experiences – largely between the 1920s and 1960s – of surgical castration with sex offenders. Surgical castration – an intrusive and irreversible procedure – was demonstrably effective in reducing sex offender recidivism rates, with studies citing reductions from more than 50 per cent pre-treatment to less than 5 per cent post-treatment. Given that the primary effect of surgery is to suppress the sexual drive by reducing testosterone levels, it was thought that pharmacological treatment approach based on a reduction of testosterone would produce the same effect. On first sight, the idea of medication which reduces the risk of sexual offending is enormously appealing – a simple, cost-effective solution which circumvents the shortcomings of psychological treatment. Inevitably, the position is far more complex. The hypothesis behind anti-libidinal medications is that the sex drive is reduced and therefore associated deviant sexual fantasies and behaviour are reduced. In fact, there is some debate as to whether it is primarily aggression, including sexual aggression, which is testosterone dependent. Some studies appear to base this medical approach on a concept of hypersexuality. Kafka (1997) went so far as to try and operationalise this concept, suggesting that a persistent total sexual outlet of seven or more orgasms per week for a minimum duration of six months be considered as the lower boundary for hypersexual desire in males. Gagne (1981) defined hypersexuality as manifested by frequent masturbation, multiple sex partners, inability to refrain from acting on deviant sexual thoughts and a high frequency of sexual fantasies and erotic dreams. Other studies seem to be less concerned with the extent of the sexual drive, but rather with the deviant outlet. It must be remembered, of course, that persistent deviant sexual interests are only found in a subgroup of sex offenders, perhaps up to 40 per cent.

Having established an excessive, or persistently deviant, sexual drive in the course of an assessment, it is extremely important to consider the motivation of the offender to engage in pharmacological therapy.

First, some high risk offenders will present an extremely 'perverse' profile, with evidence that all emotional difficulties are temporarily resolved by sexualising feelings – that is, sexual gratification as a solution to all intrapsychic conflict. Taking away the sexual solution in such offenders may lead to profound feelings of depression, and is most likely to result in non-compliance. Clearly, management strategies need to be in place to provide the offender with skills and structure in order to manage the potential vacuum. Nearly all researchers emphasise the fact that pharmacological treatments cannot stand alone – indeed, there is little evidence that they are superior to psychological therapies, but rather that they complement other treatment approaches.

Second, some high risk sex offenders are highly motivated to pursue consenting adult relationships, despite persistent deviant sexual interests. Indeed, they may view the potential success of a new relationship as a primary relapse prevention strategy. Drastically reducing the sex drive in such an instance will jeopardise the new relationship and compound pre-existing fears of sexual inadequacy and rejection within the context of adult intimacy.

Third, many of the relevant medications have significant side-effects, a few of which may be irreversible. Sex offenders, facing long prison sentences, may not be in a position to provide truly informed consent. In England and Wales, such medication can only be prescribed on a voluntary basis, whether or not the individual is subject to detention under the Mental Health Act, or a condition of treatment associated with a criminal justice disposal. Given that the majority of treatments are taken orally, there are inevitable difficulties in ensuring compliance.

The literature suggests that there are three main drug strategies:

- anti-psychotic medication;
- hormonal drugs;
- anti-depressant medication.

Neuroleptics – or anti-psychotic drugs – tend to have an anti-libidinal effect and interfere with sexual functioning in a variety of ways. Given the potential for serious side-effects, neuroleptics would only be prescribed if sexually deviant behaviours were secondary to a major psychiatric disorder such as schizophrenia. Similarly, the evidence suggests that lithium can be a successful treatment in cases of deviant sexual behaviour co-morbid with mood disorder.

The two most frequently used hormonal treatments are medroxy-progesterone acetate (MPA) and cyproterone acetate (CPA). The former is predominantly used in America, while CPA is licensed for use in Britain and Canada. Although the mechanisms of action are rather different, both ultimately reduce testosterone levels. Studies have identified that testosterone levels are significantly reduced within a few days of commencing treatment, although the full effects on libidinal functioning are not apparent for a further four to eight weeks. Initially the sexual drive is reduced or inhibited; subsequently potency, orgasm and sperm production are all affected. Subjects report reduced sexual thoughts and fantasies, frequency and pleasure of masturbation and lowered sexual frustration. With

CPA there are many reports that it brings a feeling of calm which is specifically related to a reduction of anxiety and irritability. This is of interest, particularly given practitioners' anxieties that inhibiting the sex drive may be substituted with an increase in aggressive tendencies; conversely, reducing testosterone levels may in fact reduce a propensity for violence. There are, however, a number of potentially serious side-effects to these medications, a few of which are irreversible. These include infertility and abnormal spermatozoa (slowly reversible), breast enlargement (common and may be permanent), mood changes and altered liver function. Before commencing treatment, liver function tests, serum testosterone and sperm counts need to be performed. Ongoing monitoring is required throughout treatment, including blood counts and liver function tests. While studies of MPA suggest that patients will relapse when treatment is stopped, there is evidence that after 6–12 months with CPA, dosages can be reduced and treatment stopped without a reoccurrence of the deviant sexual interests or behaviour. However, these may of course reoccur, and therefore longer-term monitoring is required. A summary of early studies examining the efficacy of anti-libidinal hormonal treatments in reducing sexual offending demonstrates greatly reduced sexual recidivism rates, where compliance with treatment was established (American Psychiatric Association 1999).

In the last ten years, there has been growing interest in the use of selective serotonergic reuptake inhibitors (SSRIs) for the paraphilias, largely based on the success of SSRIs in treating obsessional compulsive and impulse control disorders – which have similarities to the paraphilias in terms of their presentation. These medications have traditionally been prescribed for depression and premature ejaculation. A range of empirical studies would suggest that serotonergic medications – notably in relatively high doses – decrease deviant sexual interest without impairing non-deviant sexual interest. This is particularly the case where paraphilia is co-morbid with anxiety and depression. The particular advantages of this group of medications include the possibility for the offenders to retain sexual functioning while freeing themselves from intrusive deviant sexual fantasies and drives; furthermore, no specialist forensic psychiatric expertise is required to prescribe SSRIs, as they are widely prescribed within general psychiatric services. There are side-effects, which include nausea, anorexia, diarrhoea and headache, and specifically there is the possibility of sexual dysfunction such as delayed ejaculation or a lack of orgasm, which may paradoxically increase feelings of sexual frustration.

Given the above, what might be the criteria for prescribing anti-libidinal agents? A pragmatic approach would suggest that pharmacological interventions might be appropriate for sex offenders who have a persistent deviant sexual interest (whether or not they act upon it regularly or infrequently), and who experience high levels of sexual arousal and/or are distressed by frequent thoughts of acting on their sexual fantasies. There needs to be a strong motivation to comply with the medication, which is likely to be related to the perceived consequences for them or others if they should act on their sexual impulses. For those whose sexual interests are wholly deviant, or whose sexually deviant behaviour contains strong aggressive elements, hormonal agents may be the treatment of choice. However, for those offenders who seek to maintain legal, consenting intimate relationships, or whose deviant sexual interests are closely allied to anxiety and depressive disorders, anti-depressant medication (SSRIs) may be more appropriate. For adolescents who may be presenting with deviant sexual fantasies, and for whom hormonal medication is inappropriate because of the side-effects, SSRIs may provide an opportunity to attenuate the development of deviant sexual behaviour patterns.

### Psychological treatments

The 1990s were characterised by some important changes in the field of sex offender treatment. First, treatment programme became more widely available, notably within the Probation (Barker & Beech 1993) and Prison Services (Thornton & Hogue 1993). This enabled practitioners to assess which components of treatment appeared to be associated with attitudinal change and later recidivism (see Beckett *et al.* 1994 for a summary). Second, research methodology improved in the light of earlier criticisms, and addressed issues of treatment integrity, sample selection, duration of follow-up and criteria for 'success' (including survival rates). Third, techniques of meta-analysis provided researchers with identifiable base rates for recidivism in different subgroups of sex offenders against which treatment studies could measure efficacy (Alexander 1999; Hanson & Bussiere 1998).

The provision of treatment programmes for convicted sex offenders in the community has posed ethical dilemmas, particularly in those instances when a community sentence – as an alternative to custody – is being proposed to the courts. The potential availability of further victims necessitates a serious consideration of short-term as well as long-term risk, and questions of treatability are paramount. Treatment providers need to consider a number of factors:

• pragmatic considerations (e.g. whether some treatment is better than none for an offender who is being automatically released after a short prison sentence);
• which aspects of treatment programmes have been shown to be effective;
• which groups of sex offenders have been shown to respond positively to treatment;
• what are the benchmarks of success (e.g. straightforward comparison with known base rates of recidivism, or achieving harm reduction over the longer term).

The potential advantages of community treatment (if shown to be effective) are evident: not only can a risk reduction programme operate in the least restrictive environment necessary for the offender, but also there is a significant reduction in the cost implications of community treatment in comparison to custody or hospitalisation.

In the absence of large-scale randomised control studies, an examination of treatment efficacy needs to be anchored within our knowledge of overall base rate behaviours. Studies of treatment efficacy have not always described their treatment model, nor have they identified outcome by victim type. This seriously frustrates attempts to establish which programme design is most effective and for whom. Hall (1995) analysed 12 studies published since 1989: he found that a small treatment effect could be established; the highest treatment effects were in studies with the highest base rates of recidivism and longer follow-up periods of five or more years; 19 per cent of the treated samples committed further sexual offences as compared with 27 per cent of subjects in the comparison conditions; cognitive-behavioural and hormonal treatments were found to be significantly more effective than behavioural treatments, but were not significantly different from each other. He did not find a significant difference in treatment effects between rapists and child molesters.

Alexander (1999) approached the same question with different methodology, reviewing 79 sexual offender treatment outcome studies, encompassing 10,988 subjects, from 1943 to 1996. She found that, overall, 14.4 per cent of treated child molesters reoffended as compared with 25.8 per cent of untreated child molesters. Breaking down these figures further, relapse prevention treatment encompassing a cognitive behavioural model appeared to be the most effective type of intervention, with a reoffending rate of 8.1 per cent compared with 18.3 per cent in other group/behavioural interventions and 13.6 per cent in unspecified treatment modalities. There were also interesting differences in victim gender and incest/non-incest type offending: child molesters with female victims reoffended at a similar rate of 15 per cent whether they were treated or untreated, while 18.2 per cent of those treated offenders with male victims reoffended compared to 34.1 per cent of untreated child molesters with male victims. Four per cent of treated incest offenders reoffended compared to 12.5 per cent of the untreated group and 1.7 per cent of treated non-incest offenders reoffended compared to 32 per cent of untreated non-incest offenders. That is to say, the most marked treatment effects were for those child molesters who had male victims and/or who offended outside the family. This pattern of recidivism was apparent at the three-year follow-up stage.

Hanson, Gordon, Harris, Marques, Murphy, Quinsey and Seto (2002) provide the most recent data on 43 studies (n = 9,454). They confirmed that there did appear to be a significant treatment effect overall, 12.3 per cent of treated sex offenders being reconvicted compared to 16.8 per cent of non-treated sex offenders. Again, cognitive behavioural treatment was associated with the greatest reductions in reconviction.

In contrast with the above meta-analytic reviews, Marques (1999) reported preliminary results on the child sexual abusers drawn from the general prison criminal population (unselected for reasons of dangerousness or psychiatric reasons). Her study is particularly important for the attempt to provide control groups (volunteers for treatment were randomly assigned to treatment or no treatment and a non-volunteer group was also available, all groups being matched on key variables). Preliminary results from this study on child sexual abusers found the treated group sexually reoffending at 13.6 per cent (compared to 11.1 per cent of a volunteer control group and 16.6 per cent for the non-volunteers); those with male victims appeared to be doing better in the treatment group than those with female victims.

For violent offences, the treatment group reoffended at less than half the rate of the two control groups (3.6 per cent for treatment group, 7.6 per cent for volunteer controls and 8.3 per cent for the non-volunteers); the peak hazard rate for both treated and untreated child sexual abusers was around three years.

In the UK, the sex offender treatment evaluation project (STEP) has evaluated treatment programmes in the community run by probation (Beckett *et al.* 1994), and within the prison system (Beech *et al.* 1999). Treatment components are clearly described and a number of psychometric measures administered pre- and post-treatment. Preliminary outcome figures for two years following completion of treatment in the seven community programmes are encouraging (Hedderman & Sugg 1996): 8 per cent of the 133 subjects were reconvicted, six of whom (4.5 per cent) were convicted for a sexual offence, as compared to the sexual reconviction rate of 191 sex offenders given probation orders in 1990 which was 9 per cent. When controlling for differences in age, previous convictions and previous experience of youth custody, the actual rate of reconviction (9 per cent) for the STEP sample was lower than the average predicted score (13 per cent) whereas the actual rate for the general probation sample (29 per cent) was higher than the predicted rate (23 per cent). None of the 28 offenders rated as having responded well to treatment were reconvicted within the two years, compared to three recidivists out of 24 'untreated' offenders. The prison treatment sample (Beech *et al.* 1999) comprised 82 men and complete data was available on 77 of them. A treated profile was found in over two thirds of the sample in terms of a reduction in pro-offending attitudes, and one third of the sample had a treated profile in terms of a reduction in pro-offending attitudes and changes in social competency/acceptance of accountability measures.

## Treatment components

A range of treatment models have been applied to sex offenders. These include psychodynamic therapies such as individual and group psychoanalytic psychotherapy, and systemic therapy for incest offenders or those offenders wishing to be reintegrated into families (see Craissati 1998 for a full review of the models). Behavioural treatments focused specifically on problems with deviant sexual arousal are detailed in Maletzky (1991). However, the dominant mode of treatment at the present time is cognitive behavioural therapy (CBT), for which there is the most firmly established research base. This is not to undermine the potential efficacy of other models, but in terms of the accessibility of the model and its applicability, CBT is utilised by both mental health practitioners and other agencies such as probation and social services.

The CBT model is based on the premise that schemas – or core beliefs – are stable cognitive patterns which develop in early life as part of normal cognitive development, and are shaped by events and relationships. Schemas result in underlying assumptions which are conditional beliefs, and which trigger automatic thoughts – cognitions that automatically and temporarily flow through one's mind and will often reflect persistent cognitive distortions. Recidivistic sexual offenders would be expected to hold deviant schema or habitual patterns of thought and action that facilitate their offences (Hanson & Harris 2000).

There are six main components to most CBT treatment programmes, and these are detailed in Beckett *et al.* (1994):

1   *Denial and minimisation* are targeted, as breaking down denial is viewed as an important prerequisite for change and the assumption of responsibility.
2   *Victim empathy* is developed by educating perpetrators as to the harmful effect of abuse, the aim being to strengthen the motivation not to offend.
3   *Justifications and cognitive distortions* are elicited and challenged so as to stop the pattern of assuaging feelings of guilt and giving oneself permission to offend.
4   *Lifestyle and personality* addresses the issues of low self-esteem, fear of adult intimacy and inappropriate assertiveness so often found in perpetrators, with the aim of improving functioning in society.
5   *Deviant sexual fantasies* are one predictor of reoffending and are therefore targeted in order to help the perpetrator modify or control deviant arousal and develop acceptable fantasies as an alternative.
6   *Relapse prevention* aims to help perpetrators recognise risky situations, feelings, moods and thoughts, and to develop strategies to prevent relapse.

Some of these components are addressed as separate topics, while others are best incorporated into the general content. Clearly, these treatment components are closely related to the dynamic variables identified in research (Beech *et al.* 2002; Hanson & Harris 2000) which appear to predict potential change over time. It is worth highlighting that the aim of treatment may be different for different practitioners: while all agencies are concerned to prevent reoffending, mental health practitioners may equally emphasise the psychological well-being of the individual offender as a treatment aim. These concerns are not necessarily incompatible, but may influence the content and approach of different treatment programmes.

Currently, accredited programmes are running within the Prison and Probation Services. Core programmes are supplemented by extended programmes for the more 'deviant' offenders, relapse prevention (or 'Booster') programmes are widely available, and there is an adapted version of the core programme available for those offenders with low intellectual functioning.

There are few consistent exclusion criteria for cognitive behavioural treatment: total denial is inevitably problematic in an offence-focused programme, and a proportion of sex offenders will be excluded or will refuse treatment on these grounds. However, interesting anecdotal reports on the development of 'deniers' groups may produce evidence, in time, of a potentially successful treatment approach for this group. Amended treatment programmes may be necessary for those offenders with mild mental impairment and those with significant brain damage are likely to require an altogether different approach. Offenders who have killed, or who pose a high risk of immediate danger to the public, are sometimes excluded because of the destructive impact they may have on the group process. Those offenders with serious mental illness, or who present with pervasive psychological difficulties or personality dysfunction, may well be able to access standard CBT programmes, once their mental state has been stabilised or with additional psychological or psychiatric support.

High-scoring psychopaths – as measured by the Psychopathy Checklist (PCL-R, Hare 1991) – have been thought to perform poorly in therapeutic programmes, although there has been no research specific to sex offenders. More recent prison-based research (Clark 2000) found that high PCL-R scorers reoffended (after two years at risk) at a higher rate (85 per cent) if they had been in a structured offence-related programme than those high scorers who had not been treated (58 per cent). However a meta-analytic review (Salekin 2002) of 42 treatment studies on psychopathy – despite methodological limitations – suggested a more optimistic conclusion, where combined CBT and insight-oriented approaches had the highest success rate of 86 per cent. Current thinking would suggest that caution should be exercised in including this small subgroup of sex offenders in standard group treatment programmes without consideration of alternative or parallel forms of care and management.

### Measuring change during treatment

A crude, but crucial, measurement of treatment success is clearly 'outcome in terms of sexual recidivism'. However, this is a longer-term perspective which should be complemented by short-term evaluation. Clearly, any approach to measuring change should start with an identification of treatment goals, whether they be shifts in pro-offending attitudes or measures of psychological well-being and stability. Practitioner ratings of change are clearly subject to biases, unless there are clearly identified behavioural observations or standardised schedules are completed. An example of the latter would be the SONAR (Hanson & Harris 2000, detailed in Chapter 3) which suggests a simple coding system for the five components of dynamic change. Most commonly, practitioners rely upon self-report questionnaires – preferably with robust psychometric properties – which are administered before and after treatment, where comparisons can be made over time (see Beckett *et al.* 1994 and Craissati 1998 for a review of questionnaires).

## Adolescent sex offenders

The evidence base for adolescent sex offender treatment programmes is detailed in Righthand and Welch's (2001) review for the US Department of Justice. They identify that the goals of adolescent programmes generally include a need to gain control over sexually abusive behaviours and to increase prosocial interactions with peers. Treatment content tends to include addressing issues of denial and distortion, sexual education, social skills and decreasing deviant arousal and relapse prevention – the latter emphasising external controls for young people. Unlike adult sex offenders, denial in adolescents is likely to be closely linked to, and influenced by, family attitudes. Where possible, family work is advocated to address denial by providing information and education, carers' groups and family therapy (Stevenson, Castillo & Sefarbi 1990). Additional treatment components have incorporated the resolution of family dysfunction, enhancing a positive sexual identity, promoting dating skills and positive school attachments. Specialist treatment developments have included the use of vicarious sensitisation – exposure to audio-taped crime scenarios designed to stimulate arousal, followed by a video portraying the negative consequences of sexually abusive behaviour. This treatment appears to reduce deviant arousal in adolescents who are sexually aroused by prepubescent children (Weinrott, Riggan & Frothingham 1997). A teaching-family model has been developed and evaluated (Lee & Olender 1992) for specialised foster carers who are trained to use techniques for managing intense and volatile behaviours, and to use a curriculum to facilitate the skills necessary for social competence and independent living. Cognitive behavioural approaches facilitate behaviours such as impulse control and effective problem solving. In this way, adolescents receive interventions in a more naturalistic setting.

There is a lack of empirical support for the superior efficacy of groups – as with adults – despite this being the preferred mode of intervention. Practitioners have warned against a confrontational, offence-focused approach with adolescents, given that they may be more susceptible to suggestion and may feel pressurised to 'confess' to offending behaviours which they have not enacted.

The model described above is theoretically sound, but the components have not been empirically linked to reductions in recidivism. There is limited evidence to suggest that comprehensive treatment models which include group, individual and family work may be likely to reduce sexual recidivism (Bourgon *et al.* 1999). Furthermore, Borduin, Henggeler, Blaske and Stein (1990) compared multi-systemic therapy and individual treatment, following up the adolescent sex offenders for an average of 37 months. They found that the sexual recidivism rate for those in the multi-systemic therapy condition was 12.5 per cent compared to 75 per cent in the individual treatment condition. As yet, the superiority of residential versus community, or specialist versus non-specialist settings remains unclear. It seems to be the greater range and intensity of treatments which determines outcome, rather than the setting.

Given that a significant number of adolescent sex offenders present with a range of delinquent behaviours, programmes which are not sex offence specific, but which address antisocial behaviours, may be effective. Meta-analytic reviews (Izzo & Ross 1990; Lipsey &

Wilson 1998) have demonstrated the effectiveness of cognitive behavioural interventions, and those which focus on interpersonal skills and use behavioural programmes, for juvenile delinquents. Multisystemic therapy – addressing the offender's total environment, family, neighbourhood, school and community – has been validated with chronic delinquents (Borduin *et al.* 1990), which provides additional support for this promising mode of therapy.

## Female sex offenders

Few structured treatment programmes for female sex offenders are described in the literature, and inevitably much of the therapeutic work has taken place on an individual basis. In England and Wales, group work for women is in its infancy and to date has been focused within the prison system. Preliminary evaluative research is underway. In America, the major treatment programmes are in Minnesota, and include work with incarcerated female offenders and outpatients (see Atkinson 1995 for a brief description). In many ways, treatment goals are viewed as similar to those for male offenders: reducing pro-offending attitudes, enhancing intimacy deficits and developing relapse prevention skills. Some programmes emphasise a group cognitive behavioural approach as the primary treatment need, with victimisation experiences being viewed as a secondary treatment target. Others emphasise the need to engage women as victims in their own right – often in individual therapy (Saradjian & Hanks 1996) before addressing personal responsibility for offending. There are, of course, risks inherent in both approaches: offence-focused work may ignore profound individual difficulties which interfere with an offender's capacity to make use of therapy; attention to personal trauma may encourage the therapist to collude with the defensive stance of a woman who wishes to distance herself from facing up to her offending behaviour. Saradjian and Hanks (1996) point out that addressing the offender's own life history and trauma is the most effective way of effectively engaging that individual in meaningful therapeutic work and overcoming denial, and this is in line with the work on motivational interviewing with male sex offenders (see Craissati 1998).

There would appear to be considerable benefits to a programme which has multiple components, delivered in multiple modes. The Minnesota programmes have group and individual work available, based on both exploratory and educative models; furthermore, an outpatient day treatment centre, where the offender's children also attend, provides additional independent living skills training, parenting and sexuality education. Atkinson (2000) suggests that female sex offenders may well have different treatment needs according to their 'typology'. That is, she suggests that *male/lover* offenders may respond fairly quickly to offence-focused work, and the development of self-confidence and social skills/support, as long as attention is paid to any problems with substance misuse. *Predisposed* offenders may be the most difficult to treat because of the extent of their psychological disturbance, and attention will need to be paid in the first instance to their deviant sexual fantasies and subsequently to the repercussions of their childhood abuse. Atkinson does not state how this should be achieved, but it might be assumed that behavioural techniques could play a role in ameliorating fantasies in the first instance. *Male coerced/ accompanied* offenders have treatment needs in terms of reducing pro-offending attitudes and may need to address issues of victim empathy; however, these goals need to be considered in parallel with help in understanding dependency difficulties and in developing appropriate independence from abusive partners.

## Case studies

### Stephen

Stephen was willing to engage in treatment, motivated by his recent acknowledgement that he had offended against his daughter some years previously, and a desire to be allowed to continue living within his current family. There was no evidence of enduring deviant sexual interests and he presented as stable in terms of his psychological and social functioning. He received no psychiatric diagnosis. Treatment targets included pro-offending attitudes and some difficulties in relation to adult heterosexual relationships. He was considered to be rather resistant to viewing himself as a future risk, and to have a poorly developed relapse prevention strategy – given his potentially high risk living situation. He agreed to enter the group treatment programme – comprising 14 months of weekly therapy – and the three-day relapse prevention programme.

Stephen made good progress in the group treatment programme. He was a diligent attender and compliant with all tasks. His contributions were open and he engaged constructively with other group members. His insight into offence-specific issues was thought to be good. He developed an understanding of his relationship difficulties and their root in his childhood experiences, and was able to identify hostile components of his offending as well as his emotional identification with his victim, Natalie. There was some shift in his perception of himself as posing no future risk, separating out his appraisal of himself as generally low risk (which was accurate) and the potentially high risk situation in which he was placed. He developed strong relapse prevention strategies which were borne out in his behaviour at home, and confirmed by social services.

## Anthony

Given Anthony's denial in terms of the offence, it was unclear whether he needed or would cooperate with a formal treatment programme. It was decided that he should participate in an extended assessment – over five sessions – which would aim to develop a full picture of his life and difficulties with his collaboration, and in doing so utilise a motivational interviewing model to maximise the opportunities for change. By offering him some control in the process – for example, allowing him to amend the draft report – it was hoped that he would respond positively and engage. From a diagnostic point of view, antisocial personality disorder was likely to have been the primary diagnostic possibility, although recent evidence of maturation should lead to caution, despite lifestyle instability and impulsivity remaining a concern.

The underlying premise for the assessment was that denial of behaviour is not considered to be a primary risk factor for future sexual recidivism. Clarifying the assessor's stance – that he was probably guilty of rape, given the evidence and the difficulty of obtaining such a conviction in court, but his account was heard and accepted as possible – created an honest opening for discussion. Mutually acceptable goals were agreed: that he wished to stay out of prison, he wanted to maintain a relationship with his son, he wished to seek out legal means of ensuring financial stability and quality of life, and he anticipated settling in a committed relationship one day. Risks in relation to these goals were also agreed: lifestyle and peer group influences, tendencies for impulsivity and recklessness, impaired judgement due to substance misuse and his dating style/attitudes towards women.

The assessment progress, and subsequent report, was able to inform the statutory involvement of probation and the multi-agency panel, and involved ongoing consultation between the psychologist and the probation officer.

## James

At the point of assessment – some 25 years after the index offence – James was presenting with a treated profile. This was confirmed by his PPG results a few years earlier, psychometric assessments pre- and post-treatment and his presentation in interviews with numerous experienced practitioners. He had resided within a prison therapeutic community for 18 months and completed an additional 200 hours of sex offender treatment in group programmes. As well as having no identifiable pro-offending attitudes, his level of psycho-social competency was good, as far as could be measured within a secure and open prison environment; furthermore there was no evidence of impulsivity, recklessness or poor self-regulation. As with many lifers he was concerned to regulate his life, and maintained regular employment and pursued personal hobbies within prison. Sadistic sexual interests, which were so prominent in his life leading up to the index offence were thought to be either dormant or resolved. His clearly expressed aim was to seek homosexual intimacy in due course, and he had had some experience of such relationships within prison.

Determining a psychiatric diagnosis was difficult: at the time of the index offence he was considered to be psychopathic – not in itself a psychiatric diagnosis – although it would have been appropriate to diagnose him with a paraphilia (sadistic type). It was no longer clear whether this diagnosis applied. It was agreed that James was unlikely to benefit from additional cognitive behavioural group treat-ment in the community, and in any case the nature of his offence might have posed an obstacle within the group. He was offered fort-nightly individual therapy sessions with the forensic mental health team, to complement the stringent supervision plan provided by the Probation Service.

The aim of treatment was to monitor James' awareness of risk and his management of risky situations; to revisit the precursors to his offence; to assess his mental state and identify any early indications of potential relapse, including increasing withdrawal, despondency, guardedness or a resumption of former drinking habits; to support progress in his general lifestyle in terms of social contacts, coping with his living environment and seeking to establish a meaningful structure to his day; and finally, to monitor progress in his attempts at sexual intimacy and/or the re-emergence of deviant sexual interests.

James engaged willingly in treatment and was entirely compliant. He clearly thought about the sessions in-between times and brought potential risky situations and current dilemmas to the sessions. He would talk about the past, and his offence, with an appropriate level of understanding and emotional intensity. There were clearly identifiable problems for him in the community which had not been evident in open prison or the pre-release hostel. These included witnessing another long-serving lifer being recalled to prison, and facing the devastating effect the 'disclosure' of his offence had on potential employers, all of whom subsequently rejected him. He wanted to seek out social contacts but found it difficult to resolve the dilemma of when and how to disclose his past to potential friends or lovers. For a period, he became rather isolated and despondent but subsequently regained his equilibrium, found himself some meaningful voluntary work and planned to improve his social life.

## Peter

Peter clearly presented with a deviant sexual interest in boys (whether intermittent or dominant), and associated with this, a marked lack of victim empathy. There were also deficits in his psychosocial competencies, with anxieties and failures in terms of sexual orientation and sustained adult intimacy. His general level of self-regulation was good and he was likely to find work. There was no evidence of impulsivity or more pervasive psychological dysfunction. In psychiatric terms, he would have received a diagnosis of paedophilia.

Peter's motivation to seek help for his offending behaviour was thought to be ambivalent, much of his avoidance being due to feelings of shame and anxiety. This appeared to be particularly relevant in relation to his wish for individual treatment rather than group treatment. This is often the case in sex offenders who have unresolved issues concerning their own sexual victimisation by a man: they may avoid the 'claustrophobia' of group treatment programmes in prison where feelings of vulnerability in relation to intimacy can arise without the possibility of escape. A strategy was agreed with the Probation Service that group treatment in the community would be insisted upon. The rationale was to encourage a 'safe' level of intimacy within which Peter could gain confidence and make use of the social modelling function of a group.

Peter acquiesced and engaged in group treatment. Initially his progress was slow and there were concerns regarding his level of cognitive functioning which necessitated the supervising probation officer assisting with homework tasks. There were two key moments in the programme. The first related to Peter's late attendances, which resulted in written warnings, and eventually a decision to discharge him from the programme. His probation officer considered that the group therapists were being unduly punitive: 'It was his employment which prevented him attending and he was probably not able, in any case, to make much use of the treatment'. Good communication channels between the practitioners quickly identified the sado-masochistic splits in agency working – the attacking and collusive elements – which held all the anxieties regarding Peter, allowing him to avoid the issues. A compromise was found whereby he was taken out of the group, interviewed by the probation manager and given a final warning, and also recommenced the group. Re-establishing the boundaries and placing the anxiety for his future firmly within his hands appeared to assist in a re-engagement in the process.

The second key moment related to the apparent impasse regarding Peter's attitude to his own victims as having been collusive and acquiescent. It was only when discussing his own sexual victimisation in the group that he was able to disclose that he had never been brutally raped, but had in fact been persistently abused by a male neighbour over a period of months. He was profoundly distressed by his feelings of shame and guilt, believing that he was responsible for his collusion with the abuse. Whether it was this disclosure or the warm and supportive response of the other group members which effected change is not clear; regardless, this period of the programme appeared to have a cathartic effect on his own capacity to view his victims with a more accurate level of understanding and concern.

## Martin

The level of Martin's psychological disturbance, coupled with his persistent and dominant sexual interest in prepubescent boys, meant that he needed to be considered for a multimodal treatment intervention. Although a diagnosis of paedophilia would have been appropriate, the predominant diagnosis was of a personality disorder with marked antisocial and borderline features.

The aim of the group was to revisit and consolidate learning from the prison programme. Slightly to our surprise, the other group members were astute in recognising Martin's violent fantasies as a distraction from real concerns regarding likely offending. His participation was variable, sometimes demanding and self-absorbed, sometimes distracted and withdrawn. There was a deliberate strategy in the group to limit discussion of the details of his offending and fantasies and to concentrate on thoughts and feelings which were less accessible to him. He was clearly distressed by the module relating to primary relationships and victim experiences in childhood, and this coincided with him being prescribed anti-depressant medication. After Martin was recalled, his failure in the community was discussed in the group (see Chapter 5). It was normal practice for the group members to collaborate in writing a letter to prematurely discharged members, and they did so for Martin, with some care. He was clearly moved to be held in mind by others during his absence – a new experience for him – and he responded in kind, promising to seek help in prison and to rejoin the group when he was released.

Individual treatment sessions targeted deviant sexual interests and focused on risky situations, as they occurred, with an emphasis on putting relapse prevention skills into practice. It was assumed that Martin would encounter such situations, and experience urges to reoffend, thus confidentiality was extended to cover these assumptions and was agreed with the other agencies involved. Nevertheless, confidentiality was not extended to acts of abuse, clearly identified potential victims or unusually high risk situations which were unknown to other agencies. This agreement drew a delicate line between the need to protect the public and the need to encourage Martin in an open and safe discussion of his very real difficulties. It became clear that although Martin would discuss risk first in his individual sessions, he tended to discuss similar matters subsequently with the Probation Service.

# Chapter 7

# Case studies

## Introduction

The five case studies described in this chapter are discussed and quoted throughout the book. They are brought together here in their full form, combining all the extracts previously quoted. They have been edited slightly to dispense with the need for repetition of key facts, but are otherwise the same. As risk assessment procedures improve, offenders of concern can become little more than a string of identifiable risk variables. Therefore, the decision to dedicate a whole chapter to reproducing these case studies in full was made on the basis that it is important for readers to understand each case subject as a real person, whose story has a beginning, middle and end. The case studies are drawn from the author's clinical experience, each case being an amalgamation of several sex offenders. There are two reasons for this: first to preserve confidentiality and second to ensure that a wide range of risk-related issues are illustrated. The cases represent a bias towards the medium to high risk end of the spectrum which would not normally be encountered in clinical practice. However, this approach seems justified, given that most agencies – largely due to resource limitations – focus on those offenders who are most likely to pose a risk to the public. Although one case of homicide is included to illustrate particular risk conundrums, there has been a deliberate attempt otherwise to avoid cases which are unrepresentative.

## Stephen

### Referral

Stephen was a 30-year-old man, referred by social services due to concerns regarding the potential risk he might pose to his step-daughter who was currently aged 10. Four years previously, his 8-year-old biological daughter from a previous relationship alleged that he had sexually abused her while he was living at the family home. He was arrested and charged, but the case did not proceed as his daughter did not wish to give evidence against him. Three years later, he married a woman with a young daughter, but the matter did not come to social services' attention for a year until a routine police check revealed his offending background.

### Background

Stephen's personal and family history was as follows. He described himself as a rather unhappy child who had a distant relationship with his mother. His father had left when he was a baby and his mother's bitterness about the failed relationship manifested itself in repeated derogatory comments about men and a clearly stated regret that she had not had a daughter. Although Stephen was quiet and withdrawn at home, he enjoyed school and managed to achieve academically and to integrate socially. His mother did not encourage him to mix with other boys outside school hours and he could not recall an occasion when school friends came back to the house. He did, however, forge an intense friendship with the girl next door, who was his age. He perceived her as being immersed in a very loving family atmosphere and was often round at her house, receiving the interest and warmth which was lacking at home. He was distraught when she and her family moved away from the area when they were aged 12, and after initial attempts to remain in contact the children drifted apart. In retrospect, Stephen described their relationship as his 'first love'.

Stephen left school at 16 with qualifications and, after a period of apprenticeship, worked as an electrical engineer. After a period of five years, he became self-employed. There was a period of financial stress in the year leading up to the index offence, when business was slack; he kept this hidden from his partner at that time, but neverthe-less resented her spending money freely on the house and herself.

More recently his business was maintained on a stable financial footing.

Stephen met his first partner when he was 17, and she was his first sexual relationship. Prior to that, he had felt anxious about dating women, often comparing girls unfavourably to his 'first love'. His partner quickly fell pregnant, and although unplanned, Stephen felt that this new family would bring him the security he so craved. However, the relationship floundered; Stephen felt that his partner lost interest in him, sexually and emotionally, after their baby – Natalie – was born, and he resented her casual reliance on his finances. He suspected that she was having an affair, although he never dared to confront her about this. Stephen's current wife – Jane – was slightly older than him, with a daughter – Penny – from a previous relationship. He said he was attracted to Jane because of her warmth and 'motherliness', her easy nature and sense of fun. He felt they were equal partners in the relationship; she worked as well as him, and they shared care of Penny. She was a demonstrative woman, physically affectionate, and he said they had a good sexual relationship.

Stephen drank socially but had never had a difficulty with excessive use of alcohol. He had never used illicit drugs and had no psychiatric history.

### Offending behaviour

Stephen had no previous arrests, cautions or convictions prior to the allegations of sexual abuse against Natalie. Natalie disclosed the abuse to her friend's mother when she was aged 8, and the matter was immediately brought to social services' attention. Natalie said that Stephen had been coming to her bedroom in the mornings before she went to school. Initially he had wanted cuddles and affection which she had been happy to give because she felt that they were very close and she loved him. Gradually he began to make her feel uncomfortable, touching her breasts and genitalia, repeatedly asking her if she loved him and reassuring her that physical contact between people who loved each other was normal. The abuse occurred on a fortnightly basis over the period of about one year, and progressed to digital penetration and her masturbating him to the point of ejaculation. She said that she was never coerced by her father, but wanted the abuse to stop, although she still cared for him.

Stephen initially denied abusing Natalie, but when challenged more recently by social services, he admitted that she had told the truth. He felt that the abuse occurred within the context of rejection by his partner and financial stress, together with a growing feeling of closeness to Natalie; that in some ways they sought refuge in each other against his partner. He was deeply regretful about his behaviour but was confident that it would never reoccur, that Penny would never be at risk.

## Formulation

Stephen grew up without a strong sense of himself as lovable and worthy, acutely conscious of his mother's rejection of him. In his closeness to the girl next door he was able to seek out and vicariously experience the comfort and love she received. The intensity of their relationship appeared to be rather idealised, suggesting that he had never resolved his feelings of loss when she left. Although anxious about intimacy in adulthood, he did have relationships: both appeared to be characterised by an emotional neediness which was certainly unmet in the first relationship. The sexual abuse of Natalie could be understood within the context of perceived rejection by his partner, and a retreat into a non-threatening and loving relationship which mirrored his 'first love' and seemed in some ways an attempt to recapture the memory of it.

## Risk

On actuarial tools, Stephen scored as follows:

Static 99: 0 (low), 11% recidivism risk over 10 years
Risk Matrix 2000: medium (sexual)
                          medium (violent)
MnSOST-R: –7 (low), 16% recidivism risk over 6 years
SORAG: category 1; 9% recidivism risk over 10 years
PCL-R: 2 (< 4 range)

The static assessment tools generally viewed Stephen as posing a low risk in general terms. A review of possible dynamic risk variables suggested that there were some intimacy deficits in terms of his low feelings of self-esteem and insecurity in relationships. He was clearly emotionally identified with his victim at the time of the offence, but there was no suggestion of this being the case with other children. The main risk factor appeared to be the absence of a detailed and realistic relapse prevention plan, in that he viewed himself as low risk but was in fact living in a potentially high risk situation.

### Social services

A social services' assessment of Penny concluded that she was a cheerful, confident young girl who liked Stephen and had a strong and affectionate bond with her mother. Academically she was performing well at school and had a good circle of friends. The only risk factor – aside from her age and gender – was that she had no contact with her biological father and felt hurt by this; however, there was no evidence of an unhealthy attachment or dependence on Stephen as a substitute source of attention. She was consistently clear in stating to social services that she wished Stephen to return home.

Penny's mother came from a happy and loving family background. She felt she had been spoiled as a child and this was at the root of the failure of her first marriage. Her relationship with Penny's father was turbulent, largely because he was repeatedly unfaithful to Jane and drank heavily. Initially she was ashamed to admit to her family that a second relationship was failing, but eventually she accepted their support and left him. Having retrained and established herself as financially independent she met and married Stephen. She felt he lacked confidence but shared many of her interests, and they had a strong relationship. When told about the previous allegation against Stephen, she was initially furious with him for not telling her and told him to leave the family home. As Stephen admitted to the abuse she was able to believe that fondling did occur, but felt that the victim may have exaggerated or been mistaken about some of the detail; she also felt it was situational, in that he was in an unhappy relationship at the time, in which he was 'being used'. Three months after the initial disclosure, Jane made it clear to social services that she wished Stephen to be reintegrated into the family.

The following were agreed as part of the management plan, written in a contract and signed by all parties:

- Stephen would commence a community treatment programme.
- Jane would negotiate no night or weekend duties at work for the next six months.

- Jane would have six sessions with the social worker in order to understand the nature and level of risk and to put in place an effective plan for monitoring and protecting Penny.
- If a positive report were received after the first module of treatment, Stephen would return home.
- Stephen would have no unsupervised contact with Penny, despite returning home, until reassessed after one year of treatment.

## Treatment

Stephen was willing to engage in treatment, motivated by his recent acknowledgement that he had offended against his daughter and a desire to be allowed to continue living within his current family. There was no evidence of enduring deviant sexual interests and he presented as stable in terms of his psychological and social functioning. He received no psychiatric diagnosis. Treatment targets included pro-offending attitudes and some difficulties in relation to adult heterosexual relationships; he was considered to be rather resistant to viewing himself as a future risk, and to have a poorly developed relapse prevention strategy – given his potentially high risk living situation. He agreed to enter the group treatment programme, comprising 14 months of weekly therapy, and the three-day relapse prevention programme.

Stephen made good progress in the group treatment programme. He was a diligent attender and compliant with all tasks. His contributions were open and he engaged constructively with other group members. His insight into offence-specific issues was thought to be good; he developed an understanding of his relationship difficulties and their root in his childhood experiences, and was able to identify hostile components of his offending as well as his emotional identification with his victim. There was some shift in his perception of himself as posing no future risk, separating out his appraisal of himself as generally low risk (which was accurate) and the potentially high risk situation in which he was placed. He developed strong relapse prevention strategies which were borne out in his behaviour at home, and confirmed by social services.

# Anthony

## Referral

Anthony, aged 30, was referred by his probation officer for assessment and treatment shortly after his release from prison on non-parole date licence. When aged 26, he had pleaded not guilty to the rape of a 21-year-old woman, but had been found guilty and sentenced to seven years. He had served over four years, had been refused parole, and was now subject to licence for the next nine months. He had completed a thinking skills course while in prison and had attended a drug and alcohol awareness course; however, he continued to maintain that he was innocent of rape and that sexual intercourse with the victim had been consensual.

## Background

Anthony was the youngest of three boys. He described his mother as 'very loving', a soft-hearted woman who found it difficult to exert control over her children – particularly Anthony's overactive behaviour – or to protect them from her husband's fury and harsh discipline. His father was a cold and rather distant presence in the household; he worked long hours, but when at home was viewed by Anthony as excessively strict, domineering and, ultimately, physically abusive. Both Anthony's older brothers had been in trouble with school and with the police (for relatively minor matters), as adolescents and Anthony felt that his father was all the more determined to beat him into submissiveness. Their relationship was one based on fear, anger and contempt, on Anthony's part, while he believed his father viewed him as worthless.

At school, Anthony was considered to be a bright, charming and quick-witted boy. However, from primary-school years he was restless, easily distracted and disruptive in the classroom. He found it difficult to concentrate and was impulsive and reckless in his behaviour. He allied himself with other behaviourally disturbed boys and was often the centre of a disruptive group. In secondary school, he began to truant regularly with other boys. Occasionally he was embroiled in playground fights, but aggression was never noted to be a particular feature of his behaviour. After two suspensions, he eventually dropped out altogether at the age of 14, and obtained no qualifications.

In adolescence, the situation at home deteriorated as Anthony increasingly rebelled against his father's aggressive discipline to the point where his parents threw him out of the home. An aunt offered to take him in, but he ran away. For approximately two years Anthony stayed with friends, sometimes sleeping rough and always involved in a group of peers with whom he had a strong bond. He was a streetwise adolescent, popular, with a confident attitude and strong interpersonal skills. From early adolescence, he began dating girls of his age and had a number of both fleeting and sustained relationships. There was no suggestion of violence within the relationships; although affectionate towards his longer-term girlfriends, he found it difficult to sustain any commitment and was repeatedly unfaithful. However, he had cohabited for the first time for one year prior to the index offence and had a baby boy from this relationship.

Anthony had never had stable employment. He found it easy to pick up casual jobs, and had worked as a nightclub bouncer and minicab driver. He supplemented his state benefit with some earnings from limited drug dealing.

Anthony had been misusing illicit substances for many years. He was introduced to cannabis while living on the street in adolescence and had experimented with a range of Class A drugs. Although his use of cannabis was heavy – several joints daily – he maintained that he only used cocaine or ecstasy in socially appropriate settings, with others – for example, when out in a nightclub. He drank alcohol socially and sometimes to excess, although his use of alcohol had diminished in recent years. There was no evidence of alcohol dependency. He had no previous psychiatric history.

### Offending behaviour

Anthony had four previous convictions, none of which were for sexual matters. At the age of 15 he was convicted of theft and at the ages of 15 and 17 he was convicted of burglary – receiving a six-month custodial sentence on the latter occasion. All these offences were committed with others and all were motivated by financial need, particularly in the light of his homelessness and drug use. At the age of 20, Anthony was convicted of grievous bodily harm, for which he received a two-year custodial sentence. This offence related to a feud between two gangs in which Anthony became embroiled; he believed himself to be at risk of serious harm from the other gang and began to carry a knife around with him. When a fight ensued, Anthony stabbed a young man in the shoulder. The judge's comments at the time referred to Anthony's apparently sincere expression of regret, which was reflected in the relatively short sentence.

The index offence occurred one night when Anthony went out with his friends to a nightclub. Although devoted to his girlfriend, he had been feeling pressurised by the demands placed upon him as a result of cohabiting and the birth of their son. This had culminated in a row the evening of the offence. At the nightclub, the victim had 'come on to me', and Anthony responded, dancing with her and kissing her. They – and others – went back to his friend's flat, where more drinks and drugs were available. Anthony took the victim into a bedroom and they smoked cannabis together. He had been drinking and felt intoxicated but in control. He alleged that after kissing they had sexual intercourse with her full consent, whereupon they rejoined the others and had another drink. The victim maintained that she kissed Anthony but resisted his advances to have sex, whereupon he attempted to persuade her to change her mind; as she continued to resist, he became visibly angry and roughly forced himself upon her, bruising her genital area. She was frightened and did agree to have one further drink before leaving and reporting the matter to the police.

In prison, Anthony settled on the main wing and resisted all attempts to discuss his offence. However, he agreed to participate in a thinking skills course – a cognitive behavioural programme – which was not focused on the index offence. He also acknowledged that drugs and alcohol had played a part in his earlier difficulties and undertook a brief educational programme on this issue. He felt confident that he could abstain from Class A drugs and limit his use of cannabis and alcohol. He received good reports from both courses; furthermore there were no adjudications while in custody.

Anthony expressed regret that his current relationship was now over, and he clearly stated that he wished to maintain a close relationship with his son, with whom he apparently had a strong and loving bond. He was somewhat guarded in his relationship with the Probation Service, sensitive to any sign of them trying to control or dictate his future. He seemed to be most comfortable with his allocated officer when released, who was male and slightly older than him.

## Formulation

Anthony's description of himself as a restless, easily distracted child, overactive at home and unable to concentrate at school, might possibly (in retrospect) have warranted a diagnosis of Attention Deficit Hyperactivity Disorder (ADHD). Although deeply cared for by his mother, one might speculate that his feelings towards her were somewhat ambivalent, given her failure to protect him. Rejection and contempt from his father was in stark contrast to his capacity to be liked, admired and effective in the outside world. His warmth of personality and quick-witted mind brought him a sense of control and freedom which was totally absent in the home, and seemed to provide a substitute for any primary attachment. As so often occurs, Anthony's failure to identify with the primary adult male role model led to an identification in adolescence with a delinquent peer group. However, prior to the index offence, there were signs that Anthony was seeking to make some meaningful attachment and to shed some of his shallow lifestyle. The index offence occurred within the context of his difficulty in facing up to the demands of intimacy and family life, his anger not only being the result of a sexual rebuff, but related to fears that he was being controlled and demeaned.

## Risk

On actuarial tools, Anthony scored as follows:

> Static 99: 5 (medium-high), 38% recidivism risk over 10 years
> Risk Matrix 2000: high (sexual)
> high (violent)
> MnSOST-R: 3 (low), 16% recidivism risk over 6 years
> SORAG: category 6; 76% recidivism risk over 10 years
> PCL-R: 21 (15–24 range)

On actuarial tools, Anthony was predominantly scored as having a high risk of sexual recidivism. This was based on the number and range of previous convictions, as well as the victim being a stranger. In terms of dynamic factors, there are a number of areas of concern: despite recent attempts to engage in a sustained intimate relationship, there remain concerns about his capacity for commitment. This is closely related to issues of sexual entitlement and the central role that sex and dating play in maintaining his image to himself and his peers. All his offending – including his index offence – has been related to peer group influences, which are strongly implicated in the maintenance of his denial for the index offence. Although antisocial personality disorder was likely to have been the primary diagnostic possibility, recent evidence of maturation should lead to caution, although lifestyle instability and impulsivity remain a concern.

### Risk management plan

Having identified risk concerns, Anthony's strengths were thought to be his level of intelligence, his interpersonal skills and warmth, his motivation to provide a good role model for his son and evidence of maturation in his personality. Given that his period on licence was brief – nine months – a desire to control his behaviour needed to be weighed against longer-term resettlement concerns. It was decided to focus on the latter goal, particularly given that risk issues were unlikely to be immediate, but were more likely to be medium term and situational. The strategy was to enhance and consolidate internal motivation to change, actively liaise with social services in order to support an appropriate level of contact with his son and make assistance available, as required, for employment opportunities – recognising that adequate financial rewards needed to be in place in order to ensure that an illegal lifestyle was not unduly tempting. Licence conditions included a condition of psychological assessment (not treatment); residence at a probation hostel until appropriate independent accommodation could be found; and a condition to undertake a community drug team assessment, together with regular urine screening.

### Treatment

Given Anthony's denial in terms of the offence, it was unclear whether he needed or would cooperate with a formal treatment programme. It was decided that he should participate in an extended assessment – over five sessions – which would aim to develop a full picture of his life and difficulties with his collaboration, and in doing so utilise a motivational interviewing model to maximise the opportunities for change. By offering him some control in the process – for example, allowing him to amend the draft report – it was hoped that he would respond positively and engage.

The underlying premise for the assessment was that denial of behaviour is not considered to be a primary risk factor for future sexual recidivism. Clarifying the assessor's stance – that he was probably guilty of rape, given the evidence and the difficulty of obtaining such a conviction in court, but his account was heard and accepted as possible – created an honest opening for discussion. Mutually acceptable goals were agreed: that he wished to stay out of prison, he wanted to maintain a relationship with his son, he wished to seek out legal means of ensuring financial stability and quality of life, and he anticipated settling in a committed relationship one day. Risks in relation to these goals were also agreed: lifestyle and peer group influences, tendencies for impulsivity and recklessness, impaired judgement due to substance misuse and his dating style/ attitudes towards women.

The assessment progress and subsequent report informed the statutory involvement of probation and multi-agency protection, and involved ongoing consultation between the psychologist and the probation officer.

### Outcome

Anthony was compliant with the main conditions and responded well to the psychological assessment and probation supervision. He found the rules of the hostel difficult to tolerate and was aggravated by younger and more chaotic residents. Following a verbal and a written warning after returning late to the hostel on two occasions he was finally breached and recalled to prison after going out to a nightclub, taking cocaine and sleeping overnight at a friend's flat. He had remained in the community five months. His attitude to recall was, in many ways, mature: he recognised his responsibility for what had occurred and accepted he had been overconfident and somewhat dismissive of others' concerns. When released at the end of his sentence he was accepted on a voluntary basis back at the probation hostel. He subsequently moved in with his brother. Three years on, he had apparently not reoffended: he was living with his new girlfriend and contact with his son was regular and positive; he was engaged in a legitimate business with his brother which was not particularly financially successful but brought him satisfaction and allowed him to work independently; he said that he continued to smoke cannabis, but had not touched Class A drugs since his release from prison. At this point, the panel agreed that he was no longer one of the 'critical few', that the risk for all forms of recidivism was reducing, in line with his increasing levels of maturity and self-control, and that Anthony would therefore be monitored on an intermittent basis.

## James

James was referred for assessment by his probation officer prior to a Parole Board hearing, with the aim of putting together a comprehensive release plan. He was aged 58 at the point of referral, and 60 when subsequently released on life licence. He had served 25 years for the murder of a 50-year-old woman which he committed, age 35.

### Background

James was the eldest of two children, his sister being three years younger than himself. He described his parents' relationship as 'cordial', and his own childhood as 'unremarkable'. His mother was a housewife and affectionate mother; his father was strict – but certainly not physically abusive – and set high standards for his son in terms of behaviour and scholastic achievement. James said he always felt that he let his father down and was regretful that they did not manage to be closer. His mother described him as jealous of his sister, from a young age, and the sibling relationship was persistently conflictual. He was a rather withdrawn and serious child, prone to occasional but intense temper tantrums, which his mother found difficult to manage.

James encountered no particular difficulties at school, although he did not appear to make friends. He was considered to underperform academically, leaving school at 16 with a few qualifications with low grades, despite an estimated IQ of above average. He subsequently worked as a clerk in a bank; again, he was considered to be reliable but unremarkable, often passed over for promotion. He stayed in this line of work until his index offence in his mid-thirties.

James was open in describing his developing sexuality: he could recall the beginning of his deviant sexual fantasies from approximately the age of 8. This appeared to coincide with an almost total cessation of aggressive outbursts. He could only ever recall being sexually excited by the thought of strangling women – both adolescent and adult. As he attained puberty, these fantasies developed to the point where he would imagine throttling a woman with his hands while intensely sexually aroused, to the point where she lost consciousness, whereupon he would ejaculate. His fantasy figures were both women he had met and also 'pin up' figures such as film stars. He never fantasised about being physically hurt himself, nor did he imagine killing the women. The important elements of the fantasy seemed to be the power he exerted over the women and their fear of him. In reality, he made attempts in adolescence and early adulthood to date women. These encounters never progressed beyond a few dates and were not sexual. He said that he was troubled by his sadistic fantasies towards the women he dated and preferred to avoid sexual intimacy. He was not so troubled by his fantasies when they were confined to masturbatory imagery involving strangers. With time, James ceased to attempt to seek intimate relationships and spent almost all of his spare time in his room at home with his parents.

In the five years leading up to the index offence, James said that he used to drink quite heavily a few times a week. He never drank at home, but went to the pub, occasionally with work colleagues but largely alone. He had never used illicit drugs and had no previous psychiatric history.

### Offending behaviour

James had one previous conviction for indecent exposure which occurred when he was 20. He was returning from the pub one evening, having drunk five pints, and found himself walking behind a young woman who he found attractive. He followed her for a few yards, feeling sexually excited, and then as she stopped at a bus stop, he took out his erect penis and stood beside her, masturbating. The woman immediately went to call the police and he was quickly arrested. He was extremely apologetic, blamed his intake of alcohol that evening, and when he went to court he was fined.

James described a build up of a few months prior to the index offence. Although there were no discernible changes in his personal circumstances, he was aware that he was becoming more determined to act out his fantasies. He found that alcohol disinhibited him so that it was easier for him to overcome any residual inhibitions to offending. He developed offending scenarios in which he would create opportunities to be alone with a woman, and would then partially strangle her while he obtained sexual satisfaction. Again, he denied any thought of causing lasting harm or killing a potential victim. On the night of the offence, he went to the pub with the express purpose of seeking out a suitable victim. He drank three pints and managed to strike up a conversation with an older woman (aged 45). She seemed to like him and invited him back to her flat for coffee. In the kitchen, he suddenly seized a knife and grabbed the woman, threatening to harm her if she did not cooperate. He felt intensely sexually aroused at this point. The victim, in an attempt to placate him, spoke soothingly to him, attempting to maintain a sense of calm. In retrospect, James described feeling disappointed and frustrated that she was not conforming to his rehearsed fantasy: she did not appear to be dominated and terrified. He felt very angry, put his hands round her neck and strangled her. He described a sense of losing control at this point and acknowledged that he continued to asphyxiate her well beyond her loss of consciousness. He found it difficult to recall clearly his state of arousal at this point, but thought that he lost his erection as he strangled the woman. James 'came to' with a sense of numbed shock and sat by the woman's body for over two hours. Eventually he phoned the police, saying what he had done, and was arrested.

While on remand, psychiatric reports described James as 'chillingly' detached from his crime, apparently unconcerned about his future. He was thought to be psychopathic (although no formal assessment was undertaken), but no defence of diminished responsibility was put forward. After a few years, and following the death of his mother, James began to show an interest in seeking help for himself. Eventually he was transferred to a prison therapeutic community where he spent 18 months and made good progress. He went on to complete the core and extended prison sex offender treatment programme and the relapse prevention programme. Again, his progress was thought to be exemplary, probably genuinely so. During this period, James underwent a PPG assessment which yielded no significant deviant sexual interest. The turning point hinged on James' decision to 'give up' his sadistic fantasies which had become abhorrent to him, and his ability to reflect on his sexual orientation. He felt more able to contemplate his homosexuality, which he felt was his preferred sexual orientation, and went on to develop two lasting relationships with other prisoners. There were no adjudications during his 25-year stay in prison, nor had there been any concerns regarding his sexual behaviour or his conduct within the relationships.

### Formulation

Although some difficulties from James' childhood could be identified, there seemed to be no obvious trauma or markedly disturbed
attachment experiences which could account for such a striking
development of deviant sexual interests. It may be that his temperament, interacting with his early environment, led to acute anxiety in
managing his overwhelming aggressive impulses; an anxiety which
was exacerbated by a fear that he would be rejected by his father to
whom he wished to be close. The temporal link between the cessation
of aggressive outbursts and the onset of sadistic fantasies might lend
support to the premise that a withdrawal from overt violence into the
realms of sadistic control within his internal world was an attempt
to solve this emotional dilemma by means of the sexualisation of
aggression. The index offence represented a breakdown in this precarious 'solution'; that is, fantasy was no longer sufficient to maintain the status quo, and – with the disinhibiting assistance of alcohol
– James felt compelled to take the irrevocable step of putting fantasy
into action. Some might feel that James never fully accepted his
homicidal impulses, or even that he was deliberately denying such
fantasies; however, it is also possible that the failure of the offence
victim to 'play the part', triggered a loss of control and regression to
panic-stricken violence.

### Risk

On actuarial tools, James scored as follows:

Static 99: 6 (high), 45% recidivism risk over 10 years
Risk Matrix 2000: high (sexual)
                 low (violence)
MnSOST-R: 2 (low), 16% recidivism risk over 10 years
SORAG: category 3; 39% recidivism risk over 10 years
PCL-R: 10 (10–14 range)

On actuarial tools, James mainly scored high, although not universally so, the main factor being a stranger victim. There had clearly
been many changes over the years in terms of his personality and
offending attitude. At the point of release, there was no suggestion
of any problems with a capacity for intimacy, although this was
untested in the community; he no longer held any pro-offending

attitudes whatsoever, nor was there any evidence of significant deviant sexual interest either from self-report or PPG, although it was not clear whether this had dissipated or was lying dormant. He was well able to acknowledge a hypothetical risk for himself, although he felt fairly confident that he would not reoffend. His relapse prevention plan was detailed and appropriate. There was still the possibility of an acute risk factor – alcohol use – precipitating an offence, but this did not appear to be a long-term risk. The only remaining factor which was central to his risk appraisal was the long history of enduring sadistic sexual interests.

### Risk management plan

Initially James was a high priority for discussion at the multi-agency panel. However, he had a number of strengths, despite the enormity of his offending behaviour, including his mature, stable personality functioning and his capacity for reflective thought and emotional expression. Ironically, these were also the attributes most likely to be viewed suspiciously, as they could so easily mask underlying fantasies. James' relatively high profile upon release justified stringent risk management strategies. However, as an offender on life licence, the real challenge lay in pacing strategies across the long term; that is, sexual recidivism was possible over a very long time period, and risk might not be visible nor situationally triggered. All agencies agreed that the likelihood of a further offence was low, but the implications for any future victim, and for the professionals and agencies involved, were severe. The goal, therefore, was to maintain a balance between public protection and reintegration into the community for the foreseeable future. In practice, the Probation Service and forensic mental health agreed to alternate sessions, sharing similar goals achieved by slightly different means. The file was reread regularly – to hold in mind risk issues – and records were maintained to an exemplary standard. Regular risk management meetings also involved the police, although their concerns and involvement tailed off after three months when James was clearly compliant and settled. It was agreed that a meaningful structure to his day was a crucial aspect of any plan, ensuring continuity from his stable prison life, and as a primary source of self-esteem. Probation supported James in accessing employment opportunities, but they were also involved in ensuring that he developed an appropriate written disclosure regarding his offence, for prospective employers.

## Treatment

At the point of assessment James was presenting with a treated profile. This was confirmed by his PPG results a few years earlier, psychometric assessments and his presentation in interviews with numerous experienced practitioners. He had resided within a prison therapeutic community for 18 months and completed an additional 200 hours of sex offender treatment in group programmes. As well as having no identifiable pro-offending attitudes his level of psycho-social competency was good, as far as could be measured within a secure and open prison environment; furthermore, there was no evidence of impulsivity, recklessness or poor self-regulation. As with many lifers he was concerned to regulate his life. He maintained regular employment and pursued personal hobbies within prison. Sadistic sexual interests, which were so prominent in his life leading up to the index offence, were thought to be either dormant or resolved. His clearly expressed aim was to seek homosexual intimacy in due course. Determining a psychiatric diagnosis was difficult: at the time of the index offence he was considered to be psychopathic – not in itself a psychiatric diagnosis – although it would have been appropriate to diagnose him with a paraphilia. It was no longer clear whether this diagnosis applied. It was agreed that James was unlikely to benefit from additional cognitive behavioural group treatment in the community, and in any case the nature of his offence might have posed an obstacle within the group. He was offered fortnightly therapy sessions with forensic mental health, to complement the stringent supervision plan provided by the Probation Service.

The aim of treatment was to monitor James' awareness of risk and his management of risky situations; to revisit the precursors to his offence; to assess his mental state and identify any early indications of potential relapse, including increasing withdrawal, despondency, guardedness or a resumption of former drinking habits; to support progress in his general lifestyle in terms of social contacts, coping with his living environment and seeking to establish a meaningful structure to his day; and finally, to monitor progress in his attempts at sexual intimacy and/or the re-emergence of deviant sexual interests. In terms of this last point, it was hypothesised that sadistic sexual interests might be mood-related and therefore likely to re-emerge if there were signs of low or hostile mood.

James engaged well in treatment and was entirely compliant. He clearly thought about the sessions in-between times and brought potential risky situations and current dilemmas to many sessions. He would talk about the past, and his offence, with an appropriate level of understanding and emotional intensity. There were clearly identifiable problems for him in the community which had not been evident in open prison or the pre-release hostel. These included witnessing another long-serving lifer being recalled to prison and the devastating effect the 'disclosure' of his offence had on potential employers, all of whom subsequently rejected him. He wanted to seek out social contacts but found it difficult to resolve the dilemma of when and how to disclose his past to potential friends or lovers. For a period, he became rather isolated and despondent, but subsequently regained his equilibrium, found himself some meaningful voluntary work and planned to improve his social life.

### Outcome

James made exemplary progress, given his long period of incarceration and the level of scrutiny to which he was subjected. This was despite repeated rejections from prospective employers, who interviewed him but were clearly frightened away by his disclosure letter. Eighteen months after his release – still resident in the hostel, but planning a move into independent accommodation – James discussed his aim to participate in an evening course in counselling at the local college, which would be relevant to the voluntary work with ex-offenders he had recently commenced. There was some discrepancy between the mental health and the criminal justice agencies in their response: health was cautiously supportive of his approach in thinking through the issues, and concerned that he would become despondent in the face of yet more rejections. However, on balance, the risk management meeting – at which James was present – concluded that the evening course would be unwise, potentially risky, and likely to be rejected by the Home Office (in terms of licence reporting). Four days later, James was remanded into custody on a charge of attempted murder: in the evening he had carried a knife and belt up to the city centre, followed a woman down a street and stabbed her twice in the neck from behind, subsequently stabbing himself in both legs. When interviewed, James said that he was 'quietly fuming' after the risk management meeting and by the next day was indulging in sadistic fantasies (without associated feelings of sexual arousal); he deliberately planned to attack a woman, thinking to himself 'if they still think I'm high risk, I'll prove it to them'. He purchased the knife two days later, rejecting thoughts of ringing his probation officer or psychologist. He sought out a prostitute the next day and, unable to find one, followed a woman at random and attacked her. Sentenced to a second life term, James is unlikely ever to be released.

The aftermath for the professionals involved in such a major incident is considerable. The sense of disbelief at the rapidity of his decline, his refusal to make use of the support and skills easily at his disposal and his close replication of the index offence all served to undermine the confidence of the multi-agency team. In organisational terms, the Probation Service led on the incident inquiry – although all files were scrutinised by senior managers in each service – but as this was internally driven, there was no multi-agency responsibility for the conclusions and recommendations. The case was further scrutinised when James went to court. The inquiry emphasised the high quality of care and professional communication involved and there were no clear indicators that the new offence could have been prevented. In retrospect, there are perhaps two lessons to be learned. First, sadistic sex offenders – no matter how consistent their progress in treatment appears to be – pose a uniformly high risk of recidivism throughout their life. This does not necessarily lead to the conclusion that they feign improvement or change, but rather that powerful sadistic impulses may merely lie dormant, re-emerging under stress or particular triggering circumstances. Second, there is a potential paradox in rigorous and stringent risk management strategies which may in fact constrain and undermine a high risk offender to such an extent that they fear (and therefore wish to control) their failure in the community.

## Peter

### Referral

Peter, aged 25, was referred by his probation officer, prior to his discharge from prison on automatic conditional release licence. The officer wished to have Peter's suitability for community treatment assessed. Peter had served 22 months of a 44-month sentence for the indecent assault of a 14-year-old boy. He had avoided group treatment within the prison system but was concerned that his behaviour would lead to increasingly lengthy prison sentences, and he was therefore seeking help to abstain from future offending.

## Background

Peter was an only child and lived most of his childhood in the care of his father. He described his father as 'good', although it was not easy to assess the quality of the relationship. His father had met all his physical needs and had been generally caring, although he was an undemonstrative man and rather emotionally inexpressive. Peter had only vague memories of his mother, who had left the family home abruptly when he was 4. He had tried on one or two occasions to talk to his father about his mother, but soon stopped when it was clear that these conversations caused his father emotional pain. He simply knew that his mother's behaviour had been erratic and had caused his father embarrassment in the community; Peter thought she had probably been mentally ill. There were no photographs of his mother in the house and he felt there was an implicit code of silence surrounding her.

Peter found it difficult to cope with school. He had mild learning difficulties and failed academically. He was also bullied fairly persistently and only managed to make one or two friends during his education. He left aged 15 without qualifications, but nevertheless had managed to work consistently. He liked driving, and his most recent period of employment was as a long-distance lorry driver.

Peter described himself as an insecure and anxious adolescent, who was very preoccupied with his physical image, as he suffered from acne. He made no attempt to develop relationships with girls – although he would have liked to have a girlfriend – believing that he would be automatically rejected and humiliated. He was also worried at this time about his sexual orientation, as he had found himself sexually attracted to one or two boys of his own age. His first sexual experience was one of abuse: on one occasion, aged 15, he said that he had been befriended by an adult man who had bought him sweets and then brutally raped him in a car. He managed to tell his father, who told the police, and after giving a statement he thought that the perpetrator was caught and sentenced. However, he was vague about these details, not least because the matter was never again mentioned by him or his father. In late adolescence, Peter used to go to gay bars occasionally, and had two sexual encounters with adult men. He thought of himself as bisexual, but was not particularly comfortable with his homosexual inclinations.

Peter was hesitant to discuss any offence-related fantasies, but did eventually acknowledge that he was sexually attracted to adolescent boys, and that his offence victims had continued to form part of his fantasy life. However, he maintained that for at least '50 per cent' of the time he fantasised about adults.

Peter had never drunk alcohol, except for infrequent social occasions. He had never used illicit drugs and had no previous psychiatric history.

### Offending behaviour

Peter had two previous convictions for sexual assaults, when aged 18 and 20, in addition to his index offence (aged 23). He had received relatively short prison sentences on each occasion. On all three occasions the victims had been boys (aged 12, 14 and 15) with whom he had struck up a fleeting acquaintance. The offences had all occurred when he was not at work, and felt at something of a 'loose end'. He had frequented suitable places for potential victims – the seaside, the West End of London – and had engaged boys in conversation who were apparently 'hanging around'. Two of his victims were truanting from school and one – he claimed – was working as a rent boy. On each occasion, he would offer the victims cigarettes, sweets or beer, and he clearly had a capacity to relate to them at their level. He would then invite the victim into his car, or home with him, and persuade him to allow himself to be fondled, or for Peter to perform oral sex on him, or to engage in mutual masturbation.

Peter was clear that he wanted to avoid future prison sentences, and that he wanted to be 'normal'. By this he meant that he felt ashamed of being attracted to underage boys and wanted a satisfactory adult relationship with either a man or a woman. However, he found it difficult to understand that the victims were anything other than entirely cooperative, and thought that the potential for harm was greatly exaggerated.

### Formulation

There appeared to be a constellation of difficulties underpinning Peter's offending behaviour. He experienced a certain amount of emotional deprivation in childhood, given the lack of maternal care and his father's emotional reticence. This was emphasised by the lack of tangible memories or mementoes of his mother which prevented him from developing an imagined relationship with her, leaving something of a void in his life. In adolescence, he was beset with anxieties about himself, others and his capacity to be valued in relationships. He avoided women but felt guilty about any sexual feelings towards men. Clearly the rape was a traumatic experience, although Peter played this down; it seemed likely – although he denied it – that he had been troubled by irrational feelings of guilt about the attack, somehow believing himself to be culpable by having made himself vulnerable. This hypothesis was partly based on Peter's evident hostility towards his own victims and his claims regarding their responsibility within his offences – as though he was symbolically attempting to replicate and reverse his own trauma. There was some suggestion that Peter was sexually attracted to pre-pubescent boys, although whether it was his dominant sexual interest was less clear. It seemed possible that his victim choice may well have been related to emotional immaturity and an avoidance of adult intimacy.

## Risk

On actuarial tools, Peter scored as follows:

> Static 99: 6 (high), 45% recidivism risk over 10 years
> Risk Matrix 2000: very high (sexual)
> Medium (violence)
> MnSOST-R: 8 (high), 70% recidivism risk over 10 years
> SORAG: category 5; 59% recidivism risk over 10 years
> PCL-R: 7 (5–9 range)

Peter's high scores were largely related to his repeated choice of male, stranger victims. He struggled with a number of intimacy deficits in terms of avoidance of adult intimacy, emotional loneliness and low self-esteem. He also held strong victim empathy distortions and emotional identification with adolescent boys. There was some suggestion that deviant sexual activity served to mitigate life stresses and regulate his self-esteem. However, there were few antisocial features in either his background or current functioning. It was not clear that acute dynamic factors were implicated in his offending.

## Risk management plan

Peter was subject to 11 months on licence, which contained conditions to attend treatment and to reside at the hostel, prior to a move to independent accommodation. Despite concerns about risk, his strengths lay in his likely compliance with expectations of him, his strong motivation to avoid a return to prison and strengthening feelings of shame with regard to his offending behaviour. There were two agreed goals to his management plan: first, containment – physical and emotional – and second, effecting internal change by means of group treatment. Residence at the hostel stopped Peter from managing his interpersonal anxieties by means of withdrawal and avoidance, as he was encouraged to relate to the staff; regular but informal police visits reinforced his internal anxieties about his capacity to reoffend, without him feeling unduly victimised. The leaders of the group treatment programme worked closely with the supervising probation officer to provide a containing framework for addressing issues.

### Treatment

Peter clearly presented with a deviant sexual interest in boys (whether intermittent or dominant was unclear), and associated with this a marked lack of victim empathy. There were also deficits in his psychosocial competency, with anxieties and failures in terms of sexual orientation and sustained adult intimacy. His general level of self-regulation was good and he was likely to find work. There was no evidence of impulsivity or more pervasive psychological dysfunction. In psychiatric terms he would have received a diagnosis of paraphilia.

Peter's motivation to seek help for his offending behaviour was thought to be ambivalent, much of his avoidance being due to feelings of shame and anxiety. This appeared to be particularly relevant in relation to his wish for individual treatment rather than group treatment. This is often the case with sex offenders who have unresolved issues concerning their own sexual victimisation by a man: they may avoid the 'claustrophobia' of group treatment programmes in prison where feelings of vulnerability in relation to intimacy can arise without the possibility of escape. A strategy was agreed with the Probation Service that group treatment in the community would be insisted upon. The rationale was to encourage a 'safe' level of intimacy within which Peter could gain confidence and make use of social modelling.

Peter acquiesced and engaged in group treatment. Initially his progress was slow and there were concerns regarding his level of cognitive functioning, which necessitated the supervising probation officer revisiting material and assisting with homework tasks. There were two key moments in the programme. The first related to Peter's late attendance, which resulted in written warnings and eventually a decision to discharge him from the programme. His probation officer considered that the group therapists were being unduly punitive; he felt it was Peter's employment which prevented him attending and that he was probably not able, in any case, to make much use of the treatment. Good communication channels between the practitioners quickly identified the splits in agency working – the attacking and collusive elements – which held all the anxieties regarding Peter, allowing him to avoid the issues. A compromise was found whereby he was interviewed by the probation manager and given a final warning, and also recommenced participation in the group. Re-establishing the boundaries and placing the anxiety for his future firmly within Peter's hands appeared to assist in a re-engagement in the process. The second key moment related to the apparent impasse regarding Peter's attitude towards his own victims as collusive and acquiescent. It was only when discussing his own sexual victimisa-tion in the group that he was able to disclose that he had never been brutally raped, but had in fact been persistently abused by a male neighbour over a period of months; he was profoundly distressed by his feelings of shame and guilt, believing that he was responsible for his collusion with the abuse. Whether it was this disclosure or the warm and supportive response of the other group members is not clear; regardless, this period of the programme appeared to have a cathartic effect on Peter's capacity to view his victims with a more accurate level of understanding and concern.

### Outcome

Despite the formal warning Peter was able to make good progress in the group and completed it on a voluntary basis. Although he refused the offer of ongoing support thereafter, he appeared to maintain his progress three years on. He settled in his own flat and became involved in an 18-month relationship with an adult male. While he continued to be on the Sex Offenders Register and subject to police follow up, there appeared to be no evidence that he had engaged in further sexual offending.

## Martin

### Referral

Martin, aged 45, was referred for an assessment prior to his parole hearing. He was serving a five-year sentence following a conviction for indecent assault on a 9-year-old boy. He had made strenuous efforts to engage constructively in treatment during his sentence, but there were acute concerns expressed by the Probation Service and the Police Service regarding his risk. These anxieties were amplified by media interest in his case at the time of conviction and the potential for public disorder wherever he might be placed in the community.

### Background

Martin's early life was characterised, quite simply, by chaos. He was the middle child of five and both his parents were alcoholics. The children were sometimes poorly clothed and fed, often the butt of jokes by neighbourhood and school children. Martin's mother was prone to bouts of depression, at which time she would withdraw to her bed and rarely emerge. His father was often in trouble with the police and away from home. Martin described his mother as loving but unpredictable; his father was rather more consistently abusive, verbally and physically. The family were often evicted from their home, and the children were occasionally separated and placed in care.

Martin changed school on several occasions. He found it difficult to keep up with the academic work and left at 15 unable to read or write properly. Repeatedly teased, even bullied, he learned to lash out in the playground, and was sometimes suspended for fighting. He never managed to make friends, somehow losing these skills in all the moves. In late adolescence he managed to obtain a handful of short-term labouring jobs, but was usually sacked due to poor timekeeping. He had not worked – between prison sentences – for the past 15 years.

Martin's first sexual experience was one of abuse: between the ages of 8 and 12 he was sexually assaulted on a regular basis by an adult male neighbour. The abuse progressed from fondling to mutual masturbation and oral sex, culminating in an attempt at buggery, which Martin resisted. He was unclear why the abuse stopped, only that the neighbour no longer called round to invite him to his house. Martin never disclosed this abuse until his current sentence, although he was unable to explain why not. He denied that he was in any way traumatised by it, referring to the 'special attention' it afforded him and how he learnt to like it in due course, even to seek it out.

Martin described himself as exclusively heterosexual, his offences being something quite separate to his sexual orientation. He said that he had had girlfriends in adolescence and had been the lover of one of his mother's friends, in his twenties. On close questioning, it seemed that he had had sexual encounters with women, but there was no evidence of enduring affection or intimacy with his sexual partners. In terms of his fantasies, Martin was quite open in stating that 50 per cent of his fantasies were about pre-pubescent boys, 40 per cent were about adult women, and 10 per cent were about adult men. At times he had talked, rather superficially, about his concerns that he might kill a child. He showed an interest in notorious killers (including child killers) and admitted to sexual excitement at thoughts of hurting children.

Martin drank alcohol socially, occasionally to excess. He was a habitual user of cannabis but not other illicit drugs. It was not clear how important a role cannabis use may have played in his offending, given that he used a regular amount daily. He had been admitted to psychiatric hospital on three previous occasions, each brief admission precipitated by an act of deliberate self-harm. Usually he cut his wrists or took a minor overdose; however, there was a record of him having attempted to hang himself while on remand on this occasion.

### Offending behaviour

Martin had 18 previous convictions, commencing at the age of 14. They were nearly all for theft or minor driving offences. One was a burglary of industrial premises, but none were for violence. The thefts were often committed with peers, or on behalf of peers.

In terms of his sexual offending, Martin's first conviction was for the rape of a 10-year-old boy when he was aged 20, for which he received a six-year prison sentence. He was heavily intoxicated at the time and said that he felt sexually frustrated; he decided to pick a potential victim – a boy walking down the street – grabbed him and attempted to anally penetrate him, despite difficulty obtaining an erection. His second conviction was for indecent assault on a 6-year-old boy when he was aged 26, for which he received a four-year sentence. This offence involved Martin waiting outside a news-agents after school hours, offering to buy a boy sweets in exchange for touching his penis and then putting his hand down the boy's trousers. The index offence was relatively minor: Martin had been loitering in a park, watching young boys, when he decided to follow one boy as he walked home. Suddenly, in full view of passers-by, Martin impulsively ran up to the boy, smacked his bottom and asked him, 'Do you want to suck my cock?' He was subsequently assaulted by two men in the street and the police were called.

As he approached his parole date, Martin openly acknowledged that he had followed – but not assaulted – boys on other occasions. He also claimed that he had previously thrown acid into a social worker's face after she had been rude to him. He was willing to talk about his fantasies and readily explained that he felt he had the capacity to go 'completely crazy' and hurt someone. In the prison treatment programme, Martin had applied himself in a constructive manner and was thought to be sincere in his wish to change. How-ever, his reports emphasised the worrying content of his fantasies, which tended to monopolise the group process. He was thought to have poor victim empathy but a well-developed relapse prevention plan. He had received two adjudications during this sentence, both for verbal outbursts to prison staff, threatening to harm them. On both occasions he felt he had been provoked by their disrespectful behaviour.

### Formulation

Martin was clearly emotionally damaged by his childhood experi-ences which had resulted in long-term psychological dysfunction. It seemed to be, predominantly, the absence of any consistent, nurturing bonds with adults or peers which lay at the root of his failure to establish any attachments. As is so often the case, he was drawn to his sexual abuser as the sole source of attention and feelings of self-worth: if he could not be loved for himself, he could be loved for his sexual attributes. In adulthood, the only consistent relationship Martin was able to develop was with his delinquent peer group and the criminal justice system, prison containing him emotionally as the community could not. Martin's self-image appeared to be built up around his capacity to excite and interest people, and the nearer he came to release the more he needed to impress with his capacity for violence. This was amplified in the agencies' anxious response to him. His sexual offending had a compulsive, reckless quality to it – the excitement of the pursuit – which seemed to suggest a persistent need to act sexually in order to keep his own emotional neediness at bay. Psychiatrically, while deviant sexual interests warranted a diagnosis of paedophilia, the predominant diagnosis was one of a personality disorder, with marked antisocial and borderline features.

### Risk

On actuarial tools, Martin scored as follows:

> Static 99: 7 (high), 45% recidivism risk over 10 years
> Risk Matrix 2000: very high (sexual)
>                    low (violence)
> MnSOST-R: 12 (high), 70% recidivism risk over 10 years
> SORAG: category 7; 80% recidivism risk over 10 years
> PCL-R: 20 (15–24 range)

As with Peter, Martin's high scores related to his repeated choice of stranger, male victims. There were clear attachment and intimacy problems, particularly emotional loneliness and an avoidance of peer relationships, although he did not necessarily have insight into these. He was honest about marked pro-offending attitudes and emotional identification with children, as well as victim empathy distortions. There were problems with sexual self-regulation as he reported a pre-occupation with sexual matters. He believed that sexual activity increased his social status and he was prone to strong sexual urges which he wished to gratify. In addition to dominant deviant sexual interests (and arousal to violence), there were marked antisocial and borderline features to his personality, not least a problematic level of impulsivity.

### Risk management plan

Martin's pending release was highly anxiety-provoking for those responsible for his care in the community. His level of disturbance was such that there was little confidence in the potential for internal change being sufficient to contain his impulses to offend.

Nevertheless, Martin knew that he was facing a life sentence should he reoffend and was highly motivated to avoid this; he had well-developed relapse prevention skills and an interpersonal style – albeit highly dysfunctional – which was inclined to be dependent upon, rather than avoidant of, services. The primary purpose of the risk management plan was to focus on public protection by means of reliance on external rather than internal controls. To achieve this, the agencies needed to coordinate their input and agree strategies. Martin was on an extended licence period of two years, with conditions of residence at a hostel, greatly extended curfew hours (particularly around key school hours), treatment, community drug team assessment and urine testing; he was forbidden from entering areas where he had offended in the past. The emphasis on external containment included a greater role for police intelligence and a crisis plan should public interest be aroused regarding his release. The role of forensic mental health was to provide support for the hostel staff in terms of managing Martin's demands and the inevitable dynamics which would cause splits within the staff team. While the aim of treatment was to facilitate understanding and management at a psychological level, Martin's level of sexual preoccupation precluded any capacity for meaningful reflection. A referral to the prison medical staff initiated a course of anti-libidinal medication, commenced two weeks before his release. Subsequently agreeing a level of confidentiality in individual treatment aimed to allow him personal space to be viewed as an individual with psychological needs, not just a high risk offender.

## Treatment

The level of Martin's psychological disturbance, coupled with his persistent and dominant sexual interest in pre-pubescent boys, meant that he needed to be considered for both group and individual treatment. The aim of the group was to revisit and consolidate learning from the prison programme. Slightly to our surprise, the other group members were astute in recognising Martin's violent fantasies as a distraction from real concerns regarding likely offending. His participation was variable, sometimes demanding and self-absorbed, sometimes distracted and withdrawn. There was a deliberate strategy in the group to limit discussion of the details of his offending and fantasies, and to concentrate on thoughts and feelings which were less accessible to him. He was clearly distressed by the module relating to primary relationships and victim experiences in childhood, and this coincided with him being prescribed anti-depressant medication. After Martin was recalled, his failure in the community was discussed in the group. It was normal practice for the group members to collaborate in writing a letter to prematurely discharged members, and they did so for Martin, with some care. He was clearly moved to be held in mind by others during his absence – a new experience for him – and he responded in kind, promising to seek help in prison and to rejoin the group when he was released.

Individual treatment sessions targeted deviant sexual interests and focused on risky situations, as they occurred, with an emphasis on putting relapse prevention skills into practice. It was assumed that Martin would encounter such situations and experience urges to reoffend, thus confidentiality was extended to cover these assumptions and agreed with the other agencies involved. Clearly, confidentiality was not extended to acts of abuse, clearly identified potential victims or unusually high risk situations which were unknown to other agencies. This agreement drew a delicate line between the need to protect the public and the need to encourage Martin in an open and safe discussion of his very real difficulties. It became clear that although Martin would discuss risk first in his individual sessions, he tended to discuss similar matters subsequently with the Probation Service.

### Outcome

For the first two months after release, the most striking feature was the chaos which occurred in Martin's presence. He had become acutely depressed when taking anti-libidinal medication, and this together with the stress of release triggered a self-harm incident. Immediately there was a loss of confidence from the hostel and a request that mental health take over full care of Martin – rigorously resisted by health who insisted he was unsuitable for psychiatric care! Furthermore, Martin's propensity for disarming self-revelation regarding his deviant sexual fantasies was viewed by some agencies as evidence of honesty and engagement but for others was clear evidence of the need to recall him to prison immediately. No sooner had matters settled somewhat than Martin announced he had met an older woman (herself disordered and vulnerable) with whom he intended to live and forge an intimate relationship. Initially, Martin was cautioned against this relationship and this seemed to lead to a rift, in so far as he began to push boundaries and engage in conflict with professionals; the solution lay in involving his partner in the risk management plan, rather than trying to countermand her influence. During this period, Martin had ceased taking anti-libidinal medication, both because of his depressed mood and because he wished to be sexually active with his new partner. It seemed appropriate to consider relatively high dose anti-depressant medication, both for its effects in stabilising his mood and in an attempt to reduce his offence-related ruminations and fantasies.

Martin clearly struggled with urges to follow boys in the street and began to acknowledge that in many ways this activity had super-seded contact sex offending, in terms of the sense of excitement and control it afforded him. He decided to disclose this fantasy material to his probation officer and the hostel, knowing that this would be discussed at a risk management meeting. Meanwhile, attempts to find him daytime activity which would divert him from his inner world and provide meaningful structure were fruitless, given his background. The risk management meeting was split: those who felt Martin was about to commit a further sexual offence and should be recalled arguing against those who felt that his fantasies were a reflection of his personality functioning, and should be stringently responded to and contained within the community. Ultimately, Martin resolved the issue: he 'confessed' to his probation officer that he had touched a boy in the local park; his account was vague and contradictory, no corroborating details were found by the police and Martin subsequently retracted his 'confession'. Despite universal doubts that any offence had actually occurred this was sufficient to tip the balance and he was recalled.

Martin will be released shortly, bound to register with the police, but not under any statutory supervision. He aims to cohabit with his partner and is requesting further treatment. Both of these factors are likely to provide stabilising influences. However, he is refus-ing contact with either the police or the Probation Service; the latter, he says, have betrayed him. There seems little possibility of resolving the lack of daytime structure and the police will need to carefully consider the possibility of a SOO, which could restrict his movements in terms of avoiding places and activities.

# Chapter 8

# Discussion

## Introduction

The aim of this book has been to demonstrate that the risk assessment of sex offenders is not an impenetrable science. By now the reader should feel confident about the key risk variables and should be able to engage in defensible decision making in relation to each individual sex offender. Relevant legislation, as it currently stands, should be clear, and the practitioner will have the tools available to develop appropriate risk management strategies. There should be no hesitation about employing clinical judgement as such an approach will now be embedded in an appropriate evidence base. In terms of assessment, it should be easier to ensure consistency – between offenders and across agencies. Consistency in management approaches may be harder to achieve and not always desirable, as creativity in terms of an individualised approach is to be encouraged if the field of risk management is to progress. Clearly, treatment plays a role in this process, but only as part of a much broader risk management approach.

## A framework for risk assessment

The content of this book could be summarised in a simple framework for risk assessment, which comprises three strands. The first strand emphasises the role of risk – that is, the likelihood of reoffending – as only one component of broader risk assessment concerns, including victim impact and public interest (only indirectly addressed in this book). Determining risk broadly comprises two further strands – an academic and an organisational component – which are interconnected (see Figure 8.1).

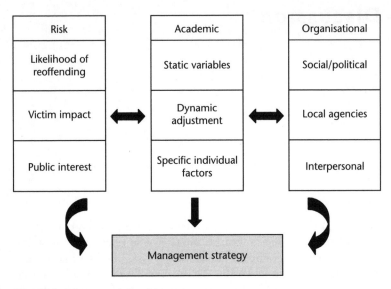

*Figure 8.1* A framework for risk assessment

The academic component has been clearly laid out in Chapters 2 and 3. Briefly, the risk posed by a sex offender first needs to be considered in terms of static factors, then adjusted to take account of key dynamic domains. Finally, there may be specific individual factors which result in a further adjustment. An example of this third level might include evidence of sadistic sexual interest, a variable which has been considered in some detail in this book because of its particular relevance to risk and victim impact. The organisational component has been alluded to throughout the book, but particularly so in Chapters 4, 5 and 6. This strand can also be thought of in terms of three levels. First, a broad social and political context or climate, which incorporates policies and legislation, and leads the public protection agenda. Clearly the media plays a role at this level. The second level is the role of agencies in risk management: professional duties, procedures and liaison at a local level, particularly in terms of the functioning of the multi-agency panels. Here, the local community may have an impact in influencing approaches to risk management procedures. The third level represents the more direct interpersonal dimension involved in individual case management, epitomised by the relationship between the offender and the practitioners involved in his care.

Ultimately, risk management approaches are shaped by all three strands of the framework. For example, the legislative background and local agency procedures may create opportunities for creative risk management, or limit the options available. At an interpersonal level, the extent to which a case manager can understand the sex offender's risks and engage him in a collaborative effort to reduce such risks may be crucial.

The nature of the interaction between the three strands needs to reflect an integrated approach; consistency is needed at the very least although, arguably, systems which are overly flexible or rigid can pose problems. For example, legislation needs to reflect the concerns of victims and the wider public as well as the differential risk posed by a range of sex offenders. Agencies need to implement policies in the light of their available resources, prioritising higher risk offenders or those with identifiable victims and taking note of the responses of the local community. Practitioners need to understand the legislation and their agency procedures; they must make evidence-based risk assessments while balancing these against the perceived needs of individual offenders.

However, rigidity in the system undoubtedly has benefits, largely because responsibility for risk management is depersonalised, approaches become consistent and the offender knows exactly where he stands. The drawbacks may include a lack of individual invest-ment in success (particularly for those offenders who tend to avoid taking personal responsibility for change) and an organisational emphasis on targeting a particularly worrying group of high risk offenders which results in over-caution or a 'false positive' approach to lower risk offenders.

## The current state of play

There seems to be little doubt that much has changed – for the better – in the last few years, in terms of risk managing sex offenders. Currently, convicted sex offenders in the community are subject to stringent supervision arrangements, including scrutiny by the multi-agency panels. There is an evidence-based approach to treatment, epitomised by the roll out of accredited sex offender treatment programmes into the community, as well as some limited specialist provision. Low base rates for reconviction may not just reflect problems with the criminal justice system, but may, more hopefully, suggest a real propensity for sex offenders to feel that they are more likely to be caught and/or to fear the personal consequences of reoffending.

There are problems, of course. Some of these are long-standing and offer no ready solutions. These include the difficulties faced by social services departments in knowing how to manage unconvicted sex offenders, and a wider problem in improving the detection and prosecution rates of sex offenders. Other problems are, paradoxically, a consequence of the benefits of improved practice. As mentioned above, the combination of low base rates for sexual reconviction and stringent risk management procedures may be leading to over-cautious practice in terms of recalls to prison, or the use of short-term custodial sentences rather than longer-term community sentences (Craissati & McClurg 1994). Such offenders may return to the community with hostile, mistrustful attitudes and no statutory obligations to comply with management approaches. Paradoxically, problems with the social exclusion of high risk sex offenders may be increasing: as better information is disseminated to a wider professional audience, local housing, employment and training opportunities may be reduced and sex offenders are stopped from forming relationships with the only other people who will accept them – fellow sex offenders.

And what does the case of James tell us? That although we should continue to strive for excellence, we are not infallible. There will always be failures – rarely so catastrophic – and therefore there need to be structures in place to manage such events: stringent supervision, high standards of record-keeping and liaison, sharing the burden of risk management and learning from mistakes with a genuine spirit of constructive enquiry.

## Risk management or psychological management?

Throughout this book, risk management has been informed by psychological principles, wherever possible. For the most part, there has been nothing inherently contradictory in these two approaches. It has been beyond the scope of this book to review the extensive work on theoretical approaches which focus on a causal explanation for sexual offending. This theoretical underpinning is reviewed briefly in Craissati (1998) and more extensively in work by Rosen (1979), Marshall, Anderson and Fernandez (1999) and others. Although the main psychological models – cognitive behavioural, systemic, and psychodynamic (including, more recently, attachment theory) – employ different terminology and applied methodology, there are inherent similarities in their understanding. Essentially, sex offenders are understood in terms of their internal emotional and cognitive lives, their relationship to particular others (including past and potential victims) and their perception of their place in the wider world. These constructs are likely to be shaped, to a greater or lesser degree, by experiences across the life span interacting with individual inherent characteristics.

For many sex offenders, possibly the majority, risk management seems to be reasonably successful, and they are able to understand – even if they do not agree with – the principles of public protection. However, for some of the case studies discussed in this book, who represent a subgroup of higher risk and more psychologically disturbed sex offenders, there is sometimes an insuperable conflict between public protection and psychological need. Take, for example, this brief description of Arthur.

*Arthur was a high risk child molester with wide-ranging psychological problems, resettling in the community after a long prison sentence. He was isolated and socially inept, but had forged a local friendship with another older, and low risk, sex offender he had met previously in prison. They planned to visit the seaside for a day trip, and Arthur – who was highly transparent – mentioned this in passing to his probation officer. There were already police concerns that Arthur, who was unoccupied during the day, was spending too much time in parks. The multi-agency panel agreed to intervene, both warning the older offender against continuing his friendship with Arthur as it might jeopardise his own resettlement, and forbidding Arthur to go on the trip. This was achieved sensitively and politely.*

Clearly, the risk management plan was aimed at preventing a potential offence, on the premise that two child molesters were likely to collude in their offending and that the seaside provided unusually high levels of opportunity to offend. Furthermore, whether or not an offence would have taken place, if the visit had come to public attention there could have been a highly destructive loss of community confidence in the agencies involved, with far reaching consequences. This reasoning seemed to be defensible and the response measured. However, the reality of the situation for Arthur, as he experienced it and discussed it in treatment, was quite different. Although unable to articulate it in sophisticated terms, he was clearly attached to his friend as a 'father figure' who was promising him a 'treat', a visit to the seaside which he had never seen. Arthur was unable to separate out the child within himself – with an overwhelming sense of emotional deprivation – from the adult offender he had become. Likewise, he was unable to separate out his experience of hostile and rejecting others as a child from the reasonable but depriving actions of the panel. Paradoxically, the sensible risk management strategy exacerbated Arthur's sense of emotional isolation, and consequently increased his propensity to withdraw into a fantasy world of deviant sexual fantasies.

Clearly, no criticism could be made of the panel's action, yet the example highlights the tensions between managing risk and meeting psychological need. There are dangers of stringent management developing into a 'risk list' which only prohibits and excludes, leading to a reduction in quality of life. More recent models, particularly that of Ward and colleagues (e.g. Ward & Stewart 2003) emphasise the role of primary goods: basic needs (such as intimacy, social roles, competency and autonomy) which are viewed as intrinsically beneficial to human beings. A suggested model of risk management, therefore, is a reframing of the problem away from avoidance goals (prohibiting risky variables) to goals which achieve primary goods and thereby enhance the offender's capacity to live a better – less impoverished – life. Thus, returning to the example of Arthur, the risk management approach might need to legitimise and emphasise friendship, intimacy and sexual satisfaction as very important primary goods for Arthur, and consequently a crucial component of any attempts to help him successfully resettle in the community. His sexual offending, and in particular his sexual interest in children have clearly been obstacles to him in achieving these goods. This may be because of Arthur's focus on sexual satisfaction, confusing it with intimacy or friendship, and perhaps because he has been unable to develop alternative sources of self-esteem and self-efficacy – through social or work roles – which would broaden his scope for achieving a 'good life' (Ward & Stewart 2003).

Such models of risk management are in their infancy and need to be tested, both practically and empirically. As practitioners evaluate the efficacy of their management practices and reflect on their successes and failures in resettling sex offenders, the integration of psychological principles into practice is likely to become more sophisticated. It seems reasonable to anticipate that we, as practitioners, will become increasingly adept at protecting the public as effectively as possible while maximising the opportunities for psychological well-being and quality of life in the offender.

# Appendix

## Minnesota Sex Offender Screening Tool – Revised

*Historical/static variables*

1 **Number of sex/sex-related *convictions* (including current conviction)**
One  0
Two or more  +2

2 **Length of sexual offending history**
Less than one year  −1
One to six years  +3
More than six years  0

3 **Was the offender under any form of supervision when they committed *any* sex offence for which they were eventually charged or convicted?**
No  0
Yes  +2

4 **Was *any* sex offence (charged or convicted) committed in a public place?**
No  0
Yes  +2

5 **Was force or the threat of force ever used to achieve compliance in *any* sex offence (charged or convicted)?**
No force in any offence  −3
Force present in at least one offence  0

6 **Has *any* sex offence (charged or convicted) involved multiple acts on a single victim within any single contact event?**
No  −1
Yes  +1

*Historical/static variables*

7   **Number of different age groups victimised across all sex/sex-related offences (charged or convicted)**
Age 6 or younger
Age 7–12 years
Age 13–15 years and the offender is more than five years older than the victim
Age 16 or older

| | |
|---|---|
| No age group or only one age group checked | 0 |
| Two or more age groups checked | +3 |

8   **Offended against a 13–15-year-old victim *and* the offender was more than five years older than the victim at the time of the offence (charged or convicted)**

| | |
|---|---|
| No | 0 |
| Yes | +2 |

9   **Was the victim a stranger in any sex/sex-related offence (charged or convicted)?**

| | |
|---|---|
| No victims were strangers | –1 |
| At least one victim was a stranger | +3 |
| Uncertain due to missing information | 0 |

10   **Is there evidence of adolescent antisocial behaviour in the file?**

| | |
|---|---|
| No indication | –1 |
| Some relatively isolated antisocial acts | 0 |
| Persistent, repetitive pattern | +2 |

11   **Pattern of substantial drug or alcohol abuse (12 months prior to arrest for the instant offence or revocation)**

| | |
|---|---|
| No | –1 |
| Yes | +1 |

12   **Employment history (12 months prior to arrest for instant offence)**

| | |
|---|---|
| Stable employment for one year or longer prior to arrest | –2 |
| Homemaker, retired, full-time student or disabled/unable to work | –2 |
| Part-time, seasonal, unstable employment | 0 |
| Unemployed or significant history of unemployment | +1 |

*Institutional/dynamic variables*

13   **Discipline history while incarcerated (does not include discipline for failure to follow treatment directives)**

| | |
|---|---|
| No major discipline reports or infractions | 0 |
| One or more major discipline reports | +1 |

*Institutional/dynamic variables*

| | | |
|---|---|---:|
| 14 | **Chemical dependency treatment while incarcerated** | |
| | No treatment recommended/not enough time/no opportunity | 0 |
| | Treatment recommended and successfully completed or in programme at time of release | −2 |
| | Treatment recommended but offender refused, quit, or did not pursue | +1 |
| | Treatment recommended but terminated by staff | +4 |
| 15 | **Sex offender treatment history while incarcerated** | |
| | No treatment recommended/not enough time/no opportunity | 0 |
| | Treatment recommended and successfully completed or in programme at time of release | −1 |
| | Treatment recommended but offender refused, quit or did not pursue | 0 |
| | Treatment recommended but terminated | +3 |
| 16 | **Age of offender at time of release** | |
| | Age 30 or younger | +1 |
| | Age 31 or older | −1 |
| | **TOTAL** | |

Reproduced with permission from Douglas Epperson (personal communication 2000)

**Notes** (see also Table 2.2)

a) The MnSOST-R was developed on a population of adult, male, incarcerated sex offenders. Any use on other populations (i.e., juveniles, females or offenders on probation) has not been validated.

b) Score all items unless there is no documented information and a reasonable approximation is not possible. If no information is available relating to an item, assume that it was not an issue.

c) 'Sex or sex-related' is defined as all sex offences by statute and any other offences clearly of a sexual nature or with a clear sexual component (e.g., kidnapping, murder, burglary that involved elements of a sex offence).

d) Item 1 measures sex/sex-related *convictions only*. Include convictions for attempted sex offences and conspiracy to commit a sex offence.

e) Items 3–9 measure sex/sex-related offences *charged or convicted*. Do *not* include charges that were withdrawn, dismissed for lack of evidence resulting in a finding of not guilty, or convictions overturned on appeal. Include attempted sex/sex related offences and conspiracy to commit a sex-related offence.

f) 'Current incarceration' includes any period of time served in prison for the instant offence. This includes the initial period of incarceration plus any returns to prison for a release violation after the initial release.

g) The MnSOST-R should *not* be used without reference to the full manual. This can be found on http://psych-server.iastate.edu/faculty/epperson/mnsost_download.htm

## Static 99 coding form

| Risk factor | Codes | | Score |
|---|---|---|---|
| | **Charges** | **Convictions** | |
| 1 Prior sex offences (excluding index) | None | None | 0 |
| | 1–2 | 1 | 1 |
| | 3–5 | 2–3 | 2 |
| | 6+ | 4+ | 3 |
| 2 Prior sentencing dates (excluding index) | 3 or less | | 0 |
| | 4 or more | | 1 |
| 3 Any convictions for non-contact sex offences | No | | 0 |
| | Yes | | 1 |
| 4 Index non-sexual violence | No | | 0 |
| | Yes | | 1 |
| 5 Prior non-sexual violence | No | | 0 |
| | Yes | | 1 |
| 6 Any unrelated victims | No | | 0 |
| | Yes | | 1 |
| 7 Any stranger victims | No | | 0 |
| | Yes | | 1 |
| 8 Any male victims | No | | 0 |
| | Yes | | 1 |
| 9 Young | Age 25 or older | | 0 |
| | Age 18–24 | | 1 |
| 10 Single | Ever lived with a lover for at least 2 years? | | |
| | Yes | | 0 |
| | No | | 1 |
| **Total score** | | | |
| **Final risk rating** | 0,1 | | Low |
| | 2,3 | | Medium-low |
| | 4,5 | | Medium-high |
| | 6+ | | High |

Reproduced with permission from David Thornton (personal communication 2000)

**Notes** (see also Table 2.3)
a) The Static 99 is designed to estimate the probability of sexual and violent recidivism among adult males who have already been convicted of at least one sexual offence against a child or non-consenting adult. It is not recommended for adolescents (less than 18 years at time of release), female offenders or offenders who have only been convicted of prostitution, pimping, public toileting or possession of indecent materials.

b)   The Static 99 can be scored from file information. If there is insufficient information to identify history of co-habitation the offender should be scored '0' on this item. The assessment should, nevertheless, be considered valid.

c)   A sexual offence is officially recorded sexual misbehaviour or criminal behaviour with sexual intent (e.g., murder, burglary etc.) which must have resulted in some form of criminal justice intervention or official sanction. This includes arrests, charges, parole violations and convictions. It may include juveniles placed into residential care for sexual aggression or members of the clergy being publicly denounced and sent to special treatment facilities. Count both juvenile and adult offences. Do not count self-reported offences.

d)   Prior sexual offences include offences which occurred prior to the index offence, even if charges are brought after the index conviction. All charges and convictions are coded even when they involve the same victim or multiple counts of the same offence.

e)   'Prior sentencing dates' refers to the number of distinct occasions on which the offender was sentenced for criminal offences. The number of charges/convictions does not matter. Do not count court appearances that resulted in a complete acquittal, nor convictions overturned on appeal. However, an official caution is equivalent to a conviction.

f)   'Index non-sexual violence' refers to convictions for non-sexual violence that are dealt with on the same sentencing occasion as the index sex offence. These may involve the same victim or a different victim.

g)   A related victim is one where the relationship would be sufficiently close that marriage would normally be prohibited (e.g., parent, uncle, grandparent, stepsister). Step relationships lasting less than two years would be considered unrelated.

h)   A victim is considered to be a stranger if they did not know the offender 24 hours before the offence. Victims contacted over the internet would not normally be considered strangers unless a meeting was planned for a time less than 24 hours after initial communication.

i)   The age of the offender refers to his age at the time of the risk assessment. If the assessment concerns an anticipated exposure to risk at some future date, the relevant age would be his age when exposed to risk.

j)   The Static 99 should not be used without reference to detailed information which can be obtained from the Solicitor General of Canada website at http://www.sgc.gc.ca/epub/corr/e199902/e199902.htm. See also Hanson and Thornton (1999, 2000) and the Coding Rules for the Static 99 (Phenix, Hanson & Thornton 2000), Corrections Research, Department of the Solicitor General of Canada.

# Risk Matrix 2000: risk of sexual reoffending

| Risk factor | Coding | Score |
|---|---|---|
| **Step 1** | | |
| 1  Age at commencement of risk | Under 18 | 0 |
| | 18–24 | 2 |
| | 25–34 | 1 |
| | Older | 0 |
| 2  Sexual appearances | 1 | 0 |
| | 2 | 1 |
| | 3,4 | 2 |
| | 5 or more | 3 |
| 3  Criminal appearances | Less than 5 | 0 |
| | 5 or more | 1 |
| **Total points** | 0 | Low |
| | 1,2 | Medium |
| | 3,4 | High |
| | 5,6 | Very high |
| **Step 2: aggravating factors** | | |
| 4  Any conviction for a contact sex offence against a male? | No | 0 |
| | Yes | 1 |
| 5  Any conviction for a contact sex offence against a stranger? | No | 0 |
| | Yes | 1 |
| 6  Single | No | 0 |
| | Yes | 1 |
| 7  Any conviction for a non-contact sex offence? | No | 0 |
| | Yes | 1 |
| **Number of aggravating factors** | 0,1 | No change |
| | 2,3 | Raise 1 risk level |
| | 4 | Raise 2 risk levels |
| **Final risk rating** | | **Low risk** |
| | | **Medium risk** |
| | | **High risk** |
| | | **Very high risk** |

Reproduced with permission from David Thornton (personal communication 2000)

# Risk Matrix 2000: risk of violent offending

| | Risk factor | Coding | Score |
|---|---|---|---|
| 1 | Age at commencement of risk | Under 18 | 4 |
| | | 18–24 | 3 |
| | | 25–34 | 2 |
| | | 35–44 | 1 |
| | | Older | 0 |
| 2 | Violent appearances | 0 | 0 |
| | | 1 | 1 |
| | | 2,3 | 2 |
| | | 4+ | 3 |
| 3 | Any burglaries? | No | 0 |
| | | Yes | 2 |
| | **Total score** | | |
| | **Final risk rating** | 0,1 | Low risk |
| | | 2,3 | Medium risk |
| | | 4,5 | High risk |
| | | 6,7 | Very high risk |

Reproduced with permission from David Thornton (personal communication 2000)

**Notes** (see also Table 2.4)

a)  The Risk Matrix 2000 is designed to estimate the sexual and violent recidivism of adult males with at least one conviction for a sexual or sex-related offence. It is not validated for use with adolescents (under the age of 18), or female offenders.

b)  The scoring rules for the Risk Matrix 2000 are similar to those of the Static 99.

c)  'Appearances' refers to an appearance at court for sentencing that includes a conviction for a sexual offence or offences with sexual intent. This should include the index offence. It does not refer to the number of charges or convictions. Violent appearances do not include sexual assaults such as rape unless there is a separate conviction for violence (on the same or a different victim). However, a violent offence must be of a kind such that a period of custody or a community supervision penalty could have been imposed. Include charges where the use of force or the threat of force is implied by the charge. The same event can be scored as both a sexual and a violent appearance if the underlying behaviour was sexual but the formal charge was violent.

d)  For sexual offences against a male, do not count illegal consenting sexual behaviour between people aged 16 or older.

e)  As for Static 99, a stranger is so defined if the victim did not know the offender 24 hours before the offence.

f)  'Single' refers to an offender who has not lived with an adult lover (male or female) on a continuous basis for at least two years.

# Sex Offender Risk Appraisal Guide (SORAG)

1 **Lived with both biological parents to age 16 (except for death of parent)**
Yes                                                                                      −2
No                                                                                       +3

2 **Elementary school maladjustment**
No problems                                                                              −1
Slight (minor discipline or attendance) or moderate problems                             +2
Severe problems (frequent disruptive behaviour and/or attendance
or behaviour resulting in expulsion or serious suspensions)                              +5

3 **History of alcohol problems**
One point allotted for each of the following: parental alcoholism,
teenage alcohol problem, adult alcohol problem, alcohol involved
in a prior offence, alcohol involved in the index offence
0                                                                                        −1
1 or 2                                                                                    0
3                                                                                        +1
4 or 5                                                                                   +2

4 **Marital status**
Ever married (or lived common law in the same home for at least
6 months)                                                                                −2
Never married                                                                            +1

5 **Criminal history score for non-violent offences (Cormier-Lang system)**
Score 0                                                                                  −2
Score 1 or 2                                                                              0
Score 3 +                                                                                +3

6 **Criminal history score for violent offences (Cormier-Lang system)**
Score 0                                                                                  −2
Score 2                                                                                   0
Score 3+                                                                                 +6

7 **Number of previous convictions for sexual offences (hands-on sexual offences prior to index offence)**
0                                                                                        −1
1 or 2                                                                                   +1
3 +                                                                                      +5

8 **History of sex offences only against girls under 14 (including index offences; if offender was less than 5 years older than victim, always score +4)**
Yes                                                                                       0
No                                                                                       +4

9. **Failure on prior conditional release (includes parole/ probation violation or revocation, failure to comply, bail violation, any new arrest while on conditional release)**
   No    0
   Yes    +3

10 **Age at index offence (at most recent birthday)**
   39+    −5
   34–38    −2
   28–33    −1
   27    0
   26 and less    +2

11 **Meets DSM-III criteria for any personality disorder**
   No    −2
   Yes    +3

12 **Meets DSM-III criteria for schizophrenia**
   Yes    −3
   No    +1

13 **Phallometric test results**
   *All* indicate non-deviant sexual preferences    −1
   *Any* test indicates deviant sexual preferences    +1

14 **Psychopathy Checklist score (PCL-R)**
   4 or less    −5
   5–9    −3
   10–14    −1
   15–24    0
   25–34    +4
   35+    +12

**TOTAL**

## Cormier-Lang Criminal History Score for non-violent and violent offences

**Non-violent offences**

| | |
|---|---|
| Robbery (bank, store) | 7 |
| Robbery (purse snatching) | 3 |
| Arson and fire-setting (church, house, barn) | 5 |
| Arson and fire-setting (garbage can) | 1 |
| Threatening with a weapon | 3 |
| Threatening (uttering threats) | 2 |
| Theft over $1,000 (includes car theft and possession of stolen property) | 5 |
| Mischief to public or private property over $1,000 | 5 |
| Break and enter and commit indictable offence (burglary) | 2 |
| Theft under $1,000 (includes possession of stolen goods) | 1 |
| Mischief to public or private property under $1,000 (also public mischief) | 1 |
| Break and enter (includes break and enter with intent) | 1 |
| Fraud (extortion, embezzlement) | 5 |
| Fraud (forged cheque, impersonation) | 1 |
| Possession of a prohibited or restricted weapon | 1 |
| Procuring a person for, or living on the avails of, prostitution | 1 |
| Trafficking in narcotics | 1 |
| Dangerous driving, impaired driving (driving while intoxicated) | 1 |
| Obstructing peace officer (including resisting arrest) | 1 |
| Causing a disturbance | 1 |
| Wearing a disguise with the intent to commit an offence | 1 |

**Violent offences**

| | |
|---|---|
| Homicide (murder, manslaughter, criminal negligence causing death) | 28 |
| Attempted murder, causing bodily harm with intent to wound | 7 |
| Kidnapping, abduction and forced confinement | 6 |
| Aggravated assault, choking, administering a noxious thing | 6 |
| Assault causing bodily harm | 5 |
| Assault with a weapon | 3 |
| Assault, assaulting a peace officer | 2 |
| Aggravated sexual assault, sexual assault causing bodily harm | 15 |
| Sexual assault with weapon | 12 |
| Sexual assault, gross indecency (vaginal, anal or oral penetration) | 10 |
| Sexual assault (attempted rape, indecent assault) | 6 |
| Gross indecency (offender fellates or performs cunnilingus on victim) | 6 |
| Sexual assault (sexual interference, invitation to sexual touching) | 2 |
| Armed robbery (bank, store) | 8 |
| Robbery with violence | 5 |
| Armed robbery (not a bank or store) | 4 |

**Notes** (see also Table 2.5)

a) The SORAG has been developed on samples of adult, male, incarcerated sex offenders. It excludes non-contact sex offenders and has not been validated for use with juveniles or females. However, a significant minority of the samples were juveniles at the time of the index offence, and the authors suggest that the predictors of recidivism among juveniles are the same as among adults.

b) The authors recommend the prediction of violent (including sexual) recidivism as the appropriate goal for sex offenders. The prediction figures all relate to violent recidivism.

c) To use the Cormier-Lang system for quantifying criminal history, score all arrests prior to the index offence separately for violent and for non-violent criminal history. Attempted offences are scored the same as if the offence had been completed with the exception of attempted murder which has a separate assigned value.

# Juvenile Sex Offender Risk Assessment Schedule

| | Variable + description | Coding | |
|---|---|---|---|
| | **Factor 1: sexual drive** | | |
| 1 | Prior charged sex offences (conviction not necessary) | None | 0 |
| | | 1 offence | 1 |
| | | >1 offence | 2 |
| 2 | History of predatory behaviour: stalking, grooming, exploitative behaviour, clear evidence of planning in sexual offence | No | 0 |
| | | Occasional | 1 |
| | | Frequent | 2 |
| 3 | Evidence of sexual preoccupation with sexual fantasies and gratification of sexual needs, compulsive masturbation, excessive use of pornography, reports frequent uncontrollable sexual urges, multiple paraphilias | No | 0 |
| | | Occasional | 1 |
| | | Frequent | 2 |
| 4 | Duration of sex offence history: only 1 known sexual offence, multiple sexual offences within 6 months, multiple sexual offences over extended period of time | 1 | 0 |
| | | multiple (<6) | 1 |
| | | multiple (>6) | 2 |
| | **Factor 2: antisocial behaviour** | | |
| 5 | Caregiver instability: lived with biological parents, one biological or step/foster parents, or multiple changes | Stable | 0 |
| | | Unstable | 1 |
| | | Highly unstable | 2 |
| 6 | Ever arrested before age of 16 | No | 0 |
| | | Once | 1 |
| | | > once | 2 |
| 7 | School behaviour problems: school failure, repeated truancy, fighting, or other serious problems | No | 0 |
| | | Mild | 1 |
| | | Severe | 2 |
| 8 | School suspensions or expulsions | No | 0 |
| | | Once | 1 |
| | | > once | 2 |
| 9 | History of conduct disorder: repetitive and persistent pattern of aggressive conduct in which the basic rights of others are violated, duration of 6+ months | No | 0 |
| | | Mild | 1 |
| | | Severe | 2 |
| 10 | Multiple types of offences: burglary, robbery, drug offences, assaults, homicide or attempted homicide, possession of a weapon, sex offences, driving offences, fraud, escape and AWOL | 1 type | 0 |
| | | 2 types | 1 |
| | | >2 types | 2 |

| Variable + description | Coding | |
|---|---|---|
| 11 Impulsivity: highly impulsive, antisocial lifestyle, including truancy, fighting, vandalism, running away from home/school/placement, drug abuse | None/minimal<br>Moderate<br>Strong | 0<br>1<br>2 |
| 12 History of alcohol abuse: no problems, or some problems associated with abuse | No/occasional<br>Moderate abuse<br>Chronic/severe | 0<br>1<br>2 |
| 13 History of parental alcohol abuse: no problems, or some problems associated with abuse | No/occasional<br>Moderate abuse<br>Chronic/severe | 0<br>1<br>2 |
| **Factor 3: clinical/treatment** | | |
| 14 Accepts responsibility for sexual offences: no evidence of minimisation/denial and full responsibility, to no acceptance of responsibility, partial denial and/or frequent minimisation | Full acceptance<br>Partial acceptance<br>No acceptance | 0<br>1<br>2 |
| 15 Internal motivation for change: distressed by offences, genuine desire to change; some degree of internal conflict mixed with a clear desire to avoid the consequences of reoffending; motivation for treatment is solely external | High<br>Mixed<br>Poor/external | 0<br>1<br>2 |
| 16 Understands sexual assault cycle<br>Including triggers and high risk situations | Good<br>Incomplete/partial<br>Poor/inadequate | 0<br>1<br>2 |
| 17 Evidence of empathy, remorse, guilt: genuine, generalisable and internalised; some degree of guilt, possibly related to shame, internalised at cognitive level; little or no evidence | Good<br>Incomplete/partial<br>Poor/inadequate | 0<br>1<br>2 |
| 18 Absence of cognitive distortions: no/occasional/ frequent expression of thoughts, attitudes or statements that are demeaning to women or children, which minimise or justify criminal conduct | None<br>Occasional<br>Frequent | 0<br>1<br>2 |
| **Factor 4: community stability/adjustment (coded for the past 6 months)** | | |
| 19 Poorly managed anger in the community: problematic physical/verbal assaults on others | None<br>Some (1 or 2)<br>Serious (3+) | 0<br>1<br>2 |

| | Variable + description | Coding | |
|---|---|---|---|
| 20 | Stability of current living situation: substance abuse by caregivers/partners, frequent changes in sexual partners, frequent moves, poor boundaries and lack of supervision of minors, frequent changes in household members, use of pornography | Stable (1)<br>Unstable (2 or 3)<br>Highly unstable (4+) | 0<br>1<br>2 |
| 21 | Stability of school: truancy, fighting, suspensions, running away, carrying weapons, use of drugs/ alcohol | Stable<br>Unstable (1 or 2)<br>Highly unstable (3+) | 0<br>1<br>2 |
| 22 | Evidence of support systems in the community: cooperation/compliance with probation, supportive family/friends, participation in organised activities (clear involvement with a delinquent peer group = score of 2) | Support (2+)<br>Some (1)<br>None | 0<br>1<br>2 |
| 23 | Quality of peer relationships: socially active, peer oriented and non-delinquent friends; a few friends and some involvement in social activities; or largely withdrawn and socially isolated, just acquaintances, or delinquent peer group | Socially active<br>Partially social<br>Poor | 0<br>1<br>2 |

### Note

a)   See Prentky et al. (2000) for a full description of the scale.

# Bibliography

Abel, G.G., Becker, J.V., Mittelman, M.S., Cunningham-Rathner, J., Rouleau, L.L. & Murphy, W.D. (1987) Self reported sex crimes of non-incarcerated paraphiliacs, *Journal of Interpersonal Violence*, 2: 3–25.

Abel, G.G., Mittelman, M., Becker, J., Rathner, J. & Rouleau, J. (1988) Predicting child molesters' response to treatment, in R.A. Prentky & V.L. Quinsey (eds) *Annals of the New York Academy of Science*, pp. 223–35. New York: NY Academy of Science.

Alexander, M. (1999) Sexual offender treatment efficacy revisited, *Sexual Abuse: A Journal of Research and Treatment*, 11, 101–16.

American Psychiatric Association (1994) *Diagnostic and Statistical Manual of Mental Disorders*, 4th edn. Washington, DC: APA.

American Psychiatric Association (1999) *Dangerous Sex Offenders: A Task Force Report*. Washington, DC: APA.

Anthony, G. & Watkeys, J. (1991) False allegations in child sexual abuse: the pattern of referral in an area where reporting is not mandatory, *Children and Society*, 5(2): 111–22.

Atkinson, J. (1995) *The Assessment of Female Sex Offenders*. Toronto: Correctional Service Canada.

Atkinson, J. (2000) *Case Studies of Female Sex Offenders in the Correctional Service of Canada*. Toronto: Correction Service Canada.

Baker, A. & Duncan, S.I. (1985) Child sexual abuse: a study of prevalence in Great Britain, *Child Abuse and Neglect*, 9: 457–67.

Balon, R. (1998) Pharmacological treatment of paraphilias with a focus on antidepressants, *Journal of Sex & Marital Therapy*, 24(4): 241–54.

Bard, L., Carter, D., Cerce, D., Knight, R., Rosenberg, R. & Schneider, B. (1987) A descriptive study of rapists and child molesters: developmental, clinical, and criminal characteristics, *Behavioral Sciences and the Law*, 5: 203–20.

Barker, M. & Beech, A. (1993) Sex offender treatment programmes: a critical look at the cognitive-behavioural approach, *Issues in Criminological and Legal Psychology*, 19: 37–42.

Bauserman, R. (1996) Sexual aggression and pornography: a review of correlational research, *Basic & Applied Social Psychology*, 18: 405–27.

Beckett, R. & Fisher, D. (1994) Assessing victim empathy: a new measure, *paper presented at the 13th Annual Conference of the Association for the Treatment of Sexual Abusers (ATSA)*. San Francisco, USA.

Beckett, R., Beech, A., Fisher, D. & Fordham, A. (1994) *Community-based Treatment for Sex Offenders: An Evaluation of Seven Treatment Programmes*. London: HMSO.

Bedarf, A. (1995) Examining sex offender community notification laws, *California Law Review*, 83(3): 885–939.

Beech, A.R. (1998) A psychometric typology of child abusers, *International Journal of Offender Therapy & Comparative Criminology*, 42: 319–39.

Beech, A., Fisher, D. & Beckett, R. (1999) *An Evaluation of the Prison Sex Offender Treatment Programme*. London: HMSO.

Beech, A., Friendship, C., Erikson, M. & Hanson, R.K. (2002) The relationship between static and dynamic risk factors and reconviction in a sample of UK child abusers, *Sexual Abuse: A Journal of Research and Treatment*, 14(2): 155–67.

Beech, A.R. & Fordham, A. (1997) Therapeutic climate of sexual offender treatment programmes, *Sexual Abuse: a Journal of Research and Therapy*, 9: 219–37.

Berliner, L & Conte, J. (1995) The effects of disclosure and intervention on sexually abused children, *Child Abuse and Neglect*, 19(3): 371–84.

Borduin, C.M., Henggeler, S.W., Blaske, D.M. & Stein, R.J. (1990) Multisystem treatment of adolescent sexual offenders, *International Journal of Offender Therapy and Comparative Criminology*, 34(2): 105–13.

Bourgon, G., Worling, J., Wormith, J. & Kulik, I. (1999) *An Evaluation of Specialized Treatment for Adolescent Sexual Offenders: An Outline for a National Multi-site Investigation*. http://qsilver.queensu.ca/rcjnet/projects/masterpr.html

Bradford, J., Bloomberg, D. & Bourget, D. (1988) The heterogeneity/homogeneity of pedophilia, *Psychiatric Journal of the University of Ottawa*, 13: 217–26.

Browne, K. & Hamilton, C. (1999) Police recognition of the links between spouse abuse and child abuse, *Child Maltreatment*, 4(2): 136–47.

Burt, M. (1980) Cultural myths and support for rape, *Journal of Personality and Social Psychology*, 39: 217–30.

Butler-Sloss, E. (1988) *The Report of the Inquiry into Child Abuse in Cleveland 1987*. London: HMSO.

Calder, M. (1997) *Juveniles and Children who Sexually Abuse: A Guide to Risk Assessment*. Lyme Regis: Russell House Publishing.

Calder, M. (2001) *Mothers of Sexually Abused Children*. Lyme Regis: Russell House Publishing.

Campbell, J. (ed.) (1995) *Assessing Dangerousness: Violence by Sexual Offenders, Batterers and Child Abusers.* Newbury Park, CA: Sage.

Ceci, S. & Bruck, M. (1993) Child witnesses, translating research into policy, *Social Policy Report, Society for Research in Child Development*, 7: 1–30.

Chaffin, M. (1992) Factors associated with treatment completion and progress among intrafamilial sexual abusers, *Child Abuse & Neglect*, 16: 251–74.

Clark, D. (2000) The use of the Hare Psychopathy Checklist Revised to predict offending and institutional misconduct in the English prison system, *Prison Research & Development Bulletin*, 9: 10–14.

Cook, D., Fox, C., Weaver, C. & Rooth, F. (1991) The Berkeley Group: 10 years experience of a group for non-violent sex offenders, *British Journal of Psychiatry*, 158: 238–43.

Cooke, D.J. (1998) Psychopathy across cultures, in D.J. Cooke, A.E. Forth & R.D. Hare (eds) *Psychopathy: Theory, Research, and Implications for Society*, pp. 13–45. Dordrecht: Kluwer.

Cooper, A. (ed.) (2002) *Sex and the Internet: A Guidebook for Clinicians.* New York: Brunner-Routledge.

Craissati, J. (1994) Sex offenders and the Criminal Justice System, *Justice of the Peace*, 158(43): 689–91.

Craissati, J. (1998) *Child Sexual Abusers: A Community Treatment Approach.* Hove: Psychology Press.

Craissati, J. & Beech, A. (2001) Attrition in a community treatment program for child sexual abusers, *Journal of Interpersonal Violence*, 16: 205–21.

Craissati, J. & Beech, A. (2003) Risk prediction and failure in a complete urban sample of sex offenders (in submission).

Craissati, J. & Beech, A. (forthcoming) The characteristics of a complete geographical sample of rapists: sexual victimization and compliance in comparison to child molesters, *Journal of Interpersonal Violence.*

Craissati, J., Falla, S., McClurg, G. & Beech, A. (2002) Risk, reconviction rates and pro-offending attitudes for child molesters in a complete geographical area of London, *Journal of Sexual Aggression*, 8: 22–38.

Craissati, J. & Hodes, P. (1992) Mentally ill sex offenders: the experience of a regional secure unit, *British Journal of Psychiatry*, 161: 846–9.

Craissati, J. McClurg, G. (1994) Sex offenders and the criminal justice system, *Justice of the Peace*, 158(43): 689–91.

Craissati, J. & McClurg, G. (1996) The Challenge Project: perpetrators of child sexual abuse in SE London, *Child Abuse and Neglect*, 20: 1067–77.

Craissati, J. & McClurg, G. (1997) The Challenge Project: a treatment programme evaluation for perpetrators of child sexual abuse, *Child Abuse and Neglect*, 21: 637–48.

Craissati, J., McClurg, G. & Browne, K. (2002a) Characteristics of perpetrators of child sexual abuse who have been sexually victimized as
children, *Sexual Abuse: A Journal of Research and Treatment*, 14(3):
225–39.

Craissati, J., McClurg, G. & Browne, K. (2002b) The parental bonding
experiences of sex offenders: a comparison between child molesters and
rapists, *Child Abuse and Neglect*, 26: 909–21.

Davis, M.H. (1980) A multidimensional approach to individual
differences in empathy, *JSAS Catalog of Selected Documents in
Psychology*, 10: 85.

Day, K. (1994) Male mentally handicapped sex offenders, *British Journal of
Psychiatry*, 165: 630–9.

Dean, K. & Malamuth, N.M. (1997) Characteristics of men who aggress
sexually and of men who imagine aggressing: risk and moderating
variables, *Journal of Personality and Social Psychology*, 72: 449–55.

Department of Health (1992) *Memorandum of Good Practice*. London:
HMSO.

Department of Health (1995) *Child Protection: Messages from Research*.
London: HMSO.

Department of Health (1996) *Childhood matters: report of the National
Commission of Inquiry into the Prevention of Child Abuse*. London:
HMSO.

Department of Health (1998) Children and young persons on Child Protection Registers year ending 31st March 1998, England, in *Department
of Health Personal Social Services Local Authority Statistics*. London:
HMSO.

Department of Health (1999) *Working Together to Safeguard Children*.
London: HMSO.

Department of Health (2000a) *The Framework for the Assessment of
Children in Need and their Families*. London: HMSO.

Department of Health (2000b) *Reforming the Mental Health Act. Part II:
High Risk Patients*. London: HMSO.

Department of Health (2002) *Reforming the Mental Health Act*. London:
HMSO.

Dhawan, S. & Marshall, W.L. (1996) Sexual abuse histories of sexual
offenders, *Sexual Abuse: A Journal of Research and Treatment*, 8: 7–15.

Douglas, K.S., Cox, D.N. & Webster, C.D. (1999) Violence risk assessment:
science and practice, *Legal and Criminological Psychology*, 4: 149–84.

Elliott, M., Browne, K. & Kilcoyne, J. (1995) Child sexual abuse prevention:
what offenders tell us, *Child Abuse and Neglect*, 19: 579–94.

Epperson, D.L., Huot, S.J. & Kaul, J.D. (1999) *Minnesota Sex
Offender Screening Tool – Revised (MnSOST-R)*. Minnesota Department of Corrections: http://psych-server.iastate.edu/faculty/epperson/
mnsost_download.htm

Epperson, D.L., Kaul, J., Huot, S., Alexander, W. & Goldman, R. (2000) *Cross-validation of the MinSOST-R*. Paper presented at the 17th Annual Research and Treatment Convention of the Association for the Treatment of Sexual Abusers, San Diego, California.

Everson, M., Hunter, W., Runyon, D., Edelsohn, G. & Coulter, M. (1989) Maternal support following disclosure of incest, *American Journal of Orthopsychiatry*, 59: 197–207.

Fedora, O., Reddon, J., Morrison, J., Fedora, S., Pascoe, H. & Yeudall, L. (1992) Sadism and other paraphilias in normal controls and aggressive and nonaggressive sex offenders, *Archives of Sexual Behavior*, 21(1): 1–15.

Feeley, M. & Simon, J. (1992) The new penology: notes on the emerging strategy of corrections and its implications, *Criminology*, 30(4): 449–74.

Finkelhor, D. & Russell, D. (1984) Women as perpetrators, in D. Finkelhor *et al.* (eds) *Child Sexual Abuse: New Theory and Research*. New York: The Free Press.

Finn, P. (1997) *Sex Offender Community Notification*. Washington, DC: National Institute of Justice, Office of Justice Programs, Research in Action.

Firestone, P., Bradford, J., Greenberg, D. & Larose, M. (1998) Homicidal sex offenders: psychological, phallometric and diagnostic features, *Journal of the American Academy of Psychiatry and Law*, 26(4): 537–52.

Firestone, P., Bradford, J., Greenberg, D. & Nunes, K. (2000b) Differentiation of homicidal child molesters, nonhomicidal child molesters, and nonoffenders by phallometry, *American Journal of Psychiatry*, 157(11): 1847–50.

Firestone, P., Bradford, J., McCoy, M., Greenberg, M., Curry, S. & Larose, M. (2000a) Prediction of recidivism in extrafamilial child molesters based on court-related assessments, *Sexual Abuse: A Journal of Research and Treatment*, 12: 203–21.

Firestone, P., Bradford, J., McCoy, M., Greenberg, D. & Larose, M. (1999) Prediction of recidivism in incest offenders, *Journal of Interpersonal Violence*, 14(5): 511–31.

Fisher, D., Beech, A. & Browne, K. (1998) Locus of control and its relationship to treatment change and abuse history in child sexual abusers, *Legal and Criminological Psychology*, 3: 1–12.

Fisher, D. & Thornton, D. (1993) Assessing risk of reoffending in sexual offenders. *Journal of Mental Health*, 2: 105–17.

Flood-Page, C. & Taylor, J. (eds) (2003) *Crime in England and Wales 2001/2002: Supplementary Volume, 01/03*. London: Research and Statistics Directorate.

Forth, A. & Kroner, D. (1995) *The factor structure of the Revised Psychopathy Checklist with incarcerated rapists and incest offenders*, unpublished manuscript.

Forth, A.E., Kosson, D. & Hare, R.D. (2003) *The Hare Psychopathy Checklist: Youth Version*. Totonto: Multi-Health Systems.

Freund, K., Chan, S. & Coulthard, R. (1979) Phallometric diagnosis with 'nonadmitters', *Behavior, Research and Therapy*, 17: 451–7.

Friendship, C. & Thornton, D. (2000) Sexual reconviction for sexual offenders discharged from prison in England and Wales: implications for evaluating treatment, *British Journal of Criminology*, 41: 285–92.

Friendship, C. & Thornton, D. (2002) Risk assessment for offenders, in K. Browne, J. Hanks, P. Stratton & C. Hamilton (eds) (2002) *Early Prediction and Prevention of Child Abuse: A Handbook*, pp. 301–16. Chichester: Wiley.

Furby, L., Weinrott, M. & Blackshaw, L. (1989) Sex offender recidivism: a review, *Psychological Bulletin*, 105: 3–30.

Furniss, T. (1991) *The Multi-professional Handbook of Child Sexual Abuse*. London: Routledge.

Gagne, P. (1981) Treatment of sex offenders with medroxyprogesterone acetate, *American Journal of Psychiatry*, 138: 644–6.

Garland, D. (1991) *Punishment and Modern Society: A Study in Social Theory*. Oxford: Clarendon Press.

Gayford, J.J. (1981) Indecent exposure: a review of the literature, *Medicine Science & Law*, 21(4): 233–42.

Giddens, A. (1990) *The Consequences of Modernity*. Cambridge: Polity Press.

Glasser, M. (1988) Psychodynamic aspects of paedophilia, *Psychoanalytic Psychotherapy*, 3: 121–35.

Goodwin, J., Sahd, D. & Rada, R. (1985) False accusations and false denials in incest: clinical myths and clinical realities, in J. Garden (ed.) *Sexual Abuse: Incest Victims and their families*. Boston, MA: John Wright.

Gratzer, T. & Bradford, M. (1995) Offender and offense characteristics of sexual sadists: a comparative study, *Journal of Forensic Sciences*, 40(3): 450–5.

Grayston, A. & De Luca, R. (1999) Female perpetrators of child sexual abuse: a review of the clinical and empirical literature, *Aggression and Violent Behavior*, 4(1): 93–106.

Griffin, D.W. & Bartholomew, K. (1994) The metaphysics of measurement: the case of adult attachment, in K. Bartholomew & D. Perlman (eds) *Attachment Processes in Adulthood*, pp. 17–52. London: Jessica Kingsley.

Gross, G. (1985) *Activities of a Development Disabilities Adult Offender Project*. Olympia, WA: Washington State Developmental Disabilities Planning Council.

Grubin, D. (1998) *Sex Offending Against Children: Understanding the Risk* (Police Research Series Paper 99). London: Home Office.

Grubin, D. & Wingate, S. (1996) Sexual offence recidivism: prediction versus understanding, *Criminal Behaviour and Mental Health*, 6: 349–59.

Hagan, M.P. & Gust-Brey, K.L. (2000) A ten-year longditudinal study of adolescent perpetrators of sexual assault against children, *Journal of Offender Rehabilitation*, 31(1–2): 117–26.

Hall, G. (1995) Sexual offender recidivism revisited: a meta-analysis of recent treatment studies, *Journal of Consulting and Clinical Psychology*, 63(5): 802–9.

Hamilton, C. and Browne, K. (1999) Recurrent maltreatment during child-hood: a survey of referrals to police child protection units in England, *Child Maltreatment*, 4(4): 275–86.

Hanson, K. (1997) *The Development of a Brief Actuarial Risk Scale for Sexual Offense Recidivism* (user report 97–04) Ottawa: Department of the Solicitor General of Canada.

Hanson, K. (2002) Recidivism and age: follow-up data from 4,673 sexual offenders, *Journal of Interpersonal Violence*, 17(10): 1046–62.

Hanson, K. & Bussiere, M. (1998) Predicting relapse: a meta-analysis of sexual offender recidivism studies. *Journal of Consulting and Clinical Psychology*, 86: 348–62.

Hanson, K., Gordon, A., Harris, A., Marques, J., Murphy, W., Quinsey, V. & Seto, M. (2002) First report of the collaborative outcome data project on the effectiveness of psychological treatment for sex offenders, *Sexual Abuse: A Journal of Research and Treatment*, 14: 169–94.

Hanson, K. & Harris, A. (1998) *Dynamic Predictors of Sexual Recidivism*. Ontario: Department of the Solicitor General.

Hanson, K. & Harris, A. (2000) *The Sex Offender Need Assessment Rating (SONAR): A Method for Measuring Change in Risk Levels, User Report 1998–01*. Ontario: Department of the Solicitor General.

Hanson, K. & Harris, A.J.R. (2001) A structured approach to evaluating change among sexual offenders, *Sexual Abuse: A Journal of Research and Treatment*, 13: 105–22.

Hanson, K., Steffy, R.A. & Gauthier, R. (1993) Long-term recidivism of child molesters, *Journal of Consulting and Clinical Psychology*, 61: 646–52.

Hanson, K. & Thornton, D. (1999) *Static 99: Improving Actuarial Risk Assessments for Sex Offenders*. Ontario: Department of the Solicitor General of Canada.

Hanson, K. & Thornton, D. (2000) Improving risk assessments for sex offenders: a comparison of three actuarial scales, *Law and Human Behavior*, 24: 119–36.

Hare, R.D. (1991) *Manual for the Revised Psychopathy Checklist*, Toronto: Multi-Health Systems.

Harris, J. & Grace, S. (1999) *A Question of Evidence? Investigating and Prosecuting Rape in the 1990s*. London: Home Office.

Hart, S.D., Cox, D.N. & Hare, R.D. (1995) *Manual for the Hare Psychopathy Checklist – Revised: Screening Version (PCL: SV)*. Toronto: Multi-Health Systems.

Hedderman, C. & Sugg, D. (1996) *Does Treating Sex Offenders Reduce Reoffending?* London: HMSO.

Her Majesty's Inspectorate of Probation (2001) *New Choreography*. London: HMSO.

Heriot, J. (1996) Maternal protectiveness following the disclosure of intra-familial child sexual abuse, *Journal of Interpersonal Violence*, 11(2): 181–94.

Home Office (1992) *Guide to the 1991 Criminal Justice Act*. London: HMSO.

Home Office (1995) *Criminal Statistics, England and Wales*. London: HMSO.

Home Office (1997) *Community Protection Order – A Consultation Paper*. London: HMSO.

Home Office (2000) *Government Proposals Better to Protect Children from Sex and Violent Offenders*. London: Home Office.

Home Office and Department of Health (1999) *Managing People with Dangerous and Severe Personality Disorder: A Consultation Document*. London: HMSO.

Horne, L., Glasgow, D., Cox, A. & Calam, R. (1991) Sexual abuse of children by children, *Journal of Child Law*, 3: 147–51.

Howitt, D. (1995) Pornography and the paedophile: is it criminogenic? *British Journal of Medical Psychology*, 68: 15–27.

Hudson, B. (2001) Human rights, public safety and the probation service: defending justice in the risk society, *The Howard Journal*, 40(2).

Hudson, S.M. & Ward, T. (1997) Intimacy, loneliness and attachment styles in sexual offenders, *Journal of Interpersonal Violence*, 12(3): 323–39.

Hunter, J.A., Goodwin, D.W. & Becker, J.V. (1994) The relationship between phallometrically measured deviant sexual arousal and clinical characteristics in juvenile sexual offenders, *Behavior Research and Therapy*, 32: 533–8.

Izzo, R. & Ross, R. (1990) Meta-analysis of rehabilitation programs for juvenile delinquents: a brief report, *Criminal Justice and Behavior*, 17(1): 134–42.

Jacobs, W., Kennedy, W. & Meyer, J. (1997) Juvenile delinquents: a between-group comparison study of sexual and nonsexual offenders, *Sexual Abuse: A Journal of Research and Treatment* 9(3): 201–17.

Johnson, J. (1992) *Mothers of Incest Survivors: Another Side of the Story*. Bloomington, IN: Indiana University Press.

Kafka, M. (1997) Hypersexual desire in males: an operational definition and clinical implications for males with paraphilias and paraphilia-related disorders, *Archives of Sexual Behavior*, 26(5): 505–26.

Kemshall, H. (2001) *Risk Assessment and Management of Known Sexual and Violent Offenders: A Review of Current Issues* (Police Research Series Paper 140). London: Home Office.

Kemshall, H. (2002) *Risk, Social Policy and Welfare*. Buckingham: Open University Press.

Kemshall, H. & Maguire, M. (2001) Public protection, partnership and risk penality: the multi-agency risk management of sexual and violent offenders, *Punishment and Society: The International Journal of Penology*, 5(2): 237–64.

Keppel, R. & Walter, R. (1999) Profiling killers: A revised classification model for understanding sexual murder, *International Journal of Offender Therapy and Comparative Criminology*, 43(4): 417–37.

Klimecki, M., Jenkinson, J. & Wilson, L. (1994) A study of recidivism amongst offenders with an intellectual disability, *Australia and New Zealand Journal of Developmental Disabilities*, 19: 209–19.

Knock, K. (2002) *The Police Perspective on Sex Offender Orders: A Preliminary Review of Policy and Practice* (Police Research Series Paper 155) London: HMSO.

Langevin, R. (1988) Defensiveness in sex offenders, in R. Rogers (ed.) *Clinical Assessment of Malingering and Deception*. New York: Guilford Press.

Langevin, R., Ben-Aaron, M., Wright, P., Marchese, V. & Handy, L. (1988) The sex killer, *Annals Sex Research*, 1: 123–301.

Lee, D. & Olender, M. (1992) Working with juvenile sex offenders in foster care, *Community Alternatives: International Journal of Family Care*, 4(2): 63–75.

Lewis, P. (1991) *The Report of the Working Party on the Assessment and Treatment of Sex Offenders at Broadmoor Hospital.*

Lindsay, W. (2002) Integration of recent reviews on offenders with intellectual disabilities, *Journal of Applied Research in Intellectual Disabilities*, 15: 111–19.

Lindsay, W., Smith, A., Law, J., Quinn, J., Anderson, A., Smith, A., Overend, T. & Allan, R. (2002) A treatment service for sex offenders and abusers with intellectual disability: characteristics of referrals and evaluation, *Journal of Applied Research in Intellectual Disabilities*, 15: 166–74.

Linehan, M.M. (1993) *The Skills Training Manual for Treating Borderline Personality Disorder*. New York: Guilford Press.

Lipsey, M. & Wilson, D. (1998) Effective intervention for serious juvenile offenders: a synthesis of research, in R. Loeber & D. Farrington (eds) *Serious and Violent Juvenile Offenders: Risk Factors and Successful Interventions*, pp. 313–45. Thousand Oaks, CA: Sage.

Lyon, E. & Kouloumpos-Lenaris, K. (1987) Clinician and state children's services worker collaboration in treating sexual abuse, *Child Welfare*, 67: 517–27.

McClurg, G. & Craissati, J. (1999) A descriptive study of alleged sexual abusers known to social services, *Journal of Sexual Aggression*, 4(1): 22–30.

MacCulloch, M.J., Snowden, P.R., Wood, P.J. & Mills, H.E. (1983) Sadistic fantasy, sadistic behavior and offending behavior, *British Journal of Psychiatry*, 143: 20–9.

Maguire, M., Kemshall, H., Noaks, L., Wincup, E. & Sharpe, K. (2001) *Risk Management of Sexual and Violent Offenders: The Work of Public Protection Panels* (Police Research Series Paper 139). London: HMSO.

Malamuth, N.M., Heavy, C.L. & Linz, D. (1993) Predicting men's antisocial behavior against women: the interaction model of sexual aggression, in G.C.N. Hall, R. Hirschman, J.R. Graham & M.S. Zaragoza (eds) *Sexual Aggression: Issues in Etiology, Assessment, and Treatment*, pp. 63–97. Washington, DC: Taylor & Francis.

Maletzky, B. (1991) *Treating the Sexual Offender*. Newbury Park, CA: Sage.

Mannarino, A. & Cohen, J. (1986) A clinical demographic study of sexually abused children, *Child Abuse and Neglect*, 10: 17–23.

Marques, J.K. (1999) How to answer the question 'Does sex offender treatment work?' *Journal of Interpersonal Violence*, 14(4): 437–51.

Marshall, P. (1997) *The Prevalence of Convictions for Sexual Offending* (No.55). London: Home Office.

Marshall, W.L. (1989) Intimacy, loneliness and sexual offenders, *Behavior Research and Therapy*, 27(5): 491–503.

Marshall, W. (1993) The role of attachments, intimacy and loneliness in the etiology and maintenance of sexual offending, *Sexual and Marital Therapy*, 8: 109–21.

Marshall, W.L., Anderson, D. & Fernandez, Y. (1999) *Cognitive Behavioural Treatment of Sexual Offenders*. Chichester: Wiley.

Marshall, W.L. & Barbaree, H. (1988) The long-term evaluation of a behavioral treatment program for child molesters, *Behaviour Research and Therapy*, 6: 499–511.

Marshall, W.L., Hudson, S.M. & Hodkinson, S. (1993) The importance of attachment bonds in the development of juvenile sex offending, in H.E. Barbaree, W.L. Marshall & S.M. Hudson (eds) *The Juvenile Sex Offender*, pp. 164–81. New York: Guilford Press.

Marshall, W.L. & Kennedy, P. (2001) Sexual sadism in sexual offenders: an elusive diagnosis, *Aggression and Violent Behavior*, 7: 1–22.

Mathews, R. (1987) *Preliminary Typology of Female Sex Offenders*. Minneapolis, MN: PHASE and Genesis 11 for Women.

Mathews, R., Hunter, J. & Vuz, J. (1997) Juvenile female sexual offenders: clinical characteristics and treatment issues, *Sexual Abuse: A Journal of Research and Treatment*, 9: 187–99.

Matthews, J., Mathews, R. & Speltz, K. (1989) Female sexual offenders: a typology, in P.Q. Patton (ed.) *Female Sexual Abuse*. New York: Sage.

Monahan, J. (1993) Limiting therapist exposure to Tarasoff liability: guidelines for risk containment, *American Psychologist*, 48(3): 242–50.

Murphy, G. & Mason, J. (1999) People with developmental disabilities who offend, in N. Bouras (ed.) *Psychiatric and Behavioural Disorders in Developmental Disabilities and Mental Retardation*, 226–45. Cambridge: Cambridge University Press.

Murphy, W.D., Haynes, M.R. & Worley, P.J. (1991) Assessment of adult sexual interest, in C.R. Hollin & K. Howells (eds) *Clinical Approaches to Sex Offenders and their Victims*. Chichester: Wiley.

Murray, G.T., Briggs, D. & Davies, C. (1992) Psychopathic disordered/ mentally ill, and mentally handicapped sex offenders: a comparative study, *Medicine, Science and the Law*, 32(4): 331–6.

Myhill, A. & Allen, J. (2002) *Rape and Sexual Assault of Women: Findings from the British Crime Survey*. London: Home Office.

Nathan, P. & Ward, T. (2002) Female sex offenders: clinical and demographic features, *Journal of Sexual Aggression*, 8(1): 5–21.

Nicholaichuk, T., Gordon, A., Gu, D. & Wong, S. (2000) Outcome of an institutional sexual offender treatment program: a comparison between treated and matched untreated offenders, *Sexual Abuse: A Journal of Research and Treatment*, 12: 139–53.

Nowicki, S. (1976) *Adult Nowicki-Strickland Internal-External Locus of Control Scale*. Test manual available from S. Nowicki, Jr., Department of Psychology, Emory University, Atlanta, GA 30322, USA.

Overholser, C. & Beck, S. (1986) Multimethod assessment of rapists, child molesters, and three control groups on behavioural and psychological measures, *Journal of Consulting and Clinical Psychology*, 54: 682–7.

Peters, J. (1976) Children who are victims of sexual assault and the psychology of offenders, *American Journal of Psychotherapy*, 30: 398–421.

Phenix, A., Hanson, K. & Thornton, D. (2000) *Coding Rules for the Static 99*. Ontario: Department of the Solicitor General of Canada.

Plotnikoff, J. & Woolfson, R. (2000) *Where are they now?: an Evaluation of Sex Offender Registration in England and Wales*. Police Research Series 126, London: Home Office.

Porter, S., Fairweather, D., Drugge, J., Herve, H., Birt, A. & Boer, D.P. (2000) Profiles of psychopathy in incarcerated sexual offenders, *Criminal Justice and Behavior*, 27: 216–33.

Pratt, J. (2000) The return of the wheelbarrow men: or, the arrival of postmodern penality, *British Journal of Criminology*, 40: 127–45.

Prentky, R. (1997) Arousal reduction in sexual offenders: a review of antiandrogen interventions, *Sexual Abuse: A Journal of Research and Treatment*, 9: 335–48.

Prentky, R.A., Harris, B., Rizzell, K. & Righthand, S. (2000) An actuarial procedure for assessing risk with juvenile sex offenders, *Sexual Abuse: A Journal of Research and Treatment*, 12(2): 71–93.

Prentky, R.A. & Knight, R.A. (1993) Age of onset of sexual assault: criminal and life history correlates, in G.C.N. Hall, R. Jirschman, J.R. Graham & M.S. Zaragoza (eds) *Sexual Aggression: Issues in Etiology, Assessment, and Treatment*, pp. 43–62. Washington, DC: Taylor & Francis.

Prentky, R.A., Lee, A., Knight, R. & Cerce, D. (1997) Recidivism rates among child molesters and rapists: a methodological analysis, *Law and Human Behavior*, 21: 635–59.

Proulx, J., Pellerin, B., McKibben, A., Aubut, J. & Ouimet, M. (1997) Static and dynamic predictors of recidivism in sexual offenders, *Sexual Abuse*, 9: 7–28.

Quinsey, V.L., Harris, G.T., Rice, M.E. & Cormier, C.A. (1998) *Violent Offenders: Appraising and Managing Risk*. Washington, DC: APA.

Quinsey, V.L., Lalumier, M., Rice, M. & Harris, G. (1995) Predicting sexual offenses, in J. Campbell (ed.) *Assessing dangerousness: Violence by Sexual Offenders, Batterers and Child Abusers*, pp. 114–37. Newbury Park, CA: Sage.

Quinsey, V.L., Rice, M. & Harris, G. (1995) Actuarial prediction of sexual recidivism, *Journal of Interpersonal Violence*, 10(1): 85–105.

Rice, M. & Harris, G. (1996) Recidivism information on 288 sexual offenders released from the Oakridge Mental Health Centre, Penetanguishene, Ontario. Unpublished data set.

Rice, M. & Harris, G. (1997) Cross-validation and extension of the violence risk appraisal guide for child molesters and rapists, *Law and Human Behavior*, 21(2): 231–41.

Rice, M., Harris, G. & Quinsey, V. (1990) A follow-up of rapists assessed in a maximum security psychiatric facility, *Journal of Interpersonal Violence*, 5: 435–48.

Rice, M., Harris, G. & Quinsey, V. (1991) Evaluation of an institutional-based treatment program for child molesters, *Canadian Journal of Program Evaluation*, 6: 111–29.

Richardson, G., Kelly, T., Bhate, S. & Graham, F. (1997) Group differences in abuser and abuse characteristics in a British sample of sexually abusive adolescents, *Sexual Abuse: A Journal of Research and Treatment*, 9: 239.

Righthand, S. & Welch, C. (2001) *Juveniles who have Sexually Offended: A Review of the Professional Literature*. US Department of Justice, Office of Juvenile Justice and Delinquency Prevention, www.ncjrs.org/html/ojjdp/report_juvsex_offend/contents.html

Rogers, D. & Rogers, R. (1995) Child sexual abuse – the interface with genitourinary medicine, *Genitourinary Medicine*, 71: 47–52.

Rosen, I. (1979) *Sexual Deviation*. London: Oxford University Press.

Rubenstein, M., Yeager, C.A., Goodstein, C. & Lewis, D.O. (1993) Sexually assaultive male juveniles: a follow-up, *American Journal of Psychiatry*, 150: 262–5.

Ryan, G. (1997) Juvenile sex offenders: development and correction, *Child Abuse and Neglect*, 11: 385–95.

Sahota, K. & Chesterman, P. (1998) Sexual offending in the context of mental illness, *Journal of Forensic Psychiatry*, 9(2): 267–80.

Salekin, R. (2002) Psychopathy and therapeutic pessimism: clinical lore or clinical reality? *Clinical Psychology Review*, 22: 79–112.

Salter, A. (1988) *Treating Child Sex Offenders and Victims: A Practical Guide*. Newbury Park, CA: Sage.

Saradjian, J. & Hanks, H. (1996) *Women Who Sexually Abuse Their Children: From Research to Practice*. Chichester: Wiley.

Schlesinger, L. & Revitch, E. (1999) Sexual burglaries and sexual homicide: clinical, forensic, and investigative considerations, *Journal of American Academic Psychiatry Law*, 27(2): 227–38.

Schram, D. & Milloy, C. (1995) *Community Notification: A Study of Offender Characteristics and Recidivism*. Seattle, WA: Urban Policy Research.

Simmons, J. & Colleagues (2002) *Crime in England and Wales 2001/2002. Findings 7/02*. London: Research, Development & Statistics Directorate, www.homeoffice.gov.uk/rds/index.htm

Sipe, R., Jensen, E.L. & Everett, R.S. (1998) Adolescent sexual offenders grown up: recidivism in young adulthood, *Criminal Justice and Behavior*, 25: 109–24.

Smallbone, S.W. & Dadds, M.R. (1998) Childhood attachment and adult attachment in incarcerated adult male sex offenders, *Journal of Interpersonal Violence*, 13(5): 555–73.

Smith, W.R. & Monastersky, C. (1986) Assessing juvenile sexual offenders' risk for reoffending, *Criminal Justice and Behavior*, 13: 115–40.

Stevenson, H., Castillo, E. & Sefarbi, R. (1990) Treatment of denial in adolescent sex offenders and their families, *Journal of Offender Counseling, Services & Rehabilitation*, 14(1): 37–50.

Street, R. (1998) *The Restricted Hospital Order: From Court to the Community* (Home Office Research Study 186). London: Home Office.

Sundram, C. (1990) *Inmates with Developmental Disabilities in New York Correctional Facilities*. New York: New York State Commission on quality of Care for the Mentally Disabled.

Taylor, M. & Quayle, E. (2003) *Child Pornography: An Internet Crime*. Hove: Brunner-Routledge.

Thornton, D. (1997) A 16-year follow-up of 563 sexual offenders released from HM Prison Service in 1979. Unpublished raw data.

Thornton, D. (2002) Constructing and testing a framework for dynamic risk assessment, *Sexual Abuse: A Journal of Research and Treatment*, 14(2): 139–53.

Thornton, D., Friendship, C., Erikson, M., Mann, R. & Webster, S. (in submission) Cross-validation of a static instrument for predicting sexual recidivism, *Law and Human Behavior*.

Thornton, D. & Hanson, K. (1996) *Do sex offenders specialise in particular forms of sexual offence?* Paper presented at the Symposium at the XXVIth International Conference of Psychology, Montreal.

Thornton, D. & Hogue, T. (1993) The large-scale provision of programmes for imprisoned sex offenders: issues, dilemmas and progress, *Criminal Behaviour and Mental Health*, 3: 371–80.

Vizard, E., Monck, E. & Misch, P. (1995) Child and adolescent sex abuse perpetrators: a review of the research literature, *Journal of Child Psychology and Psychiatry*, 36: 731–56.

Walker, N. & McCabe, S. (1968) *Crime and Insanity in England*, Vol. 1. Edinburgh: Edinburgh University Press.

Wallis, E. (2001) *A New Choreography*. London: Her Majesty's Inspectorate of Probation.

Ward, T., Hudson, S.M. & Marshall, W.L. (1996) Attachment style in sex offenders: a preliminary study, *The Journal of Sex Research*, 33(1): 17–26.

Ward, T. & Stewart, C. (2003) The treatment of sex offenders: risk management and good lives, *Professional Psychology: Research and Practice*, In press.

Wart, T. & Stewart, C. (forthcoming) Good lives and the rehabilitation of sexual offenders. In T. Ward, D. Laws & S. Hudson (eds) *Sexual Deviance: Issues and Controversies*. Thousand Oaks, CA: Sage.

Warren, J., Hazelwood, R. & Dietz, P. (1996) The sexually sadistic serial killer, *Journal of Forensic Science*, 41(6): 970–4.

Watkins, B. & Bentovim, A. (1992) The sexual abuse of male children and adolescents: a review of current research, *Journal of Child Psychology & Psychiatry*, 33(1): 197–248.

Weeks, R. & Widom, C. (1998) Self-reports of early childhood victimization among incarcerated adult male felons, *Journal of Interpersonal Violence*, 13(3): 346–61.

Weinrott, M., Riggan, M. & Frothingham, S. (1997) Reducing deviant arousal in juvenile sex offenders using vicarious sensitization, *Journal of Interpersonal Violence*, 12(5): 704–28.

Welldon, E. (1988) *Mother, Madonna, Whore: The Idealization and Denigration of Motherhood*. London: The Guilford Press.

Wilson, M. (1995) A preliminary report on ego development, in non-offending mothers of sexually abused children. *Child Abuse and Neglect*, 19: 511–18.

Wilson, R. (2002) Fractured families, fragile children – the sexual vulnerability of girls in the aftermath of divorce, *Child and Family Law*, 14(1): 1.

World Health Organisation (1994) *The International Statistical Classification of Diseases and Related Health Problems*, 10th edn. Geneva: WHO.

Young, J. (1999) *Cognitive Therapy for Personality Disorders: A Schema-focused Approach*. Sarasota, FL: Professional Resource Press.

Zevitz, R. & Farkas, M. (2000a) Sex offender community notification: managing high risk criminals or exacting further vengeance? *Behavioral Sciences and the Law*, 18: 375–91.

Zevitz, R. & Farkas, M. (2000b) Sex offender community notification: examining the importance of neighborhood meetings, *Behavioral Sciences and the Law*, 18: 393–408.

# Index